The Religion of Paul the Apostle

The Religion of Paul the Apostle

John Ashton

Yale University Press
New Haven and London

Set in Simoncini Garamond
by Northern Phototypesetting Co. Ltd, Bolton
Printed in Great Britain by St Edmundsbury Press Ltd, Suffolk

Library of Congress Catalog Card Number 00-105010

ISBN 0–300–08441–2

A catalogue record for this book is available from the British Library.

2 4 6 8 10 9 7 5 3 1

For Chris and Catherine

La vraie question n'est pas de savoir si, cherchant à comprendre, on gagne du sens ou on en perd, mais si le sens qu'on préserve vaut mieux que celui à quoi on a la sagesse de renoncer.

Claude Lévi-Strauss

Heutzutage hat kein Mensch den Paulus wirklich verstanden, der noch seiner Ansicht sein zu können meint.

Franz Overbeck

Contents

Preface

Many people have contributed to the making of this book. First I should like to acknowledge a general debt to Wolfson College, Oxford, my academic home for the last fifteen years. Wolfson is almost a mini-university on its own, and many of its Fellows, experts in an astonishing range of scholarly disciplines, have constantly stimulated my own thinking. Two in particular, a physicist (Brian Buck) and an anthropologist (Nick Allen), gave me detailed comments on an early draft of the book, and called (quite rightly) for clarity and correctness. Other friends who have performed a similar service are John Hyman, Clare Palmer, and Robert Butterworth. The last-named is one of my oldest friends, and his detailed comments, those of a trained theologian who does not fully approve of my approach, were particularly valuable.

Like many other Oxford scholars I have benefited from the patience and helpfulness of the staff of the Lower Reading Room of the Bodleian Library, and I owe just as much to the assiduous efforts of the Wolfson College librarian, Adrian Hales, to obtain books and articles not in Bodley's possession. Tracy Fuzzard, the Academic Secretary at Wolfson, has uncomplainingly sorted out my e-mail messages, and generally made my College duties easier to bear. Phil McAvoy and David O'Brien rescued me from a near-total computer illiteracy.

I should also record my indebtedness to my professional colleagues in the field of New Testament Studies: to Steve Wilson, visiting Wolfson during the period in which the book was first drafted and generously offering to read and comment on the manuscript; to Bob Morgan, who saw what was intended to be the final version and called for some last-minute emendations; to Douglas Templeton, who has forced me to rethink certain important issues; to Volker

Rabens, who read a draft of the excursus on Albert Schweitzer and made numerous valuable suggestions about how to improve it; and above all to my friend and mentor, Chris Rowland, who encouraged me to 'do my own thing' without constantly glancing over my shoulder in the fear of likely criticisms. From the moment when the lectures on which the book is based were delivered (which he chaired and introduced) he has given unstintingly of his valuable time to help me iron out many of its wrinkles. I know that he thinks the book could be improved. Yet unlike some, he agrees with the fundamental distinction between religion and theology and perhaps attaches even more importance to it than I do myself.

For helping to obtain the picture of Paul on the front cover I am grateful for the assistance of Jacques Trublet.

Readers of this book will soon become aware of my indebtedness to Ioan Lewis, whose book *Ecstatic Religion: A Study of Shamanism and Spirit Possession* provided me with an important part of my argument.

Finally I want to express my gratitude to Malcolm Gerratt for reminding me from time to time of my declared intention to write a book on Paul, for urging me to offer it in the first instance to Yale University Press, and for undertaking the difficult task of editing the finished manuscript.

I have frequently used my own translation of passages from the Bible. Other quotations, unless otherwise stated, are from the Revised Standard Version of the Bible, copyright 1946, 1952, and 1971 by the Division of Christian Education of the National Council of the Churches of Christ in the USA. Used by permission. All rights reserved.

The quotation on pp. 80–1 from *Paul*, by Hans-Joachim Schoeps, is used by permission of The Lutterworth Press.

'The Tummy Beast' from *Dirty Beasts* by Roald Dahl, copyright © 1983, is reprinted by permission of Jonathan Cape and Farrar, Straus and Giroux, LLC.

Wolfson College, Oxford
May 2000

Abbreviations

Aram	Aram periodical
CBQ	Catholic Biblical Quarterly
DACL	Dictionnaire d'Archéologie Chrétienne et de Liturgie
HTR	Harvard Theological Review
JBL	Journal of Biblical Literature
Josephus, AJ	Antiquitates Judaicae
BJ	De Bello Judaico
JSNT	Journal for the Study of the New Testament
JSS	Journal of Semitic Studies
JTS	Journal of Theological Studies
LXX	Septuagint
NT	Novum Testamentum
NTS	New Testament Studies
Philo, Agr.	De Agricultura
Cher.	De Cherubim
Migr. Abr.	De Migratione Abrahami
Sobr.	De Sobrietate
Spec.	Leg. De Specialibus Legibus
Virt.	De Virtutibus
ST	Studia Theologica
TLZ	Theologische Literaturzeitung
ZNW	Zeitschrift für die neutestamentliche Wissenschaft

Introduction

This book is a revised and expanded version of a set of eight lectures delivered in the University of Oxford between January and May 1998 as one of an annual series with the general title of The Wilde Lectures in Natural and Comparative Religion. Nobody is expected to talk about natural and comparative religion at the same time. The term 'Natural Religion' covers what is usually called the philosophy of religion. Comparative Religion is a much more problematic affair, as I discovered when I visited the dark Plutonic mills of Bodley's bookstacks to consult the trust deed of the [Henry] Wilde Lectureship, founded in 1908: 'Comparative Religion shall be taken to mean the modes of causation, rites, observances and other concepts involved in the higher historical religions, as distinguished from the naturalistic ideas and fetishisms of the lower races of mankind.'[1] Good heavens, I reflected. How could such a programme, at once so vague and so pretentious, be pursued ninety years later? Maybe it cannot. On rummaging deeper in the stacks, I discovered that this offensive rubric lasted unchanged until 1969, when the electors purged it of its egregious racism by the simple expedient of dropping the offending clause ('as distinguished from the naturalistic ideas and fetishisms of the lower races of mankind').[2] One can only sympathize with their embarrassment. And one could applaud their ingenuity in escaping from it, were it not for their failure to observe that the result of the excision was to render the rubric incoherent.

1. *Statuta et Decreta Universitatis Oxoniensis*, 1908, p. 457.
2. 1969 was clearly a year of momentous change in the University, for it was also the year in which the *Statuta et Decreta Universitatis Oxoniensis* were anglicized into *The Statutes, Decrees, and Regulations of the University of Oxford*.

For it seems to have escaped their notice that the term 'comparative' in 'Comparative Religion' derives its force from the very clause they were about to lop off. Shorn of the right to distinguish the higher from the lower religions, the rubric resembles a crab that has lost one of its claws. All it can do is to brandish its remaining pincer ineffectively in the face of the flummoxed lecturer.

The well-meaning electors were evidently anxious, no doubt in response to some query or protest, to release all subsequent lecturers from the painful obligation of endeavouring to deal with the religions of what Henry Wilde had called 'the lower races of mankind'; but I had already reached the decision to compare Paul with what I imagine he would have considered one such religion, namely shamanism. So I am in effect resurrecting Wilde's original rubric by restoring the crab's missing claw.

Such a project is not without its difficulties. In the first place I have to confront the question of my own competence. How dare a mere exegete tackle a task that lies somewhere between the sphere of the anthropologist and that of the historian of religion? In response to this objection I can only appeal to what has been called the Wisconsin principle. (For the sake of those unfamiliar with this I should add that it takes its name from a prospectus which, so it is alleged, commends the university's course in oceanography by pointing out that 'the location of the University of Wisconsin is surprisingly ideal for modern oceanographic studies. It lies midway between the Atlantic and Pacific Oceans.') But I am also embold-ened by the fact that unlike most of my academic colleagues in the United Kingdom, crouching under the shadow of university assess-ment exercises (currently conducted under the aegis of the Quality Assurance Agency), I am no longer obliged to produce at regular intervals books or articles that correspond to some abstract and ill-defined norm. Out from under the shadow, I am free to pursue my own interests, to take a generally more relaxed approach to my work, and even on occasion, as here, to trespass on the territory of others.

There are, however, theoretical difficulties too. One of these concerns the use of the word religion. When talking of Paul, most scholars prefer to speak of his *theology*, and we shall see that some claim that it is wrong to think of him as having a religion at all. So the rarer usage has to be justified as well as explained.

If the noun 'religion' poses problems, so does the adjective 'comparative'. Without being able to verify this, I suspect that the original formulation of the decree setting up the Wilde lectureship was based on the assumption of a natural progression from the 'lower' to the 'higher' religions of mankind. If that is so, then once this assumption has been called into question, then the whole enterprise, if it is not to be abandoned completely, appears to require a new and quite different kind of justification. For what is the point of comparing Buddhism with fetishism, say, or Christianity with shamanism, if no genealogical link can be established between these very different religions? Quite conceivably it was a recognition of this difficulty and not, as I first supposed, a sudden access of political correctness, that led the Wilde Electors to make such a drastic alteration to the rubrics. Before embarking on my own programme, therefore, I need to offer some reasoned defence of the practice of comparing religions as this was outlined by Henry Wilde.

One of the first scholars to apply the comparative method to the study of Paul (Adolf Deissmann) distinguished, as we shall see, between two approaches, the genealogical and the analogical. What did he mean by these terms, and is this distinction tenable? The first chapter of the present book will be itself largely introductory, and will concentrate on the practice of comparison and the nature of religion.

This comparative approach will remain present throughout the book, being especially prominent in the second chapter and in the last. But although anxious not to let go of comparison or even to lose sight of it, I have to acknowledge that there is something odd about taking the *religion* of Paul for comparison with another named religion. Unlike Buddhism or Mohammedanism (the old name for Islam), Paulinism is not really a religion at all, certainly not one that would be generally recognized as such. Yet like Buddha and Mohammed, Paul did, I think, *found* a religion, and this book is largely concerned with the question of how he came to do so. Besides being a study in comparative religion it is also proffered as a contribution towards the history of early Christianity.

This brings us to Paul himself. The task of writing a scholarly book on Paul at the end of the twentieth century is truly daunting. How is it possible to pick one's way through the innumerable essays, articles, and reviews of Paul's work, let alone all the theses, monographs and commentaries devoted to it, without being totally swamped by them?[3] On the other hand, how can one refuse to engage with the secondary literature, vast as it is, whilst continuing to aspire to academic credibility? My answer to this question is that I am venturing on something new, not previously attempted in New Testament scholarship. Moreover, despite what may seem to some readers a bewilderingly extravagant display of footnotes, this book is not intended primarily for members of the guild of biblical scholars, but for an educated lay public interested in following a rational enquiry into the origins of Christianity.

Most discussions of the apostle Paul are either (a) accounts of his life that focus predominantly on his conversion, his journeys, and his work in forming and building up Christian communities,[4] (b) systematic presentations of his thought,[5] (c) studies of his individual writings, including some, in the last twenty years or so, that have highlighted either the *rhetorical* or the *sociological* background against which they should be understood.[6] Finally (d), a few books have been published under the rubric of psychology.[7]

None of these four headings quite fits my present concerns. In the first place I am not interested in Paul's life and career as such. There are plenty of good biographies of Paul available, two of the best having appeared only very recently,[8] and I have no desire to

---

3. Joseph A. Fitzmyer's recent commentary on Romans (1993) has more than 200 pages of bibliography on this one letter alone!
4. See above all Wayne A. Meeks, *The First Urban Christians* (1983). This is an outstanding attempt to view Paul's work from the perspective of social history.
5. Most recently, J. D. G. Dunn, *The Theology of Paul the Apostle* (1998). But the most distinguished contribution to the subject is still the first volume of Rudolf Bultmann's *Theology of the New Testament*, published in German half a century earlier (Tübingen, 1948).
6. Compare for instance Hans Dieter Betz, *Galatians* (1975), emphasizing the rhetoric, with Philip F. Esler's much shorter *Galatians* (1998), stressing the relevance of sociological theory.
7. Most notably Gerd Theissen's *Psychological Aspects of Pauline Theology* (1987).
8. J. Murphy-O'Connor, *Paul: A Critical Life* (1996); A. N. Wilson, *Paul: The Mind of the Apostle* (1997). The two books are very different. The first is a scholarly study, combining a complete mastery of the primary sources with a seemingly exhaustive knowledge of the vast secondary literature, and skilfully deploying these to make a very readable book. The second is an engaging and, at times, provocative biography, written for a more general readership but manifesting an unerring eye for apposite quotations drawn from a wide variety of sources. To be

compete with them. Nor is it the purpose of this book either to discuss Paul's theology or to add to the huge and ever-growing pile of scholarly studies of his writings. Lastly, although I am indeed curious about Paul's psyche (the inner workings of his mind and his gut reactions), my perspective differs somewhat from that of the professional psychologist. No doubt much of the scholarly literature on Paul (and much else besides) is not unrelated to my own project; and that is why, eager for it to be taken seriously, I have chosen to buttress the discussion with references to a select array of earlier studies. Hence the footnotes and excursuses. Many of the footnotes are references and nothing more; others are deliberate diversions (in both senses of the word) whose bearing on the topic under review is too indirect to justify keeping them above the line: I was reluctant to side-track the reader, clutter up the main text, and overload the argument. The excursuses, like the footnotes, are intended primarily for readers who wish to dig a little deeper. It is my hope, nevertheless, that the gist of the argument will be plain enough without them.

---

added to these is Jürgen Becker's *Paul: Apostle to the Gentiles* (1993), first published in German in 1989, and rightly described in the foreword to the English edition as a 'magisterial work'. Although it includes a short sketch of Paul's life this is not, strictly speaking, a biography. Indeed, it transcends the genres, since it continues by treating each of Paul's letters in its historical context and concludes by a survey of his theology. Although his book is over 500 pages long, Becker has managed to dispense with notes and with quotations in Greek. It deserves (and will no doubt get) many readers.

1

On Comparing Religions

Comparisons and contexts

George Steiner, the first incumbent of the Weidenfeld Chair of Comparative Literature in the University of Oxford, put the title of his inaugural lecture, in 1994, in the form of a question: 'What is Comparative Literature?' He began by pointing out that 'Every act of the reception of significant form, in language, in art, in music, is comparative.... We seek to understand, to "place" the object before us – the text, the painting, the sonata – by giving it the intelligible, informing context of previous and related activity.... There is', he concluded, 'in the perception of and response to intelligibility no absolute innocence, no Adamic nakedness.'[1]

This is clearly right: anything truly unique would be, strictly speaking, incomprehensible.[2] When Paul, the subject of this book, introduced the topic of resurrection in his speech to the Athenians on the Areopagus, he was greeted, Luke tells us, with total bewilderment. Perhaps the Athenians thought he was talking about a strange new goddess: Anastasis.[3] If so, they were not just puzzled

1. *What is Comparative Literature?*, 1.
2. 'This word "unique"', writes Arnold Toynbee, 'is a negative term signifying what is mentally inapprehensible. The absolutely unique is, by definition, indescribable', *A Study of History*, vii, 255. The philosopher Hans-Georg Gadamer goes so far as to assert that 'prejudices (*Vorurteile*), in the literal sense of the word, constitute the preliminary directedness (*Gerichtetheit*) of our whole ability to experience', *Kleine Schriften*, i, 106. (Since the word *Urteil* means 'judgement' the 'literal' meaning of *Vorurteile* is 'pre-judgements'.) See too *Truth and Method*, 238–67.
3. '"He seems to be a preacher of foreign divinities" – because he preached Jesus and the resurrection' (Acts 17:18). It is worth observing that another of Paul's obsessional themes, Δικαιοσύνη, was a well-established deity in Asia Minor.

but uninterested: they had no room for Resurrection in their own pantheon. A little earlier, in Paul's only other encounter with an exclusively pagan audience, the people of Lystra were so astonished at seeing him heal a cripple that they concluded that the two strangers who had just appeared among them must be gods. Paul's companion, Barnabas, presumably a more impressive physical specimen than Paul,[4] they took to be Zeus. Paul himself, who did most of the talking, they addressed as Hermes. Realizing that what they had witnessed was in some sense a religious act, they were endeavouring to place it in the context of their own religious traditions. Luke ends the story by saying that the two men had difficulty in restraining the people from sacrificing oxen to them (Acts 14:8–18).

This story is so bizarre that many New Testament scholars, no more credulous than most of their colleagues in other disciplines, have considered it self-evidently devoid of any historical foundation. Yet not only is there abundant evidence of the association of Zeus and Hermes in Asia Minor generally, but inscriptions linking the two are especially common in the region of Lystra. Steven Mitchell, in his exhaustive study of Anatolia, contends that this concentration of evidence is highly suggestive, and 'confirms the historical precision' of this episode.[5] Perhaps just as relevant is a passage in a contemporary romance by Chariton of Aphrodisias in which the people of Miletus mistook Chariton's heroine, the fair Callirhoe, for the goddess Aphrodite. And there actually exists engraved in a stone carving from north-eastern Lydia what Robin Lane Fox calls a 'postscript to Acts and to Chariton's pastoral novel . . . the votive monument and text of a man who made his dedication "on behalf of the traces of the gods" in the year 184/5'.[6] The point is, of course, that belief in the gods in Asia Minor in this period was so strong that

---

See Stephen Mitchell, *Anatolia*, ii, 18, 26. (The word means justice, but translators of Paul's letters generally opt for 'righteousness'.)

4. Paul himself knew very well what people said of him: 'His letters are weighty and strong, but his bodily presence is weak'; and he adds, more surprisingly, 'and his speech of no account' (2 Cor 10:10).

5. *Anatolia*, ii, 24.

6. *Pagans and Christians,* 140. Chariton inserts his heroine into 'real time' by making her the daughter of Hermocrates, the Sicilian general largely responsible for ensuring the defeat of the Athenian expedition to Sicily in the middle of the Peloponnesian war. But his readers will have recognized his story as a romance, and it is not immediately obvious that ancient romances can be taken without further ado as evidence for the boundless credulity of their readers. Yet even in

from time to time people could easily be induced to affirm that they had actually put in an appearance on earth. Many people today are equally convinced of the reality of visitors from outer space.

True or not, the Lystra episode is interesting chiefly for what it tells us of our instinctive struggle for understanding when confronted by some strange new phenomenon, whether this should be a healing miracle, a report concerning a man risen from the dead, or rumours of an unidentified flying object. The response of the people of Lystra to Paul and Barnabas, as a practical example of comparative religion, involves the same kind of instinctive contextualizing that George Steiner was talking about in his lecture. Within the New Testament this episode is exceptional in making a direct comparison between the new gospel and the pagan religions it was seeking to supplant; but of course all the writers of the New Testament are endeavouring to give a meaningful context to the gospel. The difference is that they, unlike the people of Lystra, are quite confident about what this context is, namely the Hebrew, or, more accurately, the Greek Bible. What came to be thought of as a completely new religion was originally seen as a natural development of Judaism: τέλος νόμου Χριστός, as Paul succinctly puts it: Christ is the goal of the law – where it leads.[7]

Broadly speaking, this is the context in which Christianity has been regarded ever since. To apply the term 'parting of the ways' to the severance of Judaism and Christianity is undoubtedly misleading,[8] for we should be talking about a deviation on the part of Christianity rather than a bifurcation. Nevertheless, what was originally no more than a rather weird-looking branch of Judaism eventually came to be seen as a sturdy independent tree. And it is easy to see why, whenever historians and theologians have sought

---

these relatively sophisticated times people occasionally confuse fiction with fact, a propensity brilliantly exploited in Frank Marcus's play *The Killing of Sister George*, in Stephen King's novel *Misery*, and in Clint Eastwood's film *Play Misty for Me*. When a character in the very popular television soap opera, *Coronation Street*, was given an eighteen-month jail sentence for fraud in March 1998, there was a public outcry, and a backbench MP asked the Home Secretary, Jack Straw, to secure her release (as reported in *The Times* of 31 March).

7. Romans 10:4. The phrase τέλος νόμου can equally well mean the *ending* of the law. Since Paul thought this too it is impossible to be sure which of the two senses he intended. Perhaps both.
8. See Judith Lieu, 'The Parting of the Ways'.

to compare Christianity with some other religion, with rare exceptions it is to Judaism that they have turned for enlightenment. A case in point is an outstanding work of scholarship, published in 1977, in which what the author calls the *religion* of Paul is systematically compared with that found in the writings of his Jewish contemporaries or near-contemporaries. I shall return to this book, E. P. Sanders's *Paul and Palestinian Judaism*,[9] later. For the moment I want to comment briefly on Christianity's extraordinary success story in establishing, right from its inception, what may be called its contextual credentials.[10]

These are, of course, inextricably bound up with what Paul and his successors saw as God's original revelation to Israel. Without this the Christian gospel would have suffered the fate of the seed which, according to the parable, was sown on rocky or barren ground. With no soil to help it to germinate it would have withered and died.[11] As it is, Christianity continues to survive, even to thrive, in a curious and, at least until recently, inimical symbiosis with Judaism. The first to insist upon the tight link between the Old Testament and the message of the New was, we are told in a well-known story in Luke's Gospel, Jesus himself, who, 'beginning with Moses and all the prophets, interpreted to them [the two disciples who had met him on the road to Emmaus] in all the scriptures the things concerning himself' (Luke 24:27). Almost equally perplexing, until we realize that he is working from a theological agenda, is Luke's insistence that Paul, rather later, spent three successive sabbaths in the synagogue at Thessalonica explaining the scriptures to the Jewish worshippers and citing texts to show that the Messiah had to die and then rise from the dead (Acts 17:3; cf. 9:20, 22; 18:28). Christian scholars have been scratching their heads ever since in their efforts to guess the passages that Jesus and Paul were alluding to.[12]

---

9. Subtitled *A Study of Patterns of Religion*.
10. The New Testament makes a beginning, but the work was continued by the second-century apologists and later, in a very different vein, by the Alexandrians Origen and Clement.
11. See Mark 4:4–5.
12. In the earliest Christian creed, which was taken over by Paul, the phrase 'according to the scriptures' occurs twice, first to back up the assertion that 'Christ died for our sins', and then to prove that he was predicted to rise 'on the third day' (1 Cor 15:3–4). Numerous Old Testament texts have been proposed in justification.

From the Christian perspective, then, the contextual supports of Christianity, reaching deep down into Judaism, were fully formed by the time that the new writings had been given canonical status. Small wonder that the second-century heresiarch Marcion was given such short shrift when he tried to split the two Testaments apart.

Ever since the establishment, in Göttingen, in the 1880s, of the so-called history of religions school there have been sporadic attempts to prove that Pauline Christianity was heavily influenced by the pagan mystery religions. But even if we accept that Paul's theology of baptism was a kind of adaptation of rites that somehow re-enacted the dying and rising of pagan gods such as Attis or Adonis (and this is far from certain), the main burden of Paul's gospel must still find its explanatory context in the Judaism into which he was born, within which he was nurtured and educated, and which he may never have formally renounced. The most important *religious* influence upon Christianity, despite the feebleness of the actual arguments found in the New Testament and elsewhere, is what orthodox Christians have always asserted it to be: the Jewish matrix from which it sprang.

However satisfactory this answer may appear to the theologian, to other reflective people it must seem weak and insufficient. Christianity and Judaism are simply too different, too far apart. Had the Christian religion been nothing but a continuation of the message of Jesus, who proclaimed the kingdom of God, there would still have been some problem, because of the difficulty in determining precisely what this expression means. But as we know, this is not the case. Alfred Loisy stated as a historical fact: 'Jésus annonçait le royaume, et c'est l'Église qui est venue': Jesus announced the Kingdom, and what came was the Church.[13] Rudolf Bultmann's formulation was more theological: Jesus, who had been the bearer of the message, was made part of its essential content: '*the proclaimer became the proclaimed*'.[14] Among the first to proclaim him was the apostle Paul. Paul's religious message was a world apart from that of Jesus, and although we may be wrong to distinguish it too sharply from Judaism, its most important features, as we shall

---

13. *L'Évangile et l'église*, 155. The author himself referred to this book as 'ce facheux opuscule' ('this irritating little book'): *Autour d'un petit livre*, 220.
14. *Theology of the New Testament*, i, 33.

see, are not easily explained simply and solely as modifications of Jewish belief. So how *are* they to be explained? This very puzzling enigma is central to my thesis and will form the subject of the next chapter. In the remaining two sections of the present chapter I shall be considering the two concepts that go to make up the term 'Comparative Religion' (the broad topic of the lectures on which this book is based).

Comparison

We have just seen that in seeking to understand early Christianity most people are content to try and explain how and why the new religion became detached from Judaism. But in the 1880s a group of like-minded scholars in Göttingen in Germany began to shake themselves free from the theological constrictions that had up to then frequently impeded the serious study of the Bible. From now on they would attempt to treat it with the same impartiality and objectivity with which they would approach any other historical source. This group of scholars, all of them still content, despite their historical interests, to be called theologians, formed what was soon known as *die religionsgeschichtliche Schule* (literally, 'the history of religion school').[15]

In some respects this is a misleading appellation, for it conceals the predominantly Christian orientation of the group. The term 'history of religion' is in fact better suited to the kind of efforts that were already being made (especially in Britain) to trace the development, one from another, of 'natural' religions. The work of Sir John Lubbock, for instance, shows how a broadly Comtean theory of human progress linked with Darwinian evolutionism can produce a theory of the *religious* evolution of mankind.[16] Lubbock saw a progression through atheism, fetishism, nature-worship or totemism, shamanism, idolatry or anthropomorphism, to ethical

15. This is generally known in English as the history of *religions* school. But Francis Watson has pointed out to me that the use of the singular 'religion' indicates the belief of the founders of the school that religion is one dimension of human life and culture manifesting itself in a variety of different ways.
16. Sir John Lubbock, *The Origins of Civilisation*. Cf. E. J. Sharpe, *Comparative Religion*, 52.

monotheism. In Britain and America, however, the preferred term for the study of religions was Comparative Religion.[17] This differed from its German equivalent both in its origins (it arose out of a broad interest in all kinds of religion) and in its bias in favour of evolutionary theory. It is easy to see the applicability of evolutionary theory to the 'higher' religions also, at any rate where one religion can be clearly seen to have emerged from another, as Christianity did from Judaism and Buddhism from Hinduism. But in searching for explanations of Christian origins the members of the Göttingen group soon began to cast their net wider, and to try and account for certain Christian rites that have no evident origins in Judaism, above all baptism and the eucharist, by demonstrating their affinity with certain Hellenistic mystery cults.

Albert Schweitzer gives the following description of this approach: 'To pursue research along history of religion lines (*religionsgeschichtlich forschern*) involves a determination to study individual religions, not in isolation, but for the purpose of investigating the mutual influences they have openly or covertly exercised on one another';[18] and he adds that the reason for the new name (*religionsgeschichtlich*) is that for a long time theology had set its face against this method of research. Schweitzer's term 'mutual influences' (*gegenseitige Beeinflussungen*) well sums up the focus of the new method. When scholars sought for parallels between Paul's theology of baptism and Hellenistic mystery religions what they were really looking for was evidence of a direct debt. The culmination of dozens of attempts to find plausible ancestors for a variety of Christian myths and rituals was Rudolf Bultmann's notorious contention that the key to understanding John's Gospel is to be found in its debt to the myths recorded in the writings of the Mandaean Gnostics.

17. E. J. Sharpe, in his very useful and informative study, regards the two terms as equivalent, passing from one to the other without warning.
18. *Geschichte der paulinischen Forschung*, 137–8. It is significant that the English translation renders the key phrase by 'to apply the methods of Comparative Religion' (*Paul and His Interpreters*, 175). By this time (1912) the two disciplines had coalesced. Classical scholarship had been interested in the question of Christianity's debt to pagan religions from as far back as the early 17th century, when Isaac Casaubon (later to lend his name to George Eliot's dusty pedant in *Middlemarch*) attempted to show that sacramental rites in the early church were influenced by the ancient mystery religions. See Bruce M. Metzger, 'Considerations'.

What Schweitzer is talking about in the passage I have just quoted is sometimes called the *genealogical* approach, a term I want to retain because it has the advantage of highlighting the debt comparative religion owes to evolutionary theory. We shall see that this very powerful theory was enthusiastically adopted by a variety of different disciplines, though in many of these cautionary voices were soon heard, advocating an alternative approach. One such voice in the field of New Testament studies was that of Adolf Deissmann. Less famous than Schweitzer, but very influential in his day, Deissmann was the first, to the best of my knowledge, to try and shift the interest of New Testament scholars away from the study of what Schweitzer calls 'mutual influences' and thus open up an alternative to the genealogical approach. Discussing the bearing of recent papyrus findings on social and religious history, 'I find', he says, that 'the questions resolve themselves for me into the alternative: is it analogy or is it genealogy?'[19] For the latter he requires what he calls 'demonstrable borrowings'; but 'where it is a case of inward emotions and religious experience and the naïve expression of these emotions and experiences in word, symbol, and act', he prefers to think of analogy, which is what he himself focuses upon.[20]

His examples fall into two categories: first, references to social customs like manumission that throw light on Paul's letters (and occasionally upon other New Testament writings as well); and secondly, verbal reminiscences that enhance our understanding of terms such as εὐαγγέλιον (gospel), διαθήκη (testament or covenant), υἱοθεσία (adoption), and so on. But these examples have little or nothing to do with analogical parallels as he himself defines these.[21] All they show is simply Paul's imaginative use of metaphor – his skill in drawing upon customs and concepts for

19. *Light from the Ancient East*, 265. I assume, though I have not been able to verify this, that Deissmann was directly or indirectly influenced by evolutionary theory.
20. Ibid., 265–6.
21. Analogical similarities are said to be those in which 'the similarities are to be regarded as arising from more or less equal experience, due to equality of what may be called psychic pitch and equality of outward conditions' (p. 265). The German term translated by 'psychic pitch' is *Gestimmtheit der Psyche* (p. 190 in the first German edition), literally 'tunedness of the psyche'. Neither the German nor the English is very perspicuous. I shall aim for more clarity in what follows.

building a new theological language. They are such a long way from Deissmann's own complex description of what he calls religious analogy that one can only surmise that he must have set off with two quite disparate programmes and failed, without realizing it, to fit them together.

Despite this unclarity, and despite the fact that Deissmann shows no interest in the mystery religions that preoccupied many of his contemporaries, it is to his basic distinction between genealogical and analogical that Bruce Metzger turned when he came to write his classic article on methodology in the study of mystery religions nearly half a century later.[22] Deissmann had brusquely set aside the genealogical approach, saying that it was the one generally adopted by amateurs. Metzger takes a very different view: he speaks of the 'merely analogical', and says that in seeking connections between one religion and another it is not enough for one agent or institution merely to remind us of another: 'Before we assert literary or traditional connection between similar elements in story and myth, we must satisfy ourselves that such communication was possible.'[23]

It may seem surprising that having watched Deissmann shrug himself free, apparently without difficulty, from the straitjacket of the genealogical method, Metzger decided to pull it out of its drawer and to submit himself unhesitatingly to its constrictions. The truth is that Metzger, like many Christian scholars, disliked the idea of establishing any analogy between the 'historical' event of Christ's death and resurrection and the mythologically inspired mystery religions. Challenging his opponents to produce evidence of any direct debt ('we must satisfy ourselves that such communication was possible'), he felt himself on much safer ground. He could deal with and dispose of claims of direct debts. To exorcise the demon of analogy his only resource was an arbitrary dismissal.[24]

Now it is not my intention, either now or later, to join in the debate on how far if at all Paul was influenced by the mystery religions. Having followed the very detailed summary of the evidence provided by A. J. M. Wedderburn in his magisterial work *Baptism*

22. See n. 18, above. Metzger simply adopts the definition cited in the previous note without attempting to defend or criticize it, or even to explain it.
23. p. 9; Metzger is actually quoting F. C. Conybeare at this point.
24. For some perceptive comments on both Deissmann and Metzger see Jonathan Z. Smith, *Drudgery Divine,* 47–50 and 106, n. 39.

and Resurrection (487 pages),[25] I tentatively conclude that one can neither prove nor disprove any debt, either direct or indirect. If Paul did indeed draw upon the mystery religions, then he succeeded in existentializing their symbolism, by the peculiar alchemy of his Christ-inspired religious imagination, into a schematic representation of the fundamental demands of Christian belief upon Christian practice.

Samuel Sandmel, in a well-known article, has warned against the danger of what he calls parallelomania: the conviction that the existence of a similarity is enough to prove a debt. [26] Yet I believe it is important to keep both options open. The possibility of a direct debt on the part of both Judaism and Christianity to more primitive religions (genealogy) is not to be excluded a priori, and at the same time we should be on the lookout for an alternative explanation (analogy) of recognized similarities. What I mean by this will become clearer after a brief investigation of the discipline that provides the model of all evolutionary theories.[27]

(a) *Biology*. Among the many thousands of books published in the nineteenth century none has had a more profound or long-lasting influence than Charles Darwin's *The Origin of Species* (1859). To this day it continues to be the object of lively discussion. Its influence has extended far beyond its own proper sphere of plant and animal biology; and although it would be an exaggeration to say that it opened up new fields of study (anthropology and philology,[28] literary criticism and the study of religions were already well-established branches of learning), it had an extraordinary impact on these and on many other disciplines besides. Here at last was a very powerful and universally applicable scientific model that they could all adapt

---

25. Subtitled *Studies in Pauline Theology against its Greco-Roman Background*.
26. 'Parallelomania'.
27. If there are those who find the distinction between analogy and genealogy unnecessary, there are others who find it insufficient. Jonathan Z. Smith, in two brilliant papers, has defended a quadripartite distinction between (1) ethnographic, (2) encyclopaedic, (3) morphological and (4) evolutionary: 'Adde Parvum'; 'In Comparison a Magic Dwells'. Useful as this distinction may be to the historian, who has to sift through and sort out an ever-growing pile (*crescens acervus*) of complicated data, I prefer to stick with the simple distinction already outlined between genealogy and analogy.
28. For a full account of the remarkable interplay, both before and after Darwin, between philology and biology see Stephen G. Alter, *Darwinism*.

to their own programmes. Scientists had already come to suspect that, as Herbert Spencer put it, the human race had been developed 'from some lower race'.[29] Now these suspicions were confirmed and, what is more, the hypothesis was seen to hold good throughout the animal and vegetable kingdoms.

There is no need to say anything more here on the subject of *genealogical* resemblances. Even if some of the links are still missing, direct descent evidently implies direct causality. But another different kind of resemblance is also of great interest, the kind brought about through what biologists call *convergent* evolution. A wolf's skull, it seems, is scarcely distinguishable from that of a Tasmanian devil. Yet the wolf and the devil are of different families, one a dog and the other a dasyure (so named for its bushy tail). The Australian sun-bird (of the family *Nectariniidae*) looks and behaves very like an American humming-bird (of the family *Trochilidae*); and the *euphorbia canariensis* of the spurge family looks remarkably like the *sereus validus* of the cactus family. In these examples from the vegetable and animal kingdoms we have to do not just with different species but with different families.[30]

If all you are interested in is genealogy, then of course each of these instances can be accounted for individually by tracing its ancestry back in the ordinary way. But since there is no *direct* evolutionary chain linking them together, then the resemblance between them must result from their similar response to common environmental factors. Part of the explanation is still in the genes; another part must lie in the circumstances in which each of the two members of these strikingly similar pairs developed – the dry desert air, for example, in which a member of the spurge family came to resemble a cactus. Here, no less than in the case of genealogical similarities, the Darwinian theory of natural selection gives a plausible explanation of what, following the biologists, I shall call *convergent* resemblances.

(b) Let us now return to our starting-point: comparative *literature*. Towards the end of the nineteenth century this branch of study had

---

29. *An Autobiography*, i, 176. Spencer says that he first began to lean to this hypothesis in 1840, after reading Charles Lyell's *Principles of Geology*.
30. I owe these botanical examples to Roger Hall.

come to enjoy great prestige. In 1896 this led to the establishment of a chair of comparative literature in the University of Lyons (Oxford, as we know, had to wait until 1994), and shortly afterwards a certain Ferdinand Brunetière (well-known in his day) began to give lectures on this subject at the École Normale in Paris. Brunetière had come under the influence of Hippolyte Taine, who had previously advanced some amazingly outré ideas about the evolution of the arts, having actually urged art historians to approach their subject in the manner of a botanist.[31] Brunetière's contribution to an international conference held in Paris in 1900 provoked the mockery of a British critic named C. Gregory Smith who, the following year, launched a no-holds-barred attack on what I have called the *genealogical* approach. Prefacing an anonymous contribution to *Blackwood's Magazine*[32] with a phrase from Molière's *Misanthrope*: 'Mon Dieu! Laissons là vos comparaisons fades' (Let's drop your stale comparisons),[33] he went on to comment on the current tendency of history, politics, theology and ethics to relate themselves to what he called, significantly, 'their own particular ape', and to enjoy 'the new-found delights of continuity, "evolution" and natural law'. Literary criticism, he observed, 'had perforce to join in, if only to preserve its imperilled honour. Why not evolution of poetic form as well as of marsupials?'[34]

After scoffing at Brunetière's ideas concerning the genealogical approach to literature, Gregory Smith proceeded to offer a suggestion of his own: 'May there not be a comparative interest in things whose only connection is from analogy, or even in forms and motives between which there may be not only no admitted or known connection, but not even an obvious hint of likeness?'[35] It may be hard to see any advantage in comparing things 'with no obvious hint of likeness', but the proposal to adopt an analogical approach has some merit. Why, for instance, should we not compare the fate of the daughter of Jephtha in Judges 11 with that of Idomeneo, as Mozart called his version of the story, or with the similar

---

31. 'Aesthetic science is like botany …. it is a kind of botanical method, applied not to plants, but to the works of man', *Philosophy of Art*, 21. Cf. pp. 15–16.
32. 'The Foible of Comparative Literature'.
33. Act 1, Scene 1, line 101.
34. 'Foible', 39.
35. Ibid., 43.

(though not identical) legend of Iphigeneia (as Handel did in his oratorio *Jephtha* when he gave Jephtha's daughter, unnamed in the Bible, the name of Iphis)? Since we cannot reasonably suppose any knowledge of the Jewish story on the part of the author of the Greek legends, or vice versa, we must assume that the idea came to each of them independently. However that may be, there are many literary *forms* or *genres*, such as epic and comedy, the love-song and the lament, that have developed spontaneously in a variety of human societies simply in virtue of our common humanity. There is no shortage of convergent resemblances in the world of literature.

(c) For a final example of our two different kinds of resemblance we turn to *anthropology*. Since from a biologist's point of view the human race is simply the most recently evolved species of a family of apes, it is not surprising that anthropology from its inception enthusiastically adopted the principles of Darwinism. E. B. Tylor, who later, in 1884, became the first person to occupy an academic post in anthropology anywhere in the world (with the title of Reader in Anthropology in the University of Oxford), introduced his work *Primitive Culture* (1871) with the assertion that 'A first step in the study of civilization is to dissect it into details and to classify those in their proper groups.... What this task is like, may be almost perfectly illustrated by comparing those details of culture with the species of animals and plants as studied by the naturalist. To the ethnographer the bow and arrow is a species, the habit of flattening children's skulls is a species, the practice of reckoning numbers by ten is a species. The geographical distribution of these things, and their transmission from region to region, have to be studied as the naturalist studies the geography of his botanical and zoological species.'[36]

Tylor's successor, R. R. Marett, was an even more enthusiastic evolutionist. In his popularizing little book *Anthropology* he defines anthropology as 'the whole history of man as fixed and pervaded by the idea of evolution. Man in evolution – that is the subject in its full reach.'[37] He confesses that his initial description is so short that 'it is bound to be rather formal and colourless. To put some body into it,

36. *Primitive Culture*, 7.
37. *Anthropology*, 7.

however, it is necessary to breathe but a single word. That word is Darwin.' 'Anthropology', he adds, 'stands or falls with the working hypothesis, derived from Darwinism, of a fundamental kinship and continuity amid change between all the forms of human life.'[38]

The genealogical view of the role of anthropology did not go unchallenged. As early as 1896 we find the American anthropologist Franz Boas protesting against a 'new school' in Germany (followers of Adolf Bastian) and America (led by D. G. Brinton), which was interpreting identities or similarities of culture 'as results of the uniform working of the human mind'.[39] Bastian's 'much misunderstood elementary idea', he says, is that the human mind is so formed that it spontaneously invents ideas, customs and beliefs that are of universal occurrence, or accepts them whenever they are offered to it.[40] Here, applied to anthropology, we have a concept closely resembling what biologists call convergent evolution. But whereas in biology this fits comfortably within the original paradigm, the comparative method employed by anthropologists, to the evident disapproval of Boas, has broken away from evolutionary theory. Much later this method was revived and strongly urged by two twentieth-century anthropologists, very unlike but equally influential: A. R. Radcliffe-Brown and Claude Lévi-Strauss.

Besides the suggestion that the occurrence of the same custom may be ascribed to heredity, the idea that it could arise from environment is not foreign to anthropology either. Thus E. B. Tylor, in an early work, affirms that 'sometimes it may be ascribed to the working of men's minds under like conditions, and sometimes it is a proof of blood relationship or intercourse, direct or indirect, between the races among whom it's found. In the one case *it has no historical value whatever*, while in the other it has this value in a high degree, and the ever-recurring problem is how to distinguish between the two.'[41] Here is an implicit rejection of the search for what I have called convergent resemblances.

In a lecture delivered in South Africa in 1923 Radcliffe-Brown argued for a clear distinction between the goals and methods of

---

38. Ibid., 8.
39. 'Limitations', 270.
40. Ibid., 272.
41. *Researches*, 5 (my italics). Cf. pp. 125, 376ff.

ethnology and those of what he proposed to call social anthropology, leaving to the former the *historical* task of tracing the stages of the development of a culture or institution as far back as its origins, and reserving for the latter the *inductive* task of formulating 'the general laws that underlie the phenomena of culture'.[42] Nearly thirty years later, in a lecture given in London in 1951, the same scholar gave a practical instance of the inductive or comparative method. He had discovered that certain aboriginal tribes in New South Wales divided their population into two, one half named after the eagle-hawk, the other after the crow. The North American Indian tribe of the Haida similarly divides itself into two groups, named in their case after the eagle and the raven. Now there are two ways of inter-preting these data: 'If we accept the criteria formulated by the diffusionists . . . we have here what they would say is evidence of a historical connection between Australia and the Pacific coast of North America.'[43] Radcliffe-Brown himself rejected this suggestion, arguing instead that the eagle-hawk/crow division of the Darling River tribes, like the eagle/crow division of the North American Haida, represents a particular example 'of a widespread type of the application of a certain structural principle' wherein the relation between the two groups 'is one which separates and also unites, and . . . gives us a rather special type of social integration', involving 'the union of opposites'.[44] When he goes on to compare this union of opposites with the philosophical oppositions of Heraclitus or the Pythagoreans, and the Chinese principle of Yin-Yang, we may infer that from the particular instances he selects he is hoping to be able to draw much more far-reaching conclusions concerning 'the nature and functioning of social relationships and social structures based on what has here been called "opposition"'.[45]

Here and elsewhere Radcliffe-Brown's work both influences and anticipates the even more ambitious project of Claude Lévi-Strauss,

---

42. 'Methods', 8. In a lecture entitled *Concerning Parallels* H. J. Rose gives an able defence of what he calls the comparativist as opposed to the 'historical' method. 'The greatest service anthropological parallels have done us', he concludes, 'is to give a more exact and detailed meaning to the pithy maxim that men are much the same, the world over' (p. 23).
43. 'Comparative Method', 111.
44. Ibid., 123.
45. Ibid., 126–7.

as the latter generously acknowledges in his seminal study, *Anthropologie structurale*, first published in 1958. Responding, towards the beginning of this book, to the evolutionary theories of E. B. Tylor, he makes the sardonic rejoinder that whereas a horse engenders a horse, an axe never engenders another axe, and that in any case a European fork and a Polynesian fork, reserved for ritual meals, no more constitute a common species than do a European drinking straw and the tubes used for ritual drinking by certain American Indians.[46] Like Radcliffe-Brown, Lévi-Strauss wants to wriggle free from evolutionary theory, but is equally anxious to maintain the validity of a comparative method in anthropology – it will turn out to be structuralism, a method he was to employ systematically in a series of large and impressive volumes.

The debate between the early partisans of the genealogical approach and those who, intrigued by analogical resemblances between different cultures, preferred the so-called comparative method is less in evidence nowadays. Interest appears to have waned in both of these approaches. The study of origins (the historical method assigned by Radcliffe-Brown to ethnography) has been displaced by a concern to examine each culture *in situ*. And it may be partly the same concern that makes many present-day anthropologists unwilling to risk muddying the water with egregious comparisons. What is more, Lévi-Strauss's dazzlingly clever structuralist patterns, whilst continuing to impress, have ceased to convince. Broadly speaking, then, the comparative method is no longer widely favoured among social anthropologists.[47] Yet in principle the anthropologist's search for genealogical links and his quest for cultural parallels remain just as valid as the biologist's continued recognition of evolution on the one hand and of convergent evolution on the other. And the same is true of the study of religions.

Worth adding, in conclusion, is the observation that whether we are looking for genealogical links or analogical similarities, here as in all human enquiry the nature of the search is going to be determined by the kind of result we are expecting. Of course it is possible to be

---

46. *Anthropologie structurale*, 7.
47. Prominent exceptions include Nick Allen, Ioan Lewis and Jonathan Z. Smith, though the last-named might disown the appellation anthropologist. The extent of my debt to these scholars will become evident in what follows.

struck by resemblances (by the fact, say, that the bee, the bat and the budgerigar all have wings); but once you start probing for a *reason* then not only the methods you use but also the very questions you ask are going to be coloured by your own interests. Jonathan Z. Smith writes in this connection of 'the illusion of passive observation (what Nietzsche has termed "the myth of the immaculate perception")'. 'Comparison', he concludes, 'does not necessarily tell us how things "are" ' but 'how things might be conceived .... *A comparison is a disciplined exaggeration in the service of knowledge*. It lifts out and strongly marks certain features as being of possible intellectual significance, expresses the rhetoric of their being "like" in some stipulated fashion. Comparison provides the means by which we "re-vision" phenomena as *our* data in order to solve *our* theoretical problems.'[48]

Religion

(a) *Religion and revelation*. In the final section of this chapter I want to draw two distinctions, first between religion and revelation and secondly between religion and theology. 'The "Christian religion" is one predicate for a subject which may have other predicates. It is a species within a genus in which there may be other species. Apart from and alongside Christianity there is Judaism, Islam, Buddhism, Shintoism and every kind of animistic, totemistic, ascetic, mystical and prophetic religion…. From this standpoint Christianity is singular but certainly not unique.' So, rightly, Karl Barth.[49] This is the first of two meanings given to the term 'religion' in this book, meanings that are not always explicitly distinguished. It is the one employed by Henry Wilde. Wilde felt able to distinguish between the 'higher' and the 'lower' religions of mankind. Although I have no wish to preserve this particular distinction, like Karl Barth I regard Christianity and Judaism, no less than shamanism and totemism, as religions. Religion, in those societies that have one, is an integral element of people's lives, both as individuals and as members of a community. It is one of the commonest and most

48. *Drudgery Divine*, 51–2; my italics.
49. *Church Dogmatics*, i, 281.

important ways in which human beings attempt to make sense of their own existence. The term covers a variety of practices and beliefs, all relating somehow or other to unseen powers, some feared, some honoured.[50] If we leave aside the well-attested phenomenon of conversion, any particular set of such practices and beliefs is generally absorbed unreflectively by children born into the society to which it belongs and which it helps to characterize. Paul's first acquaintance with the laws, the legends and the wisdom of Israel will have been at his mother's knee. The same is true of Jesus, and also of Philo and Josephus.

Karl Barth would agree with all of this. But Barth thought that 'human' religions were all superseded by (Christian) revelation. The opening quotation comes early on in a section of his *Church Dogmatics* entitled 'The Revelation of God as the *Aufhebung* of Religion': 'For where we think that revelation can be compared or equated with religion we have not understood it as revelation. Within the problem that now engrosses us it can be understood only where *a priori* and with no possible alternative we accept its superiority over human religion, a superiority which does not allow us even to consider religion except in the light of revelation', which 'is understood only when we expect from it, and from it alone, the first and the last word about religion'.[51]

This high-handed dismissal of religion, brooking neither disagreement nor debate, could safely be ignored, were it not for the fact that Barth brings the same arrogance into his discussion of Paul, notably in the famous introduction to his commentary on Romans. Here is Barth's comment on Adolf Jülicher: 'How quick he is to treat a matter as explained, when it is said to belong to the religious

---

50. Ending a comprehensive survey of the changing meanings of the term 'religion' from the 16th century onwards, Jonathan Z. Smith concludes that 'religion' is not a native term but one created by scholars for their own purposes; it is therefore theirs to define: 'It is a second-order, generic concept that plays the same role in establishing a disciplinary horizon that a concept such as "language" plays in linguistics or "culture" plays in anthropology' ('Religion, Religions, Religious', 281–2). I am aware that my own description of religion will not please everyone, but that is beside the point.

51. *Church Dogmatics*, i, 295. In the published English translation *Aufhebung* is rendered by 'Abolition'. This, as Francis Watson has pointed out to me, is a dreadful distortion of a word that implies the raising of something up to a higher level. Nonetheless, Barth clearly regards the 'lower' religions of mankind as superseded by Christian revelation.

thought, feeling, experience, conscience, or conviction – of Paul! And, when this does not at once fit, or is manifestly impossible, how easily he leaps, like some bold William Tell, right out of the Pauline boat, and rescues himself by attributing what Paul has said, to his "personality", to the experience on the road to Damascus (an episode which seems capable of providing at any moment an explanation of every impossibility), to later Judaism, to Hellenism, or, in fact, to any exegetical semi-divinity of the ancient world!'[52] Barth clearly deplores any attempt to see Paul as a *religious* figure, and it is his powerful and authoritative rejection of religion as a fit study for Christian theology that was largely responsible for the rapid demise of the history of religions school soon after the First World War.

It might be possible to ignore Barth's arrogant refusal to allow any consideration of Paul's religion were it not for the fact that one of the most highly-respected of present-day New Testament scholars has adopted an almost identical stance in a recent commentary on Galatians.

One of J. Louis Martyn's aims in this commentary is to dispel any impression that Paul is guilty of what he calls 'anti-Judaism'. Yet according to Martyn this letter is *anti-religious* and shows that Paul is 'consistently concerned to say that the advent of Christ is the end of religion. With his call, then, he neither remained in the religion of Judaism nor transferred to a new religion, from which vantage point he could comparatively denigrate his earlier religion.'[53] So Judaism is a religion, but incipient Christianity, as represented by Paul, is not? What can this mean? Some explanation is perhaps to be found in Martyn's definition of religion as 'the various cultic means – always involving the distinction of sacred from profane – by which human beings seek to know and to be happily related to the gods or God. Religion is thus a human enterprise that Paul sharply

---

52. *Romans*, 7–8. (Note that what Barth calls 'later Judaism' we should now call early Judaism.) The extract is from the famous preface to the second German edition (1921). Barth is responding to Jülicher's review of the first edition of his *Römerbrief* in *Die Christliche Welt* 34 (1920), 453–7; 466–9. The response is curiously wide of the mark. Jülicher attacks Barth for failing to observe the most elementary rules of critical exegesis, for blatant mistranslations and misinterpretations of the Greek text, for a lack of historical sense. Most seriously, he accuses him of an actual contempt for history. There is nothing in his review to warrant the charges Barth makes in return.

53. *Galatians*, 64.

distinguishes from God's apocalypse.'[54] This is remarkably close to Barth, except that for Barth's term 'revelation' Martyn substitutes 'apocalypse' – wrongly, in my view, for by translating ἀποκάλυψις as 'apocalypse' instead of 'revelation', which is what it really means, Martyn invests the Greek word with a significance it did not have – not, at any rate, before it came to be used, later in the century, as the title of the biblical book Catholics know as *The Apocalypse*.[55]

The key phrase is 'the distinction of sacred from profane'. For Martyn what distinguishes Paul's new stance from Judaism (as well as from Christianity?) is the *absence* of this distinction, which is how human beings mark out their conceptual universe. 'In the sense in which I employ the word,' he says, 'religion is a human enterprise' – yet another Barthian sentiment.[56] By contrast, Martyn speaks of God '*calling Paul into existence* as an apostle of Jesus Christ'. This call is not, for Paul, a religious event, but 'the form taken in his own case by God's calling into existence the new creation'.[57]

This is surely nonsense. Martyn's attempt to insulate Galatians from the kind of enquiry pursued in the present book is just as arbitrary as Barth's rejection of Jülicher in his commentary on Romans. But whereas Barth is first and foremost a theologian, Martyn is an exegete. To allow one's reading of a text not only to be coloured by one's theological prejudices but to be determined and dictated by them is to abandon any pretence of scholarly objectivity.

(b) *Religion and theology*. Children soon start asking questions about what they are taught. Their questions are often quite searching. We may assume that the number of people who *never* reflect on religious matters is quite small; and anthropologists have shown that behind the beliefs and practices of what we think of as primitive societies lie complex and intricate patterns of thought. This is what Lévi-Strauss calls *la pensée sauvage*.[58] But neither this nor the children's

54. *Theological Issues*, 300.
55. See Morton Smith, 'On the History'.
56. *Galatians*, 37, n. 67.
57. *Theological Issues*, p. 164.
58. *La Pensée sauvage*. [Translated into English as *The Savage Mind* (London, 1966). 'Mind' is wrong; 'savage' as an adjective is not quite right; and, more excusably, the sly allusion to the wild pansy (prominent on the front cover) is missing altogether. Challenged to produce an alternative, the best I can offer is *The Way Savages Think* or, more simply (if we let go of 'savage'), *Primitive Thinking*.]

questioning amounts to what we call *theology*, a term that implies a more extended and (usually) systematic reflection on religious matters.

Was Paul a theologian? In one sense, yes, though his thought is a good deal less *systematic* than many New Testament scholars would have us believe. He undoubtedly reflected long and hard both upon his own experiences, and upon the problems of the various Christian communities to whom he wrote. It is not altogether wrong to speak of the outcome of his reflections as theology. But he starts out as a *religious* thinker in the more primitive sense: the *subject matter* of his reflections, above all the experience of his conversion, belongs not to theology but to religion. So this is the second sense in which I will be using the word, of Paul's religious *experiences*, and of his gut reactions to them.

The distinction between religion and theology that I wish to establish is not new. In a study devoted exclusively to Paul, Adolf Deissmann speaks of him as a 'religious genius', one of the few men to whom this much abused expression may legitimately be applied,[59] having previously declared that what is best in him 'belongs not to theology but to religion'.[60] In a later study, objecting to certain doctrinaire tendencies in nineteenth-century investigations of Paul's teaching on the grounds that they transfer Paul from what he calls 'his original sphere of vital religion' into the secondary sphere of theology, he urges that 'we must try to understand him first in his primitive religious originality'.[61]

In his book *The Mysticism of Paul the Apostle*[62] (to which the general title of my own book is intended to allude) Albert Schweitzer similarly insists on the primacy of religion over theology. Yet he shows how hard it is to maintain this stance when he compares Paul with great religious *thinkers*, and a large part of his book is taken up with an argument designed to trace the logical consequences of Paul's views on eschatology – a paradigm example of a

---

After an elaborate argument Lévi-Strauss concludes (p. 348) that 'En ce sens, on a pu la définer [sc. la pensée sauvage] comme pensée analogique': primitive peoples think *analogically*.

59. *St Paul*, 82.
60. Ibid., 6.
61. *Religion*, 154ff.
62. See Excursus IV

theological discussion. In the seminal work to which I have already alluded, *Paul and Palestinian Judaism*, E. P. Sanders takes the confusion even further. Setting out to compare Paul's *religion* with that of Palestinian Judaism, he opts for the term 'pattern of religion', which, he says, though not the same as speculative theology, '*does* have to do with *thought*, with the *understanding* that lies behind religious behaviour, not just with the externals of religious behaviour'.[63] This is tricky. Unquestionably, as I have just remarked, religion is (almost) always accompanied by thought. But the *kind* of thought Sanders focuses upon turns out to be what the scholars whom he is setting out to refute (and indeed almost everybody else) call theology. Sanders's preferred term is 'pattern of religion'. He has already admitted that this 'has largely to do with the items which a systematic theology classifies under "soteriology" [i.e. theories of salvation and redemption]',[64] although he continues to regard 'pattern of religion' as the more satisfactory expression. Yet towards the end of his book he admits that behind the differences of scheme, motif and formulation with which he has been concerned 'there may lie differences of religious experience'. However, he concludes, 'this is a matter which is much more opaque to research than is thought, and we must be content with analysing how religion appears in Jewish and Pauline thought'.[65]

Of course Sanders is right to assert that religious experience is more opaque to research than thought is; and he is right too when he implies that Paul was not a systematic theologian. But if our primary concern is with Paul's *religion* we should focus our attention not upon his published thoughts but upon the much less accessible experiences that underlie them. The bulk of what is generally thought of as his theology may be usefully regarded as his own *interpretation* of his religious experiences. I am not of course suggesting that Paul's original experiences came to him uninterpreted. One of the principal concerns of this book will be to enquire into the conditions of possibility of the experience on the Damascus road. But his letters, I would contend, are the product of subsequent reflection. In the first place, he is looking back on the Jewish tradition that

---

63. *Paul and Palestinian Judaism*, 18.
64. Ibid., 17.
65. Ibid., 549.

furnished him with the contextual grid in which his own experiences were set.[66] Secondly, he is absorbing the impact of what he himself refers to as his call but which many others see as a conversion. Finally, he is reflecting on the significance of both of these for the religious life of the new communities he had founded. This interpretative theology, or theological interpretation, is his way of making sense of his own life. So authoritative has it become that most of us accept it unquestioningly as the key, and indeed the only possible key, to understanding. We look at Paul's life through his own eyes and read it on his own terms. My intention in this book is to find an alternative key by probing beneath the standard reading in a search for a *religious* explanation of Paul's life and letters.

The distinction I want to draw between religion and theology is not intended as a slur on theology per se, or as a criticism of what seems to me to be the chief preoccupation of most present-day Pauline scholarship.[67] There can be no doubt of the theological importance of Paul's writings. Paul stands between first-century Judaism (not quite the same as it would be after it regrouped its forces in the wake of two revolts against Rome) and nascent Christianity. Between these two religions, and representing a major force in shaping the latter, lies the small but remarkable corpus of Paul's writings, which may be regarded as a kind of doctrinal blueprint of the new religion, even though it would be centuries before it was removed from the drawing-board, and even then the most famous of those who worked from it, Augustine and Luther, probably misread it. Small wonder, then, that theologians continue to pay it so much attention. But theirs is not the only possible approach.

66. This will be argued much more fully in Chapter 4.
67. I think of this as a vast ocean liner, steaming sedately onwards in the direction she has taken for the best part of the 20th century. To attempt to force her onto a different course with the power generated by one small book would be both misguided and futile. Her momentum is simply too great. (Nor is there any sign of an iceberg looming on the horizon.) And even if the skipper of the little tug-boat were to succeed in attaching a rope to her he would scarcely expect to be invited on board for drinks in the captain's cabin.

2

Paul the Enigma

This is where it all began. In 1994 I read a paper at a seminar in Wolfson College, Oxford, with the title, half-quizzical, half-whimsical, of 'Was St Paul a shaman?' Some months later, having delivered the same paper at a conference in St Andrews, I was urged by the conference organizer, Philip Esler, to allow it to be published along with the papers of the other speakers.[1] I resisted this suggestion because I knew very well how much work had to be done to make it both tough enough to deflect the barbed darts of hostile reviewers and buoyant enough to prevent it from sinking without trace to lie lost forever among the multitude of leaden works of scholarship that litter the ocean floor of academia.

Though not quite the same as the original paper, this chapter is still only a sketch of what is essentially a cumulative argument, to be built up as the book proceeds. The very first draft of the paper had an even more provocative title: 'St Paul, sham, showman or shaman?' Of course Paul was not a sham, but showman he may well have been.[2]

Much later I came to see that 'Was St Paul a shaman?', though certainly less provocative than 'Sham, showman or shaman?', still would not do. For the simple and honest answer to the question 'Was St Paul a shaman?' is 'Not really'. Shamans are not missionaries, and their authority is restricted, as Paul's was not, to the members of

---

1. See *Modelling Early Christianity*, ed. Philip F. Esler (1995).
2. Whilst preparing the talk I came across a book by Rogan P. Taylor entitled *The Death and Resurrection Show: From Shaman to Superstar*, which claimed (not very convincingly) some sort of etymological link between the word 'shaman' and the action of showing – though there is undoubtedly some affinity between showmanship and shamanship.

easily recognizable and easily circumscribed social groups – tribes, communities or villages.

On the other hand, the structural resemblances between Paul's career and that of certain shamans are, as we shall see, quite striking. Perhaps there is another, weaker way of stating the thesis, one less exposed to the objections that can be levelled against the stronger formulation.

The quest for the historical Paul

Instead of turning directly to the topic of shamanism, I want to move towards this by retracing the four steps or stages in my quest for the historical Paul.

The first is an essay by someone whom I taught over twenty years ago and who later became a distinguished anthropologist (Michael Bourdillon). The essay, dated February 1976, and entitled 'Thoughts of the spirit', begins by summarizing the work of two anthropologists, Ioan Lewis[3] and Robin Horton.[4] Basing himself on Lewis's study of affliction-cults, Bourdillon suggested that if the pattern discernible in these can be applied to belief in the Holy Spirit in New Testament times, then 'one would expect to find the concept of Spirit at first closely associated with affliction and healing, later becoming more associated with teaching and prophecy, and ultimately being dissociated from clearly visible signs'.

This essay struck me as original, disturbing, and, above all, challenging, so much so that I actually kept a copy of it (not a regular practice of mine).

Bourdillon's ideas ticked away at the back of my mind until, some ten years later, I was reminded of them by a typically provocative and acerbic lecture on 'Paul the Possessed' by the brilliant and cantankerous Morton Smith, arguing (rightly, I am convinced) in a lecture in Oxford that New Testament scholars, accustomed to thinking of Paul as a theologian, have generally failed to pay

3. *Ecstatic Religion* (1971). There is now a second, revised edition (London, 1989). See too the same author's *Religion in Context* (1986).
4. 'On the rationality of conversion'.

sufficient attention to what one might call the crudely religious elements in his life and experience.[5]

I cannot now recall whether Morton Smith alluded to the work that finally decided me to embark upon the present line of investigation. This was the first book of the great Hermann Gunkel: *Die Wirkungen des heiligen Geistes nach der populären Anschauung der apostolischen Zeit und der Lehre des Apostels Paulus*,[6] published well over a century ago in Göttingen, the birthplace of the history of religions school. One of the statements in that book is central, indeed pivotal: 'To the apostle [i.e. Paul] his life was an enigma whose solution lay for him in his teaching regarding the πνεῦμα [spirit]: to us the apostle's teaching regarding the πνεῦμα is an enigma whose solution is to be found in his life and only in his life.'[7] Although he pinpointed the enigma accurately enough (it gives the present chapter its title), Gunkel failed to pursue the solution, leaving that task to others. Yet what he does say exhibits characteristic insight. He argued that the concept of spirit that Paul inherited was of an undifferentiated supernatural force, with the emphasis upon the stunning and spectacular, but that he gradually came to place the emphasis instead upon the spirit's role in building up the Christian community. His conflict with the Corinthians was due to their persistence in laying stress on the miraculous and charismatic side of the spirit's activity. (Bourdillon had come remarkably close to this insight.)

There is nothing in Gunkel's work to suggest any connection between Paul's concept of spirit and the extraordinarily widespread religious phenomenon known as shamanism. The impulse to introduce shamanism into the equation came from the book by Ioan Lewis that Bourdillon had mentioned years earlier: *Ecstatic Religion*. On opening this I was surprised to find, embedded in a series of

5. After completing this book I was informed (by Christopher Shell) that at the time of his death Morton Smith was working on a book to be entitled 'Paul the Possessed'. The unfinished manuscript, which reportedly contains very little unpublished material, is now in the possession of the Jewish Theological Seminary, New York.

6. Göttingen, 1888. There is a rather unsatisfactory English translation: *The Influence of the Holy Spirit* (Philadelphia, 1979). ['Influence' is already wrong: the meaning of *Wirkung* is much closer to 'impact', and if a plural is required the best rendering is probably 'effects'.]

7. p. 84 (ET, pp. 105–6).

photographs of spirit possession ranging over several continents, not only a rather poor reproduction, from the *Très Riches Heures du Duc de Berry*, of a picture representing Christ casting out a devil from a possessed woman, but also a detail from a twelfth-century mosaic portraying St Paul struck blind on the road to Damascus. To the caption under this picture the author had added this comment: 'The inspired priest or shaman is usually called to his vocation by a traumatic experience.'[8]

Shamans and shamanism

The obvious next step is to try and find out something more about the phenomenon of shamanism, but here one finds oneself confronted by an impossibly vast *embarras de richesses*: like a child in a sweet shop, the most one can do here is to pick out a handful of the more succulent-looking delicacies. I propose to begin with a brief quotation from one of the acknowledged experts on the subject and follow this with some equally brief comments of my own. This will give us a start and a direction. Next I shall cite more extensively from another book, selected for some remarkable parallels with the life of Paul. In the third place I want to sketch very summarily the life and work of a Christian saint in sixth-century Anatolia, and I will conclude with some reflections on the career of a twentieth-century Christian shaman in North America.

(a) Historians of religion agree that the paradigm example of a shamanistic society is to be found among the Tungus of Eastern Siberia, to whom we owe the word 'shaman' itself. Here is what an acknowledged Russian expert has to say of them:

> the term 'shaman' refers to persons of both sexes who have mastered spirits, who at their will can introduce these spirits into themselves and use their power over the spirits in their own interests, particularly helping other people who suffer from the

---

8. Photographs between pp. 112 and 113. The mosaic in question is the first in a series on the life of St Paul that graces the Palatine Chapel, housed in the splendid royal residence of the Norman kings of Sicily.

spirits; in such a capacity they may possess a complex of special methods for dealing with the spirits.[9]

The essence of shamanhood is twofold: it has an individual aspect insofar as it involves the shaman's own experience (which is always frighteningly solitary) and a social aspect, for the shaman's authority depends upon an ability to persuade other people of his or her exceptional gifts. In both aspects the dominant characteristic, as the quotation from Shirokogoroff tells us, has to do with the world of the spirits.

Broadly speaking, the lives of shamans can be divided up into three stages or periods: first their early life; secondly their call and the experiences that accompany it, usually involving trance or ecstasy; and thirdly their subsequent career, in which they figure as people of power and authority in their own society, in control of the spirits by which they themselves used to be dominated and, frequently enough, tormented.

(b) A not untypical picture comes from a book about shamanism in Japan:

> The shaman is, first, a person who receives a supernatural gift from the spirit world. The gift is bestowed usually by a single spiritual being, who afterwards becomes his guardian and guide, sometimes even his spiritual wife. Before this critical moment in his life, the future shaman suffers for months or even years from a peculiar sickness, sometimes loosely called arctic hysteria.[10] The symptoms range from physical pains – racking headaches, vomiting, aches in the joints and back – to more hysterical or neurasthenic behaviour of wandering off into the forest, falling asleep or fainting for long periods, or hiding from the light.
>
> These symptoms usually disappear, however, at the critical moment of initiation. This violent interior experience often takes the form of a vision, in which a single supernatural being appears to him and commands him to abandon his former life and

---

9. M. S. Shirokogoroff, *The Psychomental Complex of the Tungus*, 269.
10. 'Arctic' because the phenomenon was first observed among the arctic peoples of Eastern Siberia.

become a shaman. Thereafter his soul is snatched out of his body and carried off to another realm of the cosmos, either before or above the human world. There he undergoes the fearful experience of being killed and revived. He sees his own body dismembered, the flesh scraped or boiled off the bones to the point where he can contemplate his own skeleton. He then sees new flesh and new organs clothed over his bones, so that in effect he is remade, resuscitated as a new person.

From this terrifying but characteristically initiatory experience he emerges a changed character. His former oddity and sickness gives way to a new dignity and assurance of personality, strengthened by special powers conferred by the guardian spirit who calls him to his new life and which thereafter enable him to render special services to his community.

Foremost among these powers is the ability to put himself at will into altered states of consciousness in which he can communicate directly with spiritual beings. He can fall into the state of trance, for example, in which his soul separates itself from his body and travels to realms of the cosmos inaccessible to the physical body. By travelling upwards to the multiple layers of heavens, for example, he can acquire from the spiritual inhabitants there useful knowledge of hidden things. By travelling downwards to the underworld he can rescue the souls of sick people, kidnapped and taken there by spirits. From his knowledge of the topography of these other worlds, moreover, he can act as guide to the souls of the newly dead, who without his help might well lose their way along the unfamiliar road.[11]

(c) Theodore of Sykeon, who lived as a shaman but was regarded as a saint, was born around the middle of the sixth century AD and died in 612. Sykeon is, or rather was, a village on the river Siberis in central Anatolia, about ninety kilometres west of Ankara.

Theodore lived a life of astonishing asceticism and deprivation, which started when he was twelve. For two years he managed to find time and space for periods of fasting and solitary prayer in his own

11. Carmen Blacker, *The Catalpa Bow*, 24–5. Had this book been written in these more gender-conscious days the author would undoubtedly have been on her guard against the exclusive use of the masculine pronoun.

home; but at the age of fourteen he moved out of the house to a chapel of St George nearby, where he dug himself a cave in which to live. St George soon became his spirit familiar, to whom he could turn for guidance on the path to holiness and for counsel at critical moments of his life.

At the age of sixteen Theodore left the chapel and withdrew into the wilderness, where he dug himself a larger cave on the mountainside, walled up the entrance and hid from the world, kept alive by regular visits from his only confidant, a cleric, who brought him food.

One episode during this time is particularly significant: 'Theodore had fallen ill, possessed himself by a demon. As he lay sick he was visited in a dream by St George, who asked him who had brought him to this state. Theodore pointed out the black shape of the demon standing before him. St George chased the apparition away and brought Theodore to his feet',[12] and from that moment Theodore himself had the power to expel demons and to cure the sick. In this brief episode we get a glimpse, however blurred, of the critical turning-point in Theodore's life, the one that marked his passage from the 'arctic hysteria' mentioned by Carmen Blacker to the spiritual authority that marks the true shaman.

Soon afterwards, when he was still only eighteen, Theodore was at last hunted down by his relatives and dragged from his cave, filthy, stinking and worm-ridden, looking like a corpse. Refusing to accompany his relatives home, he returned to the chapel of St George. The following day he was visited by the bishop, who with some difficulty managed to treat his horrible sores and after the briefest of preliminaries ordained him to the priesthood.

Together with his new powers, the ordination marked the conclusion of his period of initiation as a Christian shaman. It also brought him recognition by the villagers of Sykeon, who treated him as a celebrity, and later by the inhabitants of the whole region. He enjoyed immense authority, and for the remainder of his life was

12. This quotation comes from Stephen Mitchell's book on Anatolia, ii, 138. Mitchell devotes an entire chapter (the last in his book) to the life of St Theodore, which he treats with characteristic thoroughness. I am greatly indebted to it. The parallels with shamanism have not escaped him, and his notes include many valuable references to the secondary literature.

constantly being sought out with requests to cure illnesses and exorcise demons. Occasionally he even performed nature miracles, bringing rain or causing rivers to subside. I will conclude with a description of just one of his many exorcisms, far from the most spectacular: 'A cleric from a monastery in the territory of Nicomedia was seized by a demon as he emerged from the public bath-house holding a phial of oil and wrapped in towels. Catching sight of the saint in the distance, he threw the towel turban off his head, and ran up in terrible agitation. Theodore struck his chest with his hand and said, "I am speaking to you, demon; give back some sense to this body and do not occupy it, but go straightaway before me to the monastery of St Autonomus." The man was hurled to the ground, and remained possessed until the next day, continuing to rail at Theodore until the spirit admitted defeat and emerged from his victim with the words, "I am leaving him, iron-eater" (σιδηροφάγε).'[13]

(d) Granville Oral Roberts was born in 1918, just outside Bebee, Oklahoma, the fifth son, we are told, of poor but honest parents.[14] He has written a number of accounts of his healing ministry and of the events leading up to it. *The Call* (1972) is only the last of them.[15] He describes in this book how at the age of seventeen he became so severely ill with tuberculosis that he thought he was about to die. In this extremity his sister persuaded him that God would heal him, and his parents then took him to a revivalist meeting, where he experienced a dramatic cure. This was in 1935, but it was not until twelve years later, in 1947, that he received the call to become a healer himself. The following year he established Healing Waters, Incorporated, a non-taxable religious corporation,[16] and two years later he was preaching on no fewer than eighty-five radio stations. A period of intense anxiety and doubt, endured long after

13. Ibid., 142–3.
14. David Edwin Harrell, Jr, *The Healing and Charismatic Revival in Modern America*, 42.
15. His other books include *Seven Divine Aids for Your Health* (Tulsa, 1960) and *It Is Later Than You Think* (Tulsa, n.d.). For a fuller list of his published work see D. E. Harrell, Jr, *Oral Roberts*, 500.
16. Roberts describes himself as 'having been forced to become not only an evangelist but a businessman': 'Miracle Seed-Faith, Part Three', *Abundant Life*, December, 1971.

he had become an active preacher, ended when, after hearing a voice tell him to get into his car and drive home, he received the distinct message: 'From this hour your ministry of healing will begin. You will have my power to pray for the sick and to cast out devils.'[17] He is fond of recounting stories about his healing ministry. Here is how he interpreted to a religious journalist the cures he was enabled to effect: 'You must understand that I am two persons. One is just when I am myself, and the other is when the Spirit of God takes possession of me, and I feel the presence of God after my sermons. Then I can do things of which I am not normally capable. I am still in control of my faculties, you understand. I can still think and act. But there is a spirit in me that is different, using me.'[18] Demons played a large part in his healing ministry. An unusual sensitivity in his right hand gave him the power to detect 'the presence, names, and numbers of demons' in afflicted people.[19] For him a demon 'is a strange, abnormal personality of evil. He lost his celestial body, spiritual illumination, godly knowledge and balance. He is now a miserable, disfranchised, homeless, psychopathic creature.'[20]

Worth adding, finally, is the fact that among five things he believed that God had shown him Roberts numbered 'a visitation of men by angels as in Bible times' and 'a new world-wide emphasis on healing and supernatural deliverance'.[21]

The career of this American evangelist has numerous parallels with that of the typical shaman,[22] and much of what he says about his relationship with God echoes Paul's own words concerning his relation to the spirit of Jesus.

---

17. *My Story* (Tulsa/New York, 1961), 95.
18. See Will Oursler, *Healing Power*, 186.
19. Harrell, *All Things*, 50. A certain T. J. Rothke, of Cameron, Wisconsin, told Will Oursler that Oral Roberts's touch 'was like a charge of electricity. I'm an electrician and I know what that means. It starts at the top of your hand and the bottom of your feet and it goes right through your body' (W. Oursler, *Healing Power*, 183).
20. 'Demons', *America's Healing Magazine* (September, 1954), 2.
21. 'What God Has Shown to Me', *America's Healing Magazine* (October, 1954), 4–5.
22. As was observed by David Kinsley in an unpublished paper to which I am greatly indebted: 'Shamanic Tendencies in Contemporary Christian Faith Healers', 27 May, 1997.

There it is, extracts from two classic works on shamanism in Siberia and Japan, plus two individual instances: one a drastically abbreviated picture of a Christian holy man in the Byzantine era, the other remarks on the autobiography of a modern American evangelist. (It would not be hard to find examples of other Christian shamans in the centuries between.)[23] Is this enough to form the basis of an analogical comparison with the career of St Paul? I believe that it is, but before we actually turn to Paul a few further comments may be helpful.

To one coming to anthropological studies from a very different discipline, the most remarkable feature of shamanism is its extraordinary reach, both in space and time. Ioan Lewis worked in Africa, Shirokogoroff in Siberia, Carmen Blacker in Japan. Stephen Mitchell came across a striking example of shamanism whilst completing a study of Anatolia, modern Turkey. Go to India or Indonesia, South, Central or North America, and you will find other examples. The list seems endless. The Scythians in Book IV of Herodotus's *History* exhibit many of the characteristics of a shamanistic society, and so do the ancient Pythagoreans. E. R. Dodds, who cites these examples, even goes so far as to suggest, 'at the risk of being called a panshamanist,' that the mythical Orpheus was a shaman.[24]

The resemblances are manifest, and many of them may be due to direct contact. For the older period Dodds suggests 'a tentative line of descent which starts in Scythia, crosses the Hellespont into Asiatic Greece, is perhaps combined with some remnants of Minoan tradition surviving in Crete, emigrates to the Far West with Pythagoras, and has its last outstanding representative in the Sicilian Empedocles'.[25] The anthropologist Nick Allen has proposed

---

23. See for instance Carl-Martin Edsman's discussion of the life of Catharina Fager-berg in *Studies in Shamanism*, ed. C.-M. Edsman, 120–65, with some interesting methodological conclusions. I have also consulted Paul Mankowski, *Studien zur Persönlichkeit des Mystikers und des Schamanen – Ein religionsgeschichtlicher Vergleich, durchgeführt der Mystik der hl. Theresia von Avila und der Schamanen einzelner Gruppen des nordasiatischen (sibirischen) Schamanismus* (Saarbrücken, 1988). But this long title contains a promise that is not kept.

24. *The Greeks and the Irrational*, in a chapter entitled 'The Greek Shamans and Puritanism' (p.147). The other suggestions did not originate with Dodds, but his treatment is intelligent and persuasive, and includes references to much of the earlier literature.

25. Ibid., 146.

to me that the American shamans may be the descendants of northeast Asian shamans who crossed the Bering Strait and moved down the west coast of America – along the Pacific rim, like Michael Palin in his television series, though in the opposite direction, and much more slowly.[26]

Are we entitled to conclude, though, that shamanistic societies everywhere, and in every age, are thus genealogically connected? Possibly not: it would certainly be immensely difficult to construct a satisfactory genealogical tree.[27]

If, then, as is probably safest to assume, in some at least of these societies shamanism developed spontaneously, without any direct

26. This suggestion receives indirect confirmation from an article by Ryk Ward, based on a lecture given in Wolfson College in 1997 ('Language and Genes in the Americas'). During the last 50,000 years, which is when the colonization of the Americas took place, the Bering Strait was passable for two long stretches of time: first for about 15,000 years towards the beginning of this period and secondly for about 10,000 years starting around the middle (some 25,000 years ago). During these two stretches the strait will have been frozen enough to permit land access but not so much as to block the narrow ice-free passage between the Laurentide and the Cordilleran glaciers. The archaeological evidence, argues Ward, strongly favours the later stretch: from around 15,000 years ago there is an evenly discernible proliferation of [human] sites throughout North America. Study of the mitochondrial DNA of the Amerindian population in the Pacific North-West of British Columbia has shown that it was characterized from the start by some genetic diversity: 'it was by no means', as Ward puts it, 'a genetically depauperate' (p. 151). This could be explained either by a single migration of an already heterogeneous group (probably originating in Mongolia) or by a series of distinct migrations of different groups over a period of between 1,000 and 2,000 years. There is apparently no agreement whether shamans are to be found in Australia, which seems to have lost its land links with the rest of the world around 50,000 years ago. Their absence would be a further (if indirect) argument for a genealogical connection. Mircea Eliade, in his book on shamanism, does not hesitate to identify Australian medicine-men as shamans; but elsewhere (*Rites*, 101) he supports the idea that the corpus of their rites, beliefs and occult techniques 'may have taken its present form primarily under Indian influence'. Here he is following A. P. Elkin, *Aboriginal Men of High Degree* (Sidney, 1945), 76–7, who suggests the possibility of a 'historical connection between the Yoga and occult practices of India and Tibet and the practices and psychic powers of Aboriginal men of high degree'. Hinduism, he points out, 'spread to the East Indies. Yoga is a cult in Bali, and some of the remarkable feats of the Australian medicine-men are paralleled by their fellow professionals in Papua.'

27. 'There are astonishing similarities, which are not easy to explain,' writes Piers Vitebsky, 'between shamanic ideas and practices as far apart as the Arctic, Amazonia and Borneo, even though these societies have probably never had any contact with each other', *The Shaman*, 11.

dependence upon any of the others, then the question arises whether there is something in the collective psyche of human societies, the majority of which are also *religious* societies, to account for the striking behavioural similarities that we have noticed. The human race is after all a single species. We are all subject to the same emotions: fear, anger, lust, greed. Societies differ, of course, and have different ways of coping with the natural selfishness and aggressiveness of their members. Nevertheless, it is tempting to wonder whether the same concatenation of circumstances and conditions might bring out similar, that is to say convergent, responses. In that case shamanistic societies might spring up spontaneously at different times and places, like the Tasmanian devil and the wolf, the sun-bird and the humming-bird (which we noticed in the previous chapter) or the shark and the dolphin, the one a very ancient fish, the other, like the whale, a sea-mammal. In these examples from the animal kingdom we have to do not just with different species but with different families. I simply raise this question. I do not know the answer, or even how or where to look for it. But surely we should not rule out the possibility?

Paul: the evidence

In what follows I propose to treat of Paul's life in three sections, each corresponding to one of the three periods of the typical shaman's career, starting with his call, following this up with some reflections on his apostolic career, and concluding with what is surely the most intriguing question of all: Paul's experience *before* the dramatic events of the Damascus road. All of these points will be dealt with very much more fully in subsequent chapters.

(a) *Paul's call*

What exactly happened on the Damascus road we can only guess at. Up to that point, as Paul himself tells us, he had been excessively hostile towards what he calls the church (assembly/community) of God (Gal 1:13). In all probability he will have been contending for some time against an uneasy and growing conviction that the persecution in which he was engaged could not really be justified; and what the earliest Christian missionaries were saying about

Christ had already begun to cast its spell on him. This is the first of three descriptions of this event in Acts: 'As he journeyed he approached Damascus and suddenly a light from heaven flashed about him. And he fell to the ground, and heard a voice saying, "Paul, Paul, why do you persecute me?"' (9:3–4).

The narrator adds that Paul was blind when he got up and did not recover his sight for three days. Later it emerges that this event took place 'about noon' (22:6). One gets the impression from the account in Acts that the blinding light precluded vision – it sounds for all the world like a lightning flash (or possibly sunstroke) – but when Paul himself refers to the incident (Gal 1:16) he speaks of revelation, and elsewhere he insists that the Risen Christ appeared to him, last of all, after a series of other appearances. And he adds the curious expression ὡσπερεὶ τῷ ἐκτρώματι (1 Cor 15:8). The word ἔκτρωμα means literally an abortion or miscarriage, and the usual English translation ('as to one untimely born') glosses over the obscurity of the Greek. So there are lots of uncertainties here. It sometimes happens, I believe, that people recover from lightning strokes; but the anthropologist Godfrey Lienhardt told me that among the Dinka people cattle that have been struck by lightning move up in the pecking (or I suppose one should say grazing) order of the herd. If this is what happened to Paul, he interpreted it as a vision and a vocation.[28] It certainly marked the turning-point in his life (and moved him up the pecking order!). Having been temporarily blinded himself, he evidently received the power, by a typical shamanistic reversal, to inflict blindness on others; in Paul's case the victim was a fellow magician, the unfortunate Elymas (Acts 13:8), who had annoyed Paul by attempting to dissuade the proconsul in Cyprus from embracing the message of the gospel. In this he was unsuccessful, for, Luke tells us, 'the proconsul believed, when he saw what had occurred, for he was astonished at the teaching of the Lord' (Acts 13:2) – and even more astonished, we may surmise, by Paul's magical powers.

The terminology Paul uses when recounting his call is reminiscent, no doubt deliberately so, of biblical stories of prophetic

---

28. Lightning is one of the 'unusual accidents or events' that according to Mircea Eliade herald a shaman's call (*Shamanism*, 32): among the Buryat of Southern Siberia in particular, one way the gods have of choosing a future shaman is by striking him with lightning (ibid., 19).

calling. The twin themes of vocation and mission are closely inter-twined. (This point will be developed further in the next chapter.) But although the prophetic pattern is important to Paul and gives us, his interpreters, a clue to his own understanding of his experience, the close analogy with shamanistic vocations should not be overlooked. One of the commonest forms of the future shaman's election, we are informed by Mircea Eliade, is an encounter with a divine or semi-divine being 'who appears to him through a dream, sickness, or some other circumstance, tells him that he has been "chosen", and incites him thenceforth to follow a new rule of life'.[29] The experience corresponds to a rite of passage that marks the closure of one door and the opening of another, giving the indi-vidual new privileges and responsibilities in his society.

(b) *Paul's apostolic career*

Next we must consider what followed Paul's calling: his apostolic career. One of the most interesting aspects of his life from now on is his apparent mastery of spiritual phenomena. This is most apparent in his correspondence with the Corinthians, who were themselves clearly impressed by Paul's exceptional talent: his own word is χάρισμα (*charisma*). In the most important passage he resorts, with evident reluctance, to what he calls 'boasting': 'I must boast; there is nothing to be gained by it, but I will go on to visions and revelations of the Lord. I know a man in Christ who fourteen years ago was caught up as far as the third heaven – whether in the body or out of the body I do not know, God knows. And I know that this man was caught up into Paradise – whether in the body or out of the body, I do not know, God knows – and he heard things that cannot be told, which man may not utter' (2 Cor 12:1–4). The switch from the first to the third person (or the other way round) is not uncommon in this kind of account.[30] Unless this passage ('four-teen years ago') refers to his call experience (some scholars think it does, but there is no proof of this), the trance or ecstasy to which it alludes probably took place in an otherwise uncharted period of his life somewhere between the years 40 and 44, before he actually

---

29. *Shamanism*, 67.
30. R. H. Charles lists a number of examples in his edition of *1 Enoch* (pp. 57–8), and remarks that some of them are confusing.

embarked upon his missionary activity. The episode resembles mystical experiences of a kind well attested in contemporary Jewish apocalyptic literature, where heavenly journeys such as the one Paul mentions are attributed to seers or visionaries.[31] Paul speaks of this vision haltingly, even reluctantly, but lets slip the information that it was only one of a number of visions and revelations (ὀπτασίαι καὶ ἀποκαλύψεις κυρίου), and goes on to speak of an 'abundance of revelations'(12:1, 7). Since the frequency of otherworldly journeys is regarded by many historians of religion as what characterizes shamanism over against other religions,[32] this point requires emphasis here. The 2 Corinthians passage will receive fuller discussion in Chapter 4.

In 1 Corinthians there is a long section in which Paul attempts to adjudicate between what he calls spiritual gifts or charismata. This is how it begins: 'Now concerning spiritual matters, brethren, I do not want you to be uninformed. You know that when you were heathen, you were led astray to dumb idols, however you may have been moved. Therefore I want you to understand that no one speaking by the Spirit of God ever says, "Jesus be cursed" ('Ανάθεμα 'Ιησοῦς); and no one can say "Jesus is Lord" except by the Holy Spirit' (1 Cor 12:1–3). Here again we have the language and in this case surely the reality of religious experience.

At the top of the Corinthians' list of spiritual phenomena – the one to which they gave pride of place – was what, following Paul, is now called glossolalia: speaking in tongues. Paul is clearly uneasy about this but is nevertheless prepared to thank God that he himself speaks in tongues more than any of them (1 Cor 14:18). Here is one kind of spirit phenomenon that was clearly prominent – and frequent – in the Corinthian community, and in which Paul excelled. These phenomena will be discussed more fully in Chapter 7.

Another very intriguing aspect of Paul's career concerns his missionary methods, his preaching practices, his apostolic approach. Towards the beginning of the same letter he speaks of his own missionary proclamation of the gospel: 'I was with you', he says, 'in weakness and trembling, and my speech and my message were not

---

31. See Christopher Rowland, *The Open Heaven*, passim.
32. Above all Mircea Eliade in his classic *Le Chamanisme et les techniques archaïques de l'extase*.

in plausible words of wisdom, but in demonstration of the Spirit and of power, that your faith might not rest in the wisdom of man but in the power of God' (1 Cor 2:4–5). This is the RSV translation of a notoriously difficult passage, further complicated by a wide variety of manuscript variants. Elsewhere he speaks of 'the one who dispenses the spirit' (ὁ οὖν ἐπιχορηγῶν ὑμῖν τὸ πνεῦμα: Gal 3:5). We shall have to consider later the question of the identity of this 'dispenser'. (Is it God, Christ, or even Paul himself?) Paul frequently contrasts his own personal weakness (an extended example comes in 2 Cor 10–13) with the strength he derives from God. The astonishingly rapid spread of Christianity, spearheaded by Paul, is surely not to be explained, as the author of Acts would have us believe, simply on the basis of scriptural arguments that must have been incomprehensible to the majority of Paul's listeners. This argument will be developed more fully in Chapter 5.

To round off this central section on Paul's post-conversion experience, something needs to be said on the teasing but crucially important question of his relationship with Christ, or at any rate his sense of that relationship. This, after all, is the heart of the matter, for according to his own testimony it dominated his life from then on, and gave it significance and value. It is also the hardest to understand, partly because the massive structure of Christian theology bars the way, blocking progress and constricting thought. One Christian scholar who tried to find a way round the impasse was Albert Schweitzer, and I feel sympathetic to his suggestion of a Christ-centred, as opposed to a God-centred, mysticism.[33] But Schweitzer's mysticism is curiously cerebral. He betrays his intellectualist bias by aligning Paul, startlingly but significantly, alongside those towering giants of Western philosophy, Spinoza, Schopenhauer and Hegel; and at the beginning of his final chapter he calls him 'the patron saint of thought in Christianity'.

At first sight, then, the phenomenon of shamanism offers, as elsewhere, an attractive alternative to Schweitzer's approach; for Paul's language is remarkably reminiscent of the language of spirit-possession: 'it is no longer I who live but Christ who lives in me' (Gal 2:20); 'I can do all things in him who strengthens me' (Phil 4:13). Here the language of possession appears to be interchangeable with

---

33. See Excursus III, Scheitzer's *Mysticism*.

that of being possessed: one of Paul's favourite (and most opaque) phrases is 'in Christ'; yet, as we have seen, he is deeply conscious that Christ lives in him.[34] He speaks of Christ almost as of a spirit-familiar, or familiar spirit, on whom he can always rely for protection and assistance; much as the shaman feels able to turn to his spirit guide for help in dealing with the rest of the spirit world. Further consideration of this will be deferred until the last chapter.

The difference is, of course, that Christ is, or was, a human being, one whose life was just as 'shamanistic' as Paul's.[35] What makes it possible for Paul to treat Christ as a spirit is the fact, as Paul conceived it to be, of his death and resurrection, an experience somehow reproduced in Paul's own life: 'I have been crucified with Christ' (Gal 2:20) (the same passage as that quoted earlier). We have seen that the Japanese shaman whose terrifying experiences are so graphically described by Carmen Blacker conceived his traumatic initiation as a protracted death and subsequent resuscitation. A similar idea, as I will attempt to show in Chapter 4, is implicit in Paul's letters: he certainly sees Christ's dying and rising as somehow re-enacted in his own life, and the transformation that Christ underwent in a matter of days is experienced more gradually by the Christian: we are all, says Paul, 'being transformed into his likeness from one degree of glory to another; for this comes from the Lord who is the spirit' (2 Cor 3:18).

We shall have to take a closer look at some of these texts. What I want to stress here is that the conceptual tools of theology are too finely-honed to deal satisfactorily with Paul's halting attempts to put his experience of spirit-possession into words: if you try to dissect a living body you will end up with a corpse. Exegesis too stumbles and stutters at these points: it has not yet found (such at any rate is the assumption that underlies this book) the conceptual framework that is required to make sense of Paul's most intimate confessions.

---

34. 'Just as the air of life which we breathe is "in" us and fills us, and yet we at the same time live and breathe "in" this air, so it is with St Paul's fellowship of Christ: Christ in him, he in Christ.' This is a famous early attempt by Adolf Deissmann to explain Paul's meaning: *St Paul*, 128. But how much does this simile really explain?

35. See Excursus I, Jesus the Shaman

(c) *Paul before his call*

Under this heading I have but a single example, in some ways the most interesting of all, for it opens the way to an understanding of a particularly knotty exegetical problem, one for which, in my opinion, no satisfactory solution has ever been found. Let me begin with two quotations from Ioan Lewis: 'The link between affliction and its cure', he writes, 'as the royal road to the assumption of the shamanistic vocation is [thus] plain enough in those societies where shamans play the main or major role in religion and where possession is highly valued as a religious experience.'[36] And a little earlier: 'While some shamans are summoned by dreams or visions to their calling, this is by no means the universal pattern of recruitment. Very commonly, as with St Paul, the road to the assumption of the shaman's vocation lies through affliction valiantly endured, and, in the end, transformed into spiritual grace.'[37]

Lewis is clearly alluding here to a notoriously difficult passage in Romans 7 that deals with the vain attempts of the self or ego to overcome evil. According to Luther the passage concerns the constant struggle of the Christian who, though regularly overcome by temptation and burdened with guilt, finds reason nevertheless to rejoice in the saving power of Christ. This, he thought, was Paul's experience, re-enacted, he was convinced, in the life of all true believers. Most modern interpreters reject the suggestion that there is any autobiographical element here on the grounds that elsewhere (Philippians 3:6) Paul declares himself 'blameless as to the law' before he turned to Christ. But the passage gives nonetheless a disturbing impression of personal angst: 'I am', says Paul, 'carnal: sold [as a slave] to sin (ἐγὼ δὲ σάρκινός εἰμι πεπραμένος ὑπὸ τὴν ἁμαρτίαν). I do not understand my own actions. For I do not do what I want, I do the very thing I hate. Now if I do what I do not want, I agree that the law is good. So then it is no longer I that do it, but sin which dwells within me. For I know that nothing good dwells within me, that is in my flesh. I can will what is right, but I cannot do it. For I do not do the good that I want, but the evil I do not want is what I do. Now if I do what I do not want, it is no longer I that do it, but sin which dwells within me.... I see in my members', he goes

36. *Ecstatic Religion*, 70–1.
37. Ibid., 67.

on, 'another law at war with the law in my mind and making me captive to the law of sin which dwells in my members' (Rom 7:14–23).

This is the language of possession: it is not just an example of Aristotelian *akrasia*, weakness of will. The ego here is totally dominated, possessed, and occupied by an alien power. The current orthodoxy takes the ego in this passage to refer to pre-Christian man in general, not to Paul in particular. But I shall argue in the final chapter that this view is mistaken. If the account does indeed reflect Paul's own experience, and the present tense is used to heighten the effect of a story about his pre-Christian past, then it is possible to make a rough sketch of a succession of spiritual experiences in Paul's life that tallies remarkably well with Lewis's general account of the typical shamanistic career.

Paul and shamanism

In the face of all these perceived similarities – echoes of shamanism not only in Paul's life but also in the lives of two Christian healers at different times and in different places – how are we to proceed?

In the previous chapter it was suggested that there are two distinct ways of accounting for resemblances, religious and other, one genealogical and the other convergent. But there is a preliminary question to be tackled first: is shamanism really a religion at all? A full-scale review of the evidence relating to this question is beyond the scope of this book (and of its author's competence); but the anthropologist Michel Perrin, in one of the best short treatments of shamanism available, gives a considered answer:

> Yes, shamanism is a sort of religion, provided that we see religions as representations of the world inseparably attached to the acts issuing from the belief-system that they set up. For the Christian religion the relevant representation is expressed in the scriptures. The acts issuing from it are prayer, confession, the Mass, the sacraments in general, propitiatory or therapeutic rituals such as pilgrimages, the blessing of tools, occasional exorcisms. [A very Catholic list!]
>
> For shamanism the representations are found in myths that recount the origin of the world and its transfigurations and put in

place the other world (*le monde-autre*) along with its pantheon. The acts issuing from these are, as in Christianity, propitiatory rituals and therapeutic cures, but also the escorting of the souls of the dead to their final resting-place, divination, etc.[38]

A certain transference of theme or ritual, moving in either direction, is possible. 'North and South American Indian religion is pervaded with both Protestant and Catholic Christianity',[39] whilst many ostensibly Christian sects on the American continent and elsewhere that have not completely succeeded in ousting the indigenous religions still exhibit characteristics of shamanism. This is a good example of the phenomenon of *diffusion*. This may also account for the shaman-like features of the activities of Theodore of Sykeon or Oral Roberts, and conceivably for those in the career of Paul also. But we cannot simply assume this, and we are therefore confronted once again with the task of assessing which of the two causes of resemblance discussed in the previous chapter, genealogical or convergent, best accounts for the shamanistic aspects of Paul's life.

(a) *Genealogical*. As a practising Jew brought up in a Greek city, there are two possible ways in which Paul might have become acquainted with some sort of shamanistic lore. What is there in the two traditions he inherited that might have so affected his religious experiences that they came to be expressed in language reminiscent of shamanism?

At a casual glance one might be tempted to say 'very little'. But that is because of the strength of certain elements in the two cultures that tended to suppress or force underground the shamanistic tendencies present in them both.[40]

In the Jewish tradition shamanistic traits may be traced back at least as far as the period of the Judges in the eleventh century, and they surface again in the activities of Jesus and some of his contemporaries. The behaviour of the people called *nᵉbî'îm* in 1 Samuel

---

38. *Le Chamanisme*, 20–1.
39. P. Vitebsky, *The Shaman*, 133.
40. In support of this observation, Dr Allen pointed to the surprising fact that although spirit-possession is very common in India, the voluminous Sanskrit sources say virtually nothing about it.

10:5–6 was such as to render the usual translation of נְבִיאִים in this
passage ('prophets') misleading if not actually erroneous:[41] '... as
you come to the city, you [Saul] will meet a band of prophets
coming down from the high place with harp, tambourine, flute, and
lyre before them, prophesying. Then the spirit of the Lord will come
mightily upon you, and you shall prophesy with them and be turned
into another man.'[42] Much later (seventh century?) Deuteronomy
declares that 'there shall not be found among you anyone who ...
practises divination, a soothsayer, or an augur, or a sorcerer, or a
charmer, or a medium, or a wizard, or a necromancer' (18:10–11) –
which suggests that such practices were still going on. Isaiah, in the
eighth century, speaks sardonically of advisers who told people to
'consult the mediums and the wizards who chirp and mutter' (8:19);
and as late as the sixth century Jeremiah urges the exiles in Babylon:
'Do not let your prophets and your diviners who are among you
deceive you, and do not listen to the dreams which they dream'
(29:8).[43]

The most direct (and consequently the most important) evidence
of shamanistic practices in ancient Israel is to be found in the story
of King Saul's encounter with the witch of Endor. Towards the end
of his reign, when his whole world seemed to be falling apart, he felt
unable to act without some sort of divine guidance. Having
exhausted all the standard procedures, he turned in desperation to
a method he himself had outlawed:

> ... when Saul inquired of the Lord, the Lord did not answer
> him, either by dreams, or by Urim, or by prophets. Saul said to
> his servants, 'Seek out for me a woman who is a necromancer
> [אֵשֶׁת בַּעֲלַת־אוֹב, literally, 'mistress of the pit'],[44] that I may go

41. This point is more fully developed in Chapter 6.
42. It was no doubt the activity of these people, not that of the classical prophets,
    that inspired a group of late 19th-century French painters (the best-known
    being Vuillard and Bonnard) to call themselves *Nabins* after deciding to emu-
    late the violent colours and strikingly rhythmic patterns they admired in the
    work of Paul Gauguin.
43. For a much fuller account than can be given here see Arvid S. Kapelrud,
    'Shamanistic Features'.
44. The word אוֹב ('ōb) has four possible meanings: (a) a dug-out pit, used for call-
    ing spirits up from the dead; (b) a leathern bag (Job 32:19); (c) a ghost (Isa
    29:4); (d) (most commonly) a necromancer (Lev 19:31 etc.). Kapelrud suggests
    that if (b) is the meaning here, the bag in question might be a sorcery bag. But

to her and inquire of her.' And his servants said to him, 'Behold, there is a necromancer at Endor.' So Saul disguised himself and put on other garments, and went, he and two men with him, and they came to the woman by night. And he said, 'Divine for me whomever I shall name to you.' The woman said to him, 'Surely you know what Saul has done, how he has cut off the necromancers and the wizards from the land. Why then are you laying a snare for my life to bring about my death?' But Saul swore to her by the Lord, 'As the Lord lives, no punishment shall come upon you for this thing.' Then the woman said, 'Whom shall I bring up for you?' He said, 'Bring up Samuel for me.' When the woman saw Samuel, she cried out with a loud voice; and the woman said to Saul, 'Why have you deceived me? You are Saul.' The king said to her, 'Have no fear; what do you see?' And the woman said to Saul, 'I see a god coming up out of the earth.' He said to her, 'What is his appearance?' And she said, 'An old man is coming up and he is wrapped in a robe.' And Saul knew that it was Samuel, and he bowed with his face to the ground, and did obeisance. Then Samuel said to Saul, 'Why have you disturbed me by bringing me up?'…

(1 Sam 28:6–15)

As Kapelrud points out, the story shows that Saul had already condemned certain practices that were to be explicitly prohibited centuries later in the Book of Deuteronomy (18:9–10), 'but the king's own action shows how deeply rooted they were and how hard it was to have them abolished'.[45] Evidence pointing in the same direction is to be found in *Ethiopic Enoch* (of uncertain date, but possibly as early as the sixth century), which deplores the instructions given by the fallen angels in 'magical medicine, incantations, the cutting of roots' (*1 Enoch* 7–8). Much later, in the second century, the Jews are praised because 'they do not worry about …

(c) is also possible, in which case the woman is being called a mistress of ghost(s). Both these suggestions have now been overtaken by (a), a meaning that goes back to the Sumerian *ab*, found in the Gilgamesh epic. In any case meaning (d) is quite close. See Kapelrud, op. cit., 93–4, and for (a) the entry *sub voce* in *Theological Dictionary of the OT²*, edd. G.T. Botterweck and H. Ringren, i (Grand Rapids, 1977), 130–4.

45. Ibid.

portents of sneezes, nor birds of augurs, nor seers, nor sorcerers, nor the deceits of foolish words of necromancers' (*Sib. Or.* 3.220–6);[46] but it is likely that this approval masks a deep-seated *dis*approval of practices that had never been completely eliminated. One wonders too whether an author who chose to conceal his own Jewish identity by adopting the guise of a pagan oracle can have been completely insensible to the irony implicit in his condemnation of, among other things, the activities of augurs and seers.

A forbidden practice that could survive several centuries of oppression might well survive several centuries more. On the whole the biblical writers showed no eagerness to call attention to practices of which they disapproved, except of course when they felt it necessary to condemn them. Had the evidence at our disposal been limited to the Hebrew Bible we might have concluded that the 'orthodox' leaders of the Jewish community had effectively suppressed the kind of magical practices that had long ago been outlawed (but nevertheless resorted to) by King Saul. But that exorcism (if not actually necromancy) continued to be practised is indisputable: the evidence for its survival *outside* the Hebrew Bible is abundant, not least in the New Testament, both in the Gospels and in Acts.[47]

For a final confirmation of the survival of exorcism the following passage from Josephus's *Antiquities* describing the powers of King Solomon is worth quoting *in extenso*:

> God granted him knowledge of the art used against demons for the benefit and healing of men. He also composed incantations by which illnesses are relieved, and left behind forms of exorcisms with which those possessed by demons drive them out,

---

46. I have substituted 'necromancers' for 'ventriloquists' (the literal translation of the Greek ἐγγαστρίμυθοι – people who speak in the belly). This is the term chosen by the LXX to translate the Hebrew אוֹב (and, in the case of the witch of Endor, בַּעֲלַת־אוֹב), which is why, when quoting this passage, I preferred 'necromancer' to 'medium' (RSV). See Michel Lestienne's long note on this passage in his excellent edition of the *Premier Livre des Règnes*, 395–6.

47. To have dealt with these here as thoroughly as they deserve would have given this chapter an unpleasantly bloated appearance; so I have relegated them to excursuses. For the gospels see Excursus I, Jesus the Shaman; for Acts see Excursus III, The Historicity of Acts. For the abundant other material see Philip Alexander's fine contribution to the revised Schürer: 'Incantations and Books of Magic'.

never to return. And this kind of cure is of very great power among us to this day, for I have seen a certain Eleazar, a countryman of mine, in the presence of Vespasian, his sons, tribunes and a number of other soldiers, free men possessed by a demon, and this was the manner of the cure: he put to the nose of the possessed man a ring which had under its seal one of the roots prescribed by Solomon, and then, as the man smelled it, drew out the demon through his nostrils, and, when the man at once fell down, adjured the demon never to come back into him, speaking Solomon's name and reciting the incantations which he had composed. Then wishing to convince the bystanders and prove to them that he had this power, Eleazar placed a cup or foot-basin full of water a little way off and commanded the demon, as it went out of the man, to overturn it and make known to the spectators that he had left the man. And when this was done, the understanding and wisdom of Solomon were clearly revealed, on account of which we have been induced to speak of these things, in order that all men may know the greatness of his nature and how God favoured him, and that no one under the sun may be ignorant of the king's surpassing virtue of every kind.

A.J. 8.45–9 (tr. Marcus)[48]

It makes no difference to my argument whether the story of Solomon's seal reflects an authentic tradition that had been somehow smuggled through the official censors (it is not found in the Bible) or simply, as Geza Vermes clearly supposes, a current (first century AD) practice that Josephus is projecting back into the time of Solomon.[49]

48. The tradition of Solomon's magical powers persisted, most notably in the extraordinary *Testament of Solomon* (3rd or 4th century AD), although it was suppressed in official rabbinic circles until the 12th century (another example of official censorship). (Following Kapelrud I have restricted my discussion of the Old Testament evidence to exorcism and necromancy. But a lot more could have been said. The career of the prophet Elijah is full of shamanistic traits. The visions of the prophets, especially Isaiah, Ezekiel and Daniel, deserve comment. So do the detailed descriptions of the ecstatic trances of pseudoepigraphic seers such as Enoch, Baruch and Ezra. Some of this material is briefly alluded to in the conclusion of Excursus II, Merkabah Mysticism.)

49. 'As a Hellenistic historian', he comments, Josephus 'describes the Israelite king as a model of wisdom, but accompanies this approach with the more popular ideas of a Palestinian Jew': *Jesus the Jew* (London, 1973), 62.

The *Antiquities* of the Jewish Josephus, written in Greek for mostly Roman readers, illustrates how readily Paul's three worlds, as they have been called,[50] brush against one another, cling, and gather, like gigantic bubbles. Of these three worlds, Jewish, Greek and Roman, it is to the second that we must now turn.

The Greek evidence differs from the Jewish in that instead of being largely confined to historical sources it is found predominantly in myth and ritual. E. R. Dodds, as we have already seen, was willing to risk being tarred with the brush of panshamanism by venturing to call Orpheus a shaman. But Orpheus, whose visit to Hades to rescue his beloved Eurydice is marvellously recounted by Virgil in a passage of the *Georgics* (4.453–525) and has been from then on a favourite topos in Western song and story, is only the best-known of a number of shaman-like figures who have found a place in Greek legend. Probably the most obscure is Phormio, the hero of *Trophonius*, a lost comedy by the Sicilian playwright Cratinus that does not even rate a mention in the new (1996) edition of the *Oxford Classical Dictionary* (1,640 pages).

Walter Burkert, following the lead of Dodds and, rather earlier, Karl Meuli,[51] has tried to establish a link between on the one hand a variety of Greek legends concerning visits to the underworld and magical metamorphoses, and on the other hand rituals whereby shamanistic priests summon up souls from the underworld or guide dead souls to their new home. He argues that there is much valuable evidence in Greek texts that has been rejected, neglected or completely ignored because, embedded as it is in artistic prose and poetry, it has assumed the colours of its environment and thus acquired a kind of invisibility. This seems to me a brilliant insight, not sufficiently stressed in Burkert's own dryly academic prose. For it leads to the realization that even Homer, whom we read as much as anything else for his sheer humanity, may be transforming into story magical rites and practices that in real life he may have scorned or scoffed at. At the beginning of the last book of the *Odyssey* he exercises his own magic to conjure up a picture of Hermes summoning the souls of Penelope's suitors and guiding them with his beautiful golden rod until they eventually reach the Elysian fields,

50. Richard Wallace and Wynne Williams, *The Three Worlds of Paul of Tarsus*.
51. 'Scythica'.

the home of the dead, carpeted with asphodels – a host of golden daffodils. 'It is not over-venturesome (*nicht zu kühn*)', observes Burkert, 'to see in the details of the myth the reflection of a rite: the picture of Hermes, escort of souls, with his rod and his winged sandals, is a projection of the actual praxis of a γόης, a soul-escorting shaman.'[52]

Homer, then, reveals the human rather than the magical (*an Stelle des Magischen*).[53] (But at the same time he conceals the magical beneath the human.) 'Literally speaking,' Burkert concludes, 'Homer's world may be full of gods; but these gods have been stripped – to an astonishing extent – of anything demonic or numinous: their epiphany has nothing of the *mysterium tremendum*. Similarly, the world of the dead has been robbed of its power, and Demeter, Dionysus and the Furies receive only incidental mention. It is clear nevertheless than these dark powers are present throughout: the world of the epic is in this respect infinitely many-layered.'[54]

(One literary source of particular interest to the Pauline scholar that Burkert does *not* mention is Euripides' *Alcestis*, in which Heracles volunteers to descend into the underworld 'the sunless abodes' of Persephone and Pluto – to fetch back the dead queen for

---

52. 'ΓΟΗΣ', 46. Burkert remarks that Homer (*Od.* 24.1) uses (though in the middle voice) the verb ἐκκαλεῖν, the technical term for the summoning of the dead. Among other examples he reminds us that in Euripides' *Bacchae* (234) King Pentheus calls Dionysus a γόης ἐπῳδός, a chanting shaman; similarly, in Aeschylus's *Persae* (687), the dead king Darius demands to be called out of Hades by ψυχαγωγοὶ γόοι. Ψυχαγωγία, another technical term, denotes the escorting of dead souls, and Burkert suggests that the term γόης, which he wants to translate as 'shaman', comes from the word Aeschylus uses to mean a chant summoning up the dead, but whose first meaning was probably a dirge helping to lay the dead to rest, a kind of requiem. Such a rite is especially necessary when the standard funerary arrangements are not available. The Argonaut Phrixus, having died in a distant land, visits Pelias in a dream, and begs him to come and bring his soul (and the golden fleece) back home. Since such a journey was obviously impossible there was a need for a γόης ψυχαγωγός, able to undertake an 'ecstatic journey' so as to find the dead man's soul and lead it to rest (p. 47). Although the 'ecstatic' journey to the other world that is one of the hallmarks of shamanism is never mentioned in direct connection with the γόης 'the frequently evoked art of self-metamorphosis is a partial equivalent [cf. Herodotus (4.105) on the Scythians]: this is precisely where the Greeks speak of ἔκστασις' (p. 45).
53. Ibid.
54. Ibid., 52.

her distraught husband, Admetus.[55] Heracles was the patron deity of Paul's birthplace, Tarsus, which honoured him as its founder and saviour.)[56]

More generally, Burkert comments that 'the Greek sense for moderation and order has the effect of repressing uncontrollable upsurges of emotion and ecstatic, magical rites'.[57] Much of the success of this repression, he thinks, is due to the rise of the city state, the polis: Γόης and the order of the polis are polar opposites.'[58] Shamanism surfaces in the fifth century in the guise of Pythagoreanism, as Dodds had already seen, and as Burkert argues much more fully in an important book whose original German edition appeared the same year as the fascinating article on which I have drawn for my information in this section.[59]

Comparing the two sets of evidence, Jewish and Greek, we may find them surprisingly, even disconcertingly, complementary. Both show clear signs that oppressive forces have been at work, religious in the one case, rationalist in the other, the Jewish evidence coming from historical, the Greek from literary sources. And whereas, apart from the single – though highly significant – incident of the witch of Endor, what the Jewish sources reveal is mostly a strong tradition of exorcism, the Greek sources, once subjected to Burkert's penetrating analysis, indicate the existence of other shamanistic practices, magical transformations, otherworldly journeys, the escorting of dead souls to their final resting-place.

In fact, as Burkert shows, these practices apparently faded out towards the end of the fifth century, whereas once we direct our gaze to Paul's contemporaries we find plenty of evidence for the survival of exorcism and of other magical practices besides. But exorcism is not the problem. If this alone were enough to prove shamanism we could rest our case. Many of the early followers of Jesus were

---

55. Perhaps the omission is due to the fact that Heracles rejects the appellation ψυχαγωγός in this play, claiming to have brought back the real Alcestis, not just an underworld phantom (φάσμα νερτέρων).
56. Andrew Wilson, following Hans-Joachim Schoeps, plausibly imagines Paul as a young boy watching in fascination the annual ceremony in which the god was ritually cremated with a view to his resurrection in the spring: *Paul*, 26–7.
57. Burkert, 55.
58. Ibid., 53.
59. Finely translated into English as *Lore and Science in Ancient Pythagoreanism* (Cambridge, 1972).

exorcists, and Paul was one of them. But although, as we have already seen, Paul's career exhibits many shamanistic traits, there is no evidence to suggest that he had somehow picked these up from another shaman whom he had come across in his early life, either Jewish or Greek. There is a remote possibility, which cannot altogether be ruled out, that Paul inherited his shamanism from Jesus himself.[60] Some people, Andrew Wilson among them, believe that Paul must have known Jesus in his lifetime, though what evidence we have tells against this suggestion. Sufficiently far-out to appeal to the enthusiastic amateur, it is by no means as crazy as some of the theories that have recently excited so much interest, such as the idea that Jesus was a practising homosexual, or a divorcee with several children. But it is surely incapable of proof.

(b) *Convergent.* Most of the scholars who first took an interest in comparative religion were looking for genealogical explanations. If we abandon the search for these on the grounds that, at least where shamanism is concerned, they are simply not available, we may wish to reconsider the alternative explanation: *convergent* resemblances. There remains the possibility that the shamanistic pattern of Paul's life is to be explained by a concatenation of circumstances that caused him to react in the way he did. The anguished self-questioning which, I shall argue, preceded his conversion is analogous to the shaman's 'arctic hysteria'; the call itself is decidedly shamanistic in character; and so is the relation to the Spirit that followed it; while the 'ecstatic' rapture of which Paul writes so guardedly to the Corinthians was only one of a multiplicity of such revelations. I have made these points before and will be considering each of them more fully as the book proceeds. The convergent explanation, in which both *heredity* and *environment* may have played a part, cannot be ruled out. But it is hard to see even in principle how to set about proving it. So we are left with the uncomfortable perception that neither of the two kinds of explanation that biologists (and, to a lesser extent, philologists and anthropologists) find so useful – genealogical or convergent – is available to us.

What promised at the outset, then, to be a radically bold and innovative investigation seems to have petered out in what some

---

60. See Excursus I, Jesus the Shaman.

may think a disappointingly lame, not to say tame, conclusion. We are, it seems, in an impasse. This outcome (if that is the right word) is likely to prove welcome to many Christian theologians, uncomfortable as they are with any suggestion of possible pagan influences upon the true religion. Is there any way out of the impasse?

It should first be emphasized that the impossibility of establishing a satisfactory evolutionary tree is in no sense a *refutation* of the theory in either of its modes, genealogical or convergent. When Charles Lyell first used the term 'missing links' of fossil species in chalk in the third edition of his *Elements of Geology* (1851) it was to express the hope that these might some day be supplied, and 'the break in the chain' repaired.[61] There remains, however, one final avenue yet to be explored. Any investigation of observed similarities (whether in the human or the natural sciences) must begin with a search for the causes of these. Only when all conceivable causes have been ruled out will the investigator turn to the sole remaining explanation: coincidence, that unaccountable surd. (The clearest example of coincidence that I know comes from philology. The English word for bad is the same as the Persian, the German word for barn the same as the Coptic. Why? No reason.)[62] Some might say (though I would disagree) that this must be the case with the similarities I have detected between Paul's life and that of the typical shaman. But even if this were so, there might still be some advantage in stressing the similarities simply as a way of highlighting the *religious* features of Paul's career. In that case we would be using shamanism as a model or a metaphor. We may recall what Jonathan Z. Smith says about comparison, that it is *a disciplined exaggeration in the service of knowledge*: it is a heuristic device.

Even in the natural sciences it is not possible to give an accurate account of physical phenomena in straightforwardly literal language. That is why scientists resort to models. Models are not far from metaphors.[63] Like metaphors, they have the advantage of drawing attention to some particular feature of whatever it is that they are

---

61. *Elementary Geology*[3], 220.
62. I owe these examples to David Langslow. I used to think it a coincidence that the word for sack is virtually the same in all the languages I know; but Professor Langslow tells me that in all likelihood it was carried to Europe by Eastern traders, along with the rough cloth bag the word denotes.
63. See Max Black, *Models and Metaphors*.

focused on without involving any claim, either explicit or implicit, that this is the *only* way of looking at them. It could be waves at one moment, particles the next. Good metaphors are equally instructive: Aristotle goes so far as to say that a command of metaphor is a mark of native intelligence (εὐφυΐα), for to use metaphors well you need an eye for resemblances (τὸ ὅμοιον θεωρεῖν): *Poetics* 22.17. Somewhere in the first chapter of the second book of *The Mill on the Floss* George Eliot apostrophizes him thus: 'if you had had the advantage of being "the freshest modern" instead of the greatest ancient would you not have mingled your praise of metaphorical speech as a sign of high intelligence, with a lamentation that intelligence so rarely shows itself in speech without metaphor, – that we can so seldom declare what a thing is, except by saying that it is something else?'

For an example I will turn to poetry, taking a leaf from Murphy-O'Connor's book in which, starting with a famous passage from *As You Like It*, he argues, with breathtaking bravura, to the conclusion that Paul must have been an old man (around sixty!) by the time he wrote his letter to Philemon in AD 53.[64]

This is the passage (which I will turn to a rather different use):

> All the world's a stage
> And all the men and women merely players;
> They have their exits and their entrances;
> And one man in his time plays many parts,
> His acts being seven ages.

Now suppose that in response to a teacher's question, 'Is this true? Is all the world a stage?', a child simply said , 'No, not really', we might express some surprise at his or her literal-mindedness. It is the kind of reply we would expect from a Mr Spock, looking at the world dispassionately from outer space, but not from a human being, however young.[65] Yet this is precisely the reply I myself gave

64. *Paul*, 1–4.
65. Yet a sociologist, temporarily deserting his own profession for a sortie into New Testament scholarship, comes close: 'The problem with metaphors is not that they are false, but that they are *empty*. Many of them do seem to ooze profundity, but at best metaphors are merely definitions [!]': Rodney Stark, *The Rise of Christianity: A Sociologist Reconsiders History* (Princeton, 1996), 23–4. I prefer

to the question, 'Was St Paul a shaman?' on the first page of this chapter. What is the difference? The difference is that the children in the classroom know, or should know, what Jacques is about. He is speaking as a character of one of Shakespeare's plays, and all the characters in Shakespeare's plays, even the humblest, speak in metaphor. Exegetes, on the other hand, do not, at any rate not often. (Some might say not often enough.)

Since even scientists, as we have just noted, cannot express their hypotheses in ordinary language without resorting to models, exegetes too may consider themselves entitled to build upon the resemblances so heavily underlined in this chapter between the career of Paul and that of the typical shaman, so as to construct a sustained *metaphor,* leaving on one side the possibility that the genealogical or convergent explanation that has so far eluded us may be tucked away somewhere in an unvisited nook or unexplored cranny. This will enable us to concentrate upon *religious* features of Paul's life that have been largely ignored by modern scholarship. Model, metaphor, or heuristic device, shamanism can still play a part in this enquiry: we are not obliged to bin it in order to preserve any shred of professional integrity.

Conclusion

Jonathan Z. Smith is fond of quoting a passage from William James's *Varieties of Religious Experience* that expresses the resentment people feel when they hear an object that is 'infinitely important' to them classified along with something else: 'Probably a crab would be filled with a sense of personal outrage if it could hear us class it without ado or apology as a crustacean, and thus dispose of it. "I am no such thing," it would say: "I am *myself, myself* alone."'[66] The truth is, however, that there are millions of crabs, and it takes an expert to distinguish one *species*, let alone a single individual, from another. So the crab's brazen claims have to be dismissed.

---

to side with Aristotle and Eliot: oozing profundity, however this is conceived, is certainly not something I would claim for (or wish upon) any metaphor of mine.

66. W. James, *Varieties of Religious Experience*, 10. See J. Z. Smith, *Drudgery Divine*, 37; *Imagining Religion*, 6; *Map is Not Territory*, 242–3.

How then should we proceed when we are dealing with individual human beings, in this case with the apostle Paul? Since the whole point of this chapter has been to assert the essential *comparability* of Paul's experiences with those of men and women representing an astonishing variety of human societies throughout the ages, I would obviously want to resist J. Louis Martyn's efforts to insulate Paul against what he would regard as the impertinent and inappropriate intrusions of historians of religion. By placing Paul in the company of other Christian shamans who, like him, professed allegiance to Christ and had a career structure very like his own, we can overcome the awkwardness of having to compare the experiences of a single individual with the vast array of phenomena that emanate from and characterize a whole religion – in this case the religion of shamanism. No doubt Paul would retain a certain prominence, but though singular he would no longer be single, still less unique. Nor need we have any scruple about comparing *Christian* shamanism with all or any of the various other kinds of shamanism that have been highlighted in this chapter, or indeed with the many that have not.

To establish the legitimacy of such a comparison, though, is only one of the aims of this book. The other (complementary) aim is to put forward, however tentatively, a theory concerning the actual genesis of the Christian religion. To do this we have to hand back to Paul, as it were, the individuality we have just denied him, and to abandon, at least for the time being, the discipline of comparative religion in favour of *history*.

Of all the human sciences history is probably the one most resistant to the comparative-studies virus that swept through Western universities towards the end of the nineteenth century. Writing in 1905, the indefatigable Louis H. Jordan, eager as ever to grant Comparative Religion greater respectability by setting it in the context of more senior academic disciplines that had already been infected by the bug, lists over two dozen of these, starting with Anatomy and Philology, moving through Literature and History, adding Art, Architecture, Ethnology and Mythology, taking in Zoology towards the end, and adding for good measure Civics, Politics, Symbolics (!) and Liturgics (!!).[67] The subject that fits least

---

67. L. H. Jordan, *Comparative Religion*, 31–51.

comfortably in the whole of this long list is surely History. It is not that historians are averse in principle to making comparisons between events from different periods and people from different lands. Plutarch's *Parallel Lives* is only the first of many such comparisons. Nevertheless, 'The Arnold Toynbee Chair in Comparative History' has an odd ring to it. For the most part historians agree with Aristotle in distinguishing the individuality of history from the universality of philosophy; and their reactions to Toynbee's own monumental efforts range from wary respect to thinly disguised contempt. When historians do engage in comparisons it is generally not in the service of some ambitious and long-ranging theory but in order to illuminate part of a quite narrowly focused argument.

In the chapters that follow I shall be focusing primarily on Paul's individual experience, the most important evidence, I am convinced, at the disposal of anyone attempting to comprehend the first and most decisive breakaway from its Jewish matrix of the new and as yet unnamed religion – the Jesus movement – that was soon to be called Christianity. Right at the end I shall be returning to the shamanistic comparison that has been the main preoccupation of the present chapter. But it is now time to turn to the event on the Damascus road. Should we think of it as a call – or as a conversion?

EXCURSUS I
Jesus the Shaman

The suggestion that Jesus was a shaman is bound to cause offence. It is arguably a good deal less offensive, and, historically speaking, very much more probable than the recently floated theory that Jesus saw his own death as an atonement for the sins of Israel; but many more people are likely to resist it because it *sounds* derogatory. It is not meant to be.

To mitigate any possible offence let me start by admitting that Jesus' shamanism was by no means the most important aspect of his life. From the point of view of its impact upon subsequent history (*Wirkungsgeschichte*) it was the least important. Its relevance to this book is that if I am right about Jesus I am more likely to be right about Paul, because of the real possibility of an inherited debt.

If shamans are what you are looking for, Jesus is a much stronger candidate than Paul. Paul was a missionary with a message, whereas Jesus was a healer. No doubt he too had a message to proclaim (the Kingdom of God), but no agreement has ever been reached on what precisely that message was. Moreover, the life-style of a wandering healer ('the Son of Man has nowhere to lay his head') demands just the kind of environment in which shamans are usually found: not the highly organized city state which, if Burkert is right, is what ensured the demise of the shaman (γόης) in ancient Greece, but field or forest, hills or tundra, tribal village and local settlement.

Although of subordinate interest in the context of this book, the whole subject of Jesus' shamanism clearly deserves a much lengthier treatment than it can be given here.[1] In fact almost all the

---

1. The first reason for relegating this important subject to an excursus is that my discussion is too long for a footnote. A second reason is that the argument,

material included in this excursus has been comprehensively discussed in a recent book by Bernd Kollmann.[2] But since Kollmann concludes that Jesus was *not* a shaman I need to explain why I disagree.

The argument will be divided into three parts, concerning (a) exorcisms and kindred topics; (b) the temptation and baptism narrative; (c) the transfiguration scene.

Exorcisms and kindred topics

That Jesus was an exorcist is one of the most secure elements in the whole tradition; but in the majority of the lives of Jesus that have appeared in the last two centuries it is a fact in search of a context.[3] A salient exception is Geza Vermes's *Jesus the Jew*.[4] The third chapter of this book, entitled 'Jesus and charismatic Judaism', is a landmark in New Testament scholarship. Setting Jesus alongside other Jewish charismatics like Honi the Circle-Drawer and Hanina ben-Dosa, Vermes succeeds in dispelling the aura of uniqueness surrounding Jesus that makes so much of the gospel evidence so hard to evaluate.[5] In any case the fact that Jesus was an exorcist is not in dispute. I will comment here on two scenes in Mark's gospel and on one in Luke's.

Mark 1:21–27

And they went into Capernaum; and immediately on the sabbath he entered the synagogue and taught. And they were astonished

---

being somewhat technical and compressed, may not be easy to follow.

2. *Jesus und die Christen*.

3. When Jesus' exorcisms *are* discussed it is generally apropos of his eschatology: how far can they be regarded as signs of the coming of the kingdom? This question is usually treated without reference to the kind of social conditions that encourage the practice of exorcism. It is perhaps no accident that when he comes to draw up his list(s) of what can be said with certainty about the historical Jesus, Ed Sanders fails to include his activities as an exorcist [see *Jesus and Judaism*, 11 and 326], unlike Rudolf Bultmann who puts it first in his very different list: 'The Historical Jesus and the Risen Christ', 22.

4. G. Vermes, *Jesus the Jew*.

5. Vermes's discussion of Hanina has been expanded and refined by Seán Freyne: 'The Charismatic'.

at his teaching, for he taught them as one who had authority, and not as the scribes. And immediately there was in their synagogue a man with an unclean spirit; and he cried out, 'What have we to do with one another (Τί ἡμῖν καὶ σοί;) Jesus of Nazareth? Have you come to destroy us? I know who you are, the Holy One of God.' But Jesus mastered (ἐπετίμησεν) it, saying, 'Hold your tongue (Φιμώθητι), and come out of him!' And the unclean spirit, convulsing him and crying with a loud voice, came out of him. And they were all amazed, so that they questioned among themselves, saying, 'What is this? A new teaching! With authority he commands even the unclean spirits, and they obey him.

Jesus' first recorded public act (if we except the scene in Luke in which he teaches in the temple whilst still a child) is an exorcism. Like the other evangelists, Mark has his own agenda, and quite often adjusts his material for his own purposes. In this story, however, he sticks close to the source, as can be seen from the fact that *he does not understand it*.

Two verbs are important: ἐπιτιμᾶν, generally translated 'rebuke', one of its meanings in classical Greek, and φιμοῦν. Found here in the imperative mood, this is generally translated 'Be silent!' but it really means 'to muzzle'. It occurs only once in the LXX as a translation of the Hebrew, in Deut 25:4, where it refers to the muzzling of an ox (cf. 1 Tim 5:18); but in ancient magical texts it is used as a synonym of καταδεῖν ('to bind') to signify the fettering of the unruly or obstreperous.[6] In the context of an exorcism both these verbs are used in connection with the exercise of control over the demonic world: mastery in the one case, muzzling in the other.

The verb ἐπιτιμᾶν corresponds to the Hebrew (or Aramaic) גער. This occurs 28 times in the Bible, 21 of them with reference to the overcoming of the enemies of God.[7] The word is also found in the Genesis Apocryphon from Qumran (a haggadic midrash on the story of Abram's hazardous journey to Egypt with his wife Sarai in Genesis 12:10–20). At some point Abram is called in to exorcise a

---

6. See Erwin Rohde, *Psyche*, 424.
7. These figures are taken from an article by Howard Clark Kee, 'Terminology', in which he gives a full treatment of גער, without mentioning φιμοῦν. Like many others, he is chiefly interested in establishing the eschatological import of Jesus' exorcisms.

demon that has been afflicting Pharaoh and the male members of his household. Telling of his success, he reports: 'I prayed . . . and laid my hands on his [head]; and the scourge departed from him and the evil [spirit] was rebuked away (ואתגערת) [from him], and he recovered' (20.29).[8]

This is already enough to place Jesus in among first-century Palestinian exorcists. But Mark himself has no interest in this, as we can see from the way he comments on his own exorcism stories: 'whenever the unclean spirits beheld him, they fell down before him and cried out, "You are the Son of God." And he would strictly order them (πολλὰ ἐπιτίμα αὐτοῖς) not to make him known' (3:11–12). The unfamiliar name 'Holy One of God' is replaced by the more familiar 'Son of God'; the word ἐπιτιμᾶν is re-employed with a much feebler meaning; and the muzzling of the demon is re-interpreted in the service of Mark's secrecy theory.

The next passage shows a remarkable similarity in vocabulary and theme:

Mark 4:35–41

On that day, when evening had come, he said to them, 'Let us go across to the other side.' And leaving the crowd, they took him with them in the boat, just as he was. And other boats were with him. And a great storm arose, and the waves beat into the boat, so that the boat was already filling. But he was in the stern, asleep on the cushion; and they woke him and said to him, 'Teacher, do you not care if we perish?' And he awoke and mastered (ἐπετίμησεν) the wind, and said to the sea, 'Be silent! Muzzle yourself! (πεφίμωσο).' And the wind ceased, and there was a great calm. He said to them, 'Why are you afraid? Have you no faith?' And they were filled with awe, and said to one another, 'Who then is this, that the wind and sea obey him?'

In ancient Jewish mythical thinking the sea was regarded as the haunt of demons, and the term גער is often used of the mastery

---

8. This is Vermes's translation in *Jesus*, 66, following the standard dictionary rendering of גער. In his more recent translation, *The Complete Dead Sea Scrolls*, 455, he prefers 'expelled'. But even this is too weak. In a fragment from the War Scroll (4Qmᵃ) the word is used of the defeat of 'the gods'.

exercised over these malign sea-devils.[9] So it is surprising that Kollmann, who knows this perfectly well, detects a Hellenistic influence at this point and refuses to give this story a place among the authentic traditions of Jesus' exorcisms. To have done so would have meant associating him with the truly shamanic activity of direct interference with natural phenomena.

The next passage is very different:

Luke 10:17–20

The seventy returned with joy, saying, 'Lord, even the demons are subject to us in your name!' And he said to them, 'I was watching (ἐθεώρουν) Satan fall like lightning from heaven. Behold I have given you the power (τὴν ἐξουσίαν) to tread upon serpents and scorpions,[10] and over all the power of the enemy; and nothing shall hurt you. Nevertheless, do not rejoice in this, that the spirits are subject to you; but rejoice that your names are written in heaven.'

Kollmann does not question the authenticity of the saying concerning Satan's fall but states (as often, without argument) that it does not belong in its present context. He thinks it likely that it was spoken when Jesus began his own preaching career after dissociating it from that of John the Baptist. He ends with the grudging admission (tucked away in a footnote) that 'from the perspective of the phenomenology of religion (*religionsphänomenologisch*) we might recall in this connection the visions of the spirits that mark the outset of shamans' activity,' and he refers in conclusion to Eliade's work on shamanism.[11]

---

9. E.g. 2 Sam 22:16; Isa 17:13; 50:3; Nahum 1:4; Job 26:11; Ps 18:16, 104:7; 106:9. Kee comments interestingly on all these texts, 'Terminology', 236–7.
10. There is a close parallel here with an episode in the life of Hanina ben Dosa. A snake that had bitten him whilst he was engaged in prayer was soon after found dead near the entrance to its hole: ' "Woe to the man", they exclaimed, "bitten by a snake, but woe to the snake which has bitten Rabbi Hanina ben Dosa" ' (bBer 33a). (See Vermes, *Jesus*, 73.)
11. *Jesus und die Christen*, 194, n. 88.

The temptation and baptism narrative

Mark 1:12–13

The spirit immediately flung him out (αὐτὸν ἐκβάλλει) into the wilderness. And he was in the wilderness forty days, tempted by Satan; and he was with the wild beasts; and the angels ministered to him.

What we have seen to be the characteristic threefold division of a shaman's career is much more readily detectable in Jesus than in Paul. In the first place, the traumatic experience that precedes the shaman's call is not easy to discern in Paul's letters (though I shall be arguing that it can be found if one looks hard enough), whereas what is generally called the temptation narrative takes place in all three synoptic gospels immediately after Jesus' baptism and before the commencement of his healing ministry. In Matthew and Luke, admittedly, there is now no trace of a struggle; but Mark's account, according to which Jesus spent forty days in the wilderness after being flung out there by the spirit, invites a reading as a shaman's trial: 'And he was with the wild beasts'; the story concludes, 'and the angels ministered to him'. Could the spirits tormenting Jesus have assumed the form of savage animals, as is the case in many accounts of shamans' trials, and once he had overcome them was he comforted by the angels? This is apparently how Matthew and Luke read the story, though they soften Mark's 'flung out by the spirit' into 'led' (ἀνήχθη/ἤγετο), substitute the devil for Mark's wild beasts, and make the story into a kind of midrash upon the temptations of Israel in the wilderness of Sinai. (Jesus' clever responses to the devil's suggestions are drawn from different episodes in Deuteronomy.) Reading the story as an admittedly slightly sanitized version of a shaman's trial makes much more sense of it than simply dismissing it, as Bultmann does, as a 'legend'.[12] Putting it in a cupboard out of harm's way and then throwing away the key is not an explanation but a refusal to explain.

An alternative way of looking at the wild beasts is to see them as friendly spirits, like the angels that succeeded them. This is how

---

12. Bultmann, *Geschichte*[7], 1967, 270.

Morton Smith interprets the story. After inviting us to compare it with Eliade's account of the shaman's deliberate withdrawal into solitude to prepare himself for his career by a preliminary period of self-torture, he continues: '[The shaman] is supposed to be tested, subjected to terrible ordeals, or even killed by evil or initiatory spirits, but is helped by friendly spirits who appear in the form of animals. The statement that the spirit *drove* Jesus into the wilderness accords with rabbinic reports of demonic compulsion and suggests that Jesus was "possessed", although elsewhere it is claimed that he "had" the spirit.'[13]

Kollmann clearly has no patience with any of this and summarily disposes of Smith's view with the dismissive comment that he takes the story at face value (*für bare Münze*).[14] He himself takes it for granted that Mark is drawing upon the tradition of the trial of the just man (Wisd 2:10) and of Israel's forty-year sojourn in the desert (Exod 16:35; Deut 1:3). But this is itself just an assumption, and one that needs to be called into question. We should recall here two passages from the Books of Kings. First there is the episode in which Elisha is being urged to send for his master Elijah: 'it may be that the spirit of the Lord has caught him up and cast him upon some mountain or into some valley' (2 Kings 2:16).[15] Secondly there is the story of Elijah's long journey to Mount Horeb, on which he fasted for forty days and forty nights (1 Kings 19:8). A writer aware of an earlier tradition may of course borrow from this either to emphasize the connection with the past or simply to add an extra resonance to his own story, as both Matthew and Luke have done (independently?) by filling out Mark's spare narrative with detailed allusions to the people's temptations during their forty-year trek. Quite probably it was Mark's precise 'forty days' that prompted this move. But is it so obvious that Mark invented the whole story for the sake of a literary allusion? It is quite conceivable that Jesus himself, impressed by the account in 1 Kings 19:4 of how Elijah prepared for his ministry by a forty-day fast in the desert, decided to follow his example. He certainly attached no less importance to Jewish traditions than the evangelists. In that case there will have been an

---

13. *Jesus the Magician* [2], 104.
14. *Jesus und die Christen*, 271, n. 1.
15. In the LXX the word translated 'cast' here is rendered by ῥίπτειν ('toss').

authentic tradition behind the story. Nor should we assume, as Kollmann does, that the stilling of the storm in Mark 4 results from a combination of literary reminiscence and a desire not to allow Jesus to be seen to be outshone by contemporary Hellenistic wonder-workers. Ancient, authoritative texts have always been read in ways that issue in practical consequences: most liturgies point to a desire for remembrance that goes beyond the bounds of the purely literary. What else is the institution of Lent but a practical application of the tradition of Jesus' forty-day fast?

Mark 1:9–11

In those days Jesus came from Nazareth of Galilee and was baptized by John in the Jordan. And when he came up out of the water, immediately he saw the heavens opened and the Spirit descending upon him like a dove; and a voice came from heaven, 'Thou art my beloved Son (Σὺ εἶ ὁ υἱός μου ὁ ἀγαπητός); with thee I am well pleased.'

In all three synoptic accounts the baptism story immediately precedes the temptation narrative. It would be easier for my case if the order were reversed, for then it would be possible to argue that Jesus had undergone the typical shamanic sequence (struggle followed by call). Nevertheless, the conjunction may be significant, and in any case the most plausible interpretation of the baptism scene is that Jesus, like Paul, first became aware that he was being called by God on the occasion of a heavenly vision. Both Justin Martyr (*Dial.* 88.3, 8; 103.6) and the Gospel of the Ebionites (closer to the story than we are) associate God's words to Jesus with God's enthronement of King David in Psalm 2:7 ('this day I have begotten thee'); and it may be that the term ἀγαπητός, in spite of the literal meaning ('beloved'), is intended to convey the sense of 'doomed to death', since the term it generally translates in the Hebrew Bible, יָחִיד (literally, 'only child'), is virtually always used of an only child either recently dead or just about to die.[16]

---

16. See my note on Mark 12:6 in *Understanding*, 320, n. 68, and, for a defence of the view that a genuine visionary experience is being recalled here, C. Rowland, *Open Heaven*, 358–64.

The transfiguration scene

Mark 9:2–8

And after six days Jesus took with him Peter and James and John, and led them up a high mountain apart by themselves; and he was transfigured (μετεμορφώθη) before them, and his garments became glistening, intensely white, as no fuller on earth could bleach them. And there appeared to them Elijah with Moses; and they were talking to Jesus. And Peter said to Jesus, 'Master, it is well that we are here; let us make three booths, one for you and one for Moses and one for Elijah.' For he did not know what to say, for they were exceedingly afraid. And a cloud overshadowed them (καὶ ἐγένετο νεφέλη ἐπισκιάζουσα αὐτοῖς) and a voice came out of the cloud, 'This is my beloved Son; listen to him.' And suddenly looking around they no longer saw any one with them but Jesus only.

This is a scene that baffles biographers, which is no doubt why most of them leave it severely alone. But it offers plenty of scope to redaction critics, interested in tracking the theological preoccupations of each evangelist. Matthew and Luke have modified Mark's account; but the similarities between this episode and the baptism story suggest that Mark too has already adjusted elements of the tradition for his own purposes. The early form critics regarded the story as a kind of anticipatory resurrection appearance, displaced from its original position.[17] Like their treatment of the temptation narrative, this is a non-solution, and in any case, as Morton Smith cogently observes, 'if it is difficult to believe that a man's disciples saw him transfigured while he was still alive, it is yet more difficult to believe that they saw him so after he had been arrested, "crucified, dead, and buried"'.[18]

---

17. So Bultmann, *Geschichte*[7], 278, n. 1, following Wellhausen, Loisy and Bousset: 'that Jesus should have been seen in a vision (*das visionäre Schauen Jesu*) whilst still corporally present is scarcely credible (*eine kaum glaubliche Sache*)' – on which Morton Smith comments sardonically (and a trifle unfairly) that what is really *kaum glaublich* is 'that such a statement should have been made by a modern teacher of religion, even if only of New Testament, who might have been expected to know something of the phenomena of ecstatic cults': 'Origin', 41.
18. 'Origin', 41.

Alan Segal, noticing that the word used for transfiguration is the same as that used by Paul to indicate the (gradual) transformation of his converts into a fully Christian existence, thinks that the scene may be intended as a model for the gospel reader, 'as well as a sign of Jesus' own identity as God's principal angelic manifestation'. He also finds an 'unmistakable' connection with the heavenly journey motif in Jewish mystical apocalypticism.[19] The heavenly journey is a motif that Jewish apocalypticism has in common with shamanism,[20] so it may be that Jesus' ability to transform himself into a heavenly being by donning angelic clothes is a final indication of his own shamanism. Morton Smith emphasizes that the scene was interrupted by a passing cloud that blotted out the vision: 'the familiar story of the magical séance that ends abruptly when the spell is broken by an inauspicious act.... So widespread a story', he concludes, 'probably reflects a common experience in hallucinative rites.'[21]

Elsewhere Morton Smith argues more extensively in favour of the proposition that Jesus experienced mystical ascents in his own lifetime. Among other texts he appeals to the Philippians hymn and, much more plausibly in my opinion, to Jesus' saying in John 3:13: 'Nobody has ascended into heaven except the one who descended from heaven, the son of Man.'[22] Most intriguingly he takes Paul's phrase 'I know a man in Christ' or 'I know in Christ a man' (2 Cor 12:2) to refer, not to Paul himself (which is the way almost all scholars take it), but to Jesus! He makes things easier for himself by mistranslating Paul's οἶδα as 'I knew' (even the 'fourteen years ago' does not make this possible), and in spite of a brave try he does not really manage to give a convincing explanation of how Paul could have spoken of knowing *Jesus* 'in Christ'.[23] Nevertheless, the more general proposition that the *evangelists* told the story of Jesus' transfiguration 'because it was basically a report of something that once happened' should, I think, be accepted.[24]

---

19. *Paul the Convert*, 111–12.
20. On this topic see especially Susan Niditch, 'The Visionary'.
21. *Jesus the Magician*, 122.
22. On this verse see especially Hugo Odeberg, *The Fourth Gospel*, 72; and my *Understanding*, 348–56.
23. 'Ascent to the Heavens'. For a fuller discussion of this important text see Chapter 4, 'Paul the Mystic'.
24. 'Origin and History', 43. See too C. Rowland, *Open Heaven*, 364–8.

All in all, the historical figure of Jesus exhibits so many of the characteristic features that we have seen to be generally associated with shamanism that he should, surely, be given the title too. Even if it is hard to agree with Morton Smith (and A. N. Wilson) that Paul knew Jesus in his lifetime, the similarities in their experiences give an additional edge of probability to the proposition that Paul too was a shaman.

3
Paul the Convert

The barge she sat in, like a burnished throne
Burned on the water: the poop was beaten gold;
Purple the sails, and so perfumèd that
The winds were lovesick with them; the oars were silver,
Which to the tune of flutes kept stroke and made
The water which they beat to follow faster,
As amorous of their strokes. For her own person,
It beggared all description: she did lie
In her pavilion, cloth-of-gold of tissue,
O'er picturing that Venus where we see
The fancy outwork nature: on each side her
Stood pretty dimpled boys, like smiling Cupids,
With divers-coloured fans, whose winds did seem
To glow the delicate cheeks which they did cool,
And what they undid did.

So spoke Shakespeare's Enobarbus, describing Cleopatra's first meeting with Mark Antony, when 'she pursed up his heart, upon the river of Cydnus'. What Shakespeare does not tell us, nor Plutarch, for that matter, from whom he borrowed his description,[1] needing only a few delicate touches to transform it into poetry, is that the place of this encounter was none other than the town in which, maybe half a century later (the year of this meeting was 41 BC), the apostle Paul was born: Tarsus in Cilicia, 'no mean city', as Paul himself told the tribune who arrested him in Jerusalem (Acts 21:39).

---

1. *Life of Antony*, 26.1–2. The quotation is from Act 2, Scene 2 of *Antony and Cleopatra*.

And he told no more than the truth. The geographer Strabo, whose life overlapped Paul's (he died around AD 24), says of the people of Tarsus that they 'have devoted themselves so eagerly, not only to philosophy, but also to the whole round of education in general, that they have surpassed Athens, Alexandria, or any other place that can be named where there have been schools and lectures of philosophers' (*Geography* 14.5.13). But he adds that few foreigners were inclined to stay there, and when the natives of the city went abroad to complete their education most of them never went back.[2] We should remember, however, that when Paul visited Athens, he must have done so in the knowledge that it was by now well down on the university league table.

In this chapter I shall make a few tentative dabs at ideas that will have to be sketched in more fully later. Paul was a mystic, an apostle, a prophet, a charismatic. As we consider what is commonly called his conversion we shall catch glimpses of all these varied facets of his eventual self, before even he had begun to reflect on them. When he did they would be built into what is called his theology; but they have their beginnings as part of his religion.

The three questions to be addressed in this chapter are these: (1) Should we speak of Paul's *conversion* or not rather refer to his *call* (as apostle or prophet)? (2) What exactly happened on the Damascus road? (3) How are we to explain the transformation of a zealous Jew into a Jesus movement missionary? Did this happen suddenly, 'brim, in a flash, full', in the striking phrase of Gerard Manley Hopkins, or had Paul already been 'mined with a motion, a drift'? Was the revelation perceived instantaneously as a vocation, or did the conviction of his mission to the Gentiles reach him later, with the benefit of hindsight? In other words, is the key to the

2. Paul himself returned at least once (Gal 1:21). Richard Wallace and Wynne Williams remark that although Tarsus was famous for its philosophers, 'there is no reason to suppose that a Jewish tentmaker born in Tarsus would therefore have a better than average knowledge of philosophical ideas, any more than we would expect someone who worked in a car factory in Oxford to have for that reason a better knowledge of Wittgenstein than one whose workplace was in Coventry': *Three Worlds*, 133. But then Paul was not just your common or camp-site tentmaker. Rudolf Bultmann showed long ago in his first published book, *Der Stil der paulinischen Predigt und der kynisch-stoische Diatribe* (Göttingen, 1910), that he had a real knowledge of rhetorical techniques. Just how much, though, is still disputed.

explanation to be sought before the event, after the event, or in the event itself?

The first of these questions is the easiest. The second is a problem for which no definitive solution is available, but I shall introduce the topic here, continue the discussion in the following chapter, and return to it, from a different perspective, in the last chapter of the book. The third, really a series of questions, contains one of the most intriguing puzzles in current New Testament scholarship, how to account for the increasing importance assumed by the *Gentiles* in the missionary activity of what was still just a Jewish sect, now proclaiming its recently executed teacher to be the Jewish Messiah. Paul and his first biographer, Luke, disagree on many things, but they are united on one key issue: Paul had received a summons from God to carry the new message concerning Jesus the Messiah beyond the bounds of Jewry to the furthest reaches of the Gentile world. Anyone content to accept their reports at face value has no problem. Visited from heaven by a special revelation, Paul was told to preach to the Gentiles, and that is what he did. But why the Gentiles? The historian, trying to probe beneath the surface, cannot rest content with an answer that does little more than restate the problem.

Why is it, we might ask, that the urgency of this problem has not been appreciated until quite recently? Probably, as Terence Donaldson argues, because Paul's concern for the Gentiles was considered hitherto 'not as a "topic" or a "problem" – an aspect of his life and thought requiring reflection and explanation – but as axiomatic – a basic assumption about his life and thought that formed part of the framework for reflection on and explanation of the rest'.[3] The recognition of Paul's work among the Gentiles as a problem rather than an axiom is one of a number of major changes in recent approaches to Paul that justify Donaldson in speaking of a 'paradigm shift'. (He goes on to align this with Thomas Kuhn's *Structure of Scientific Revolutions*.)

Call or conversion?

Of all the headings I have given to the chapters in this book, 'convert' is the one that would have caused Paul the most trouble. Any

3. T. L. Donaldson, *Paul and the Gentiles*, 4.

suggestion that he had abandoned the Judaism of his youth to take up another *religion* would have left him utterly bewildered. And since this is the inference any present-day listener or reader would draw from this term, then we should either hedge it around with protective thorns or give it up completely. Jerome Murphy-O'Connor asserts in his recent biography that in view of 'the radical shift in Paul's perception of God and of the divine plan of salvation' it is simply pedantic to refuse to call him a convert.[4] But this is to read Paul's life through heavily-tinted Christian spectacles. The radical shift in perception of which Murphy-O'Connor speaks did indeed take place. But the inference that it is consequently mere pedantry to deny Paul the title of convert is an over-simplification. Either he is being disingenuous or he has failed to appreciate the real difference between admitting that Paul's religious beliefs underwent a dramatic change and seeing this change as an immediate conversion. For the language of conversion cannot but suggest that Paul, from being a Jew, became a Christian.[5] If so, then Christianity must have been in place before Paul embraced it, and such a thesis puts too great a strain on our credulity. There simply was not time for those who had begun to proclaim Jesus to their fellow Jews to think of themselves as anything other than as his disciples, as they had been during his lifetime. They certainly proclaimed him to be Messiah; but there is no reason to suppose that they had begun to draw the kind of radical conclusions from their own message that were eventually to force the new movement out of Judaism. Their name for themselves, seemingly, was 'the Way' (Acts 9:2; 19:9, 23; 22:4; 24:14, 22), which suggests that though conscious of following a new path, they had as yet no sense that it was a new religion.[6]

As for Paul, although he had actually persecuted the followers of Jesus for some time before the incident on the Damascus road

---

4. *Paul*, 70, n. 2.
5. See Krister Stendahl, *Paul among Jews and Gentiles*, 7–23
6. Luke tells us that it was in Antioch, some time after Gentiles had begun to be admitted into the church, that 'the disciples were for the first time called Christians' (Acts 11:26). Paul – or rather Saul – was in Antioch when the name was first introduced, but he never uses the word in his own letters. Apart from Acts 26:28, where King Agrippa ironically accuses Paul of trying to make him a Christian, there is only one other instance of the word in the New Testament, in 1 Pet 4:16.

dramatically changed his life, he may never have fully sensed that the movement he had joined had become a new religion. At all events he continued throughout his life to think of himself as a Jew. I have already remarked that his letters constitute a kind of doctrinal blueprint of Christianity; but if the plans were already on the table in Paul's lifetime, the work of construction had scarcely begun. The so-called Pastoral Letters, no longer ascribed to Paul except by a handful of extreme conservatives, give us some idea of the way Paul's inspired vision was beginning to harden into something resembling the institutional church. But these must be dated some decades after Paul's death.

To conclude: this is one of those questions that can legitimately be answered by a cliché: it all depends on what you mean by.... If, in saying Paul was a convert you simply mean that his life was radically changed, the answer is yes; but if you mean that from being a Jew he immediately became a Christian (surely the way most people would take it), then the answer is no. Whenever I myself allude to Paul's conversion in this book it will always be simply in the sense of radical change.

One of the problems we have here is that at this period the Greek word Ἰουδαῖος, which could be used either as an adjective or as a noun, had two possible references: it could refer either to a *Judaean*, someone belonging to the quite small region of Palestine still known as Judaea, or to a *Jew* living in one of a very large number of communities known collectively as the diaspora. The adjectival rendering, *Jewish*, had then, as now, both a religious and a racial connotation. The distinction between these could not easily be drawn by people thinking, speaking or writing in Greek.[7] It could be argued that since Paul unquestionably ended his life as a Christian, the need to find some way of making the distinction (since he continued to assert his Jewishness) arose in the first place from his life and writings. (Nowadays, perhaps, he might be called a 'reconstructed' or 'recentred' Jew.)

Before proceeding, something needs to be said about the three accounts of the event in the Book of Acts. Purists are reluctant to muddy the exegetical waters by mingling Paul's own spare and

---

7. The problem is even more pressing and troublesome in John's gospel. On this topic see my *Studying John*, 36–70.

reticent reference to his call with Luke's more dramatic account in Acts 9, plus the even more colourful stories Paul told, so Luke informs us, on separate occasions before two different audiences. Evidently these cannot be taken to be faithful renderings of Paul's own words. Whether or not Luke, as some have argued, had access to the letter to the Galatians, and added a little artistic verisimilitude to Paul's terse summary, the particular details in all three chapters in Acts are his own. If he had access to an early narrative of the incident, close enough to one (probably the first) of his three versions, then the extraneous details in the other two must be attributed to his own historical (and theological) imagination. But for my purposes, I want to insist, *this does not matter.*[8] Having already argued that Paul's theology is best regarded as an *interpretation* of his experiences, I can consistently maintain that his interpretation, however privileged (and a Wittgensteinian might refuse even this concession),[9] is by no means the only possible one. And in Luke we have a precious witness of how Paul's fellow-believers, contemporaries and quite possibly personal friends, interpreted an event which they too saw as absolutely pivotal in the history of the early church. The fact that Luke chooses to include three separate versions of Paul's call proves that what matters for him most is what the three versions have in common.

Galatians 1:11–17

For I would have you know, brothers and sisters, that the gospel which was preached by me is not man's gospel. For I did not receive it from man, nor was I taught it, but it came through a revelation of Jesus Christ. For you have heard of my former life in Judaism, how I persecuted the church of God to an extreme

8. Mark Goodacre has reminded me that there is nothing in the Galatians passage to show that the vision took place on the Damascus road. This could be just an inference of Luke, based solely on Paul's statement that he returned to Damascus after his sojourn in Arabia. Interesting things happen on roads in Luke, such as the Samaritan's mugging on the descent to Jericho (Luke 10) or Jesus' appearance to the disciples journeying to Emmaus (Luke 24). Yet 'the Damascus road incident' has become a virtually universal synonym for Paul's conversion or call, and the adoption of this convention does not affect my argument. Moreover, if John Bowker is right (see n. 35) the road is relevant.
9. Wittgenstein denied that individual human beings have what he called 'privileged access' to their own feelings.

degree and tried to destroy it; and I advanced in Judaism beyond many of my own age among my people, so extremely zealous was I for the traditions of my fathers. But when he who set me apart from my mother's womb, and had called me through his grace was pleased to reveal his Son in me (ἐν ἐμοί), in order that I might preach him among the Gentiles, I did not confer with flesh and blood, nor did I go up to Jerusalem to those who were apostles before me, but I went away into Arabia; and again I returned to Damascus.

Acts 9:1–9

But Saul, still breathing threats and murder against the disciples of the Lord, went to the high priest and asked him for letters to the synagogues at Damascus, so that if he found any belonging to the Way, men or women, he might bring them bound to Jerusalem. Now as he journeyed he approached Damascus, and suddenly a light from heaven flashed about him. And he fell to the ground and heard a voice saying to him, 'Saul, Saul, why do you persecute me?' And he said, 'Who are you, Lord?' And he said, 'I am Jesus, whom you are persecuting; but rise, and enter the city, and you will be told what you are to do.' The men who were travelling with him stood speechless, hearing the voice but seeing no one. Saul arose from the ground; and when his eyes were opened, he could see nothing; so they led him by the hand and brought him into Damascus. And for three days he was without sight, and neither ate nor drank.

Acts 22:5–11

… and I journeyed to Damascus to take those also who were there and bring them in bonds to Jerusalem to be punished. As I made my journey and drew near to Damascus, about noon a great light from heaven suddenly shone about me. And I fell to the ground and heard a voice saying to me, 'Saul, Saul, why do you persecute me?' And I answered, 'Who are you, Lord?' And he said to me, 'I am Jesus of Nazareth, whom you are persecuting.' Now those who were with me saw the light but did not hear the voice of the one who was speaking to me. And I said, 'What shall I do, Lord?' And the Lord said to me, 'Rise and go into Damascus, and there you will be told all that is appointed for you to do.' And when I could not see because of the brightness of that light, I was led by the hand by those who were with me, and came to Damascus.

Acts 26:12–18

Thus I journeyed to Damascus with the authority and commission of the chief priests. At midday, O king, I saw on the way a light from heaven, brighter than the sun, shining round me and those who journeyed with me. And when we had all fallen to the ground, I heard a voice saying to me in the Hebrew language, 'Saul, Saul, why do you persecute me? It hurts you to kick against the pricks.' And I said, 'Who are you, Lord? And the Lord said, 'I am Jesus whom you are persecuting. But rise and stand upon your feet; for I have appeared to you for this purpose, to appoint you to serve and bear witness to the things in which you have seen me and to those in which I will appear to you, delivering you from the people and from the Gentiles – to whom I send you to open their eyes, that they may turn from darkness to light and from the power of Satan to God, that they may receive forgiveness of sins and a place among those who are sanctified by faith in me.'

What happened?

Few professional commentators are willing to tackle this question directly. It may be fairly called an academic storm-centre from which most people prudently run for cover, taking shelter under an assemblage of those knotty little puzzles so beloved of exegetes which, however interesting in themselves, leave students bewildered and frustrated, unable to comprehend why the commentator to whom they have turned for assistance has not only given no satisfactory answer to the one question they want solved, but has failed to address it at all. Ferdinand Christian Baur, who gave the problem its classic formulation as long ago as 1845, had no such inhibitions. The main emphasis, he says, must be put on the question whether what happened on the Damascus road is to be regarded as an interior reality or an exterior one ('eine äußere oder innere Tatsache').[10] In other words, did it really happen as a physical reality, or was it a vision or hallucination?

(a) Let us start with Hans-Joachim Schoeps. Schoeps is interesting because besides offering what he claims to be the first comprehensive study of Paul for a generation (he is writing in 1959), he claims an advantage in approaching Paul 'as an impartial historian of religion',[11] a claim he often repeats in the course of his book. Speaking of the 'Damascus event', he says:

> Discussions have taken place as to how far it was psychologically prepared, as to whether it sprang from an ecstatic visionary disposition, as to whether its objectivity is reliable, and so on. It is difficult to get anywhere in this way. If we adopt this approach and explain away the vision on a psychological basis, so that it becomes but the subjective vision of an ecstatic in a state of tension, then to be consistent we should have to adopt the same method of easy explanation – which is only an explaining away – for Moses' vision of God at the burning bush, while the divine voice to the patriarchs and prophets would have to be similarly explained as subjective and fanciful. If we wish to understand

10. F. Ch. Baur, *Paulus*, 64.
11. *Paul*, xi.

what happened at this point in the life of the apostle, and what were its consequences, then we must accept fully the real objectivity of the encounter as it is testified in the letters and in Acts. It is assumed of the theologian that in his own existence he becomes the contemporary of Paul,[12] that with Paul he believes in Jesus as the manifested and risen Son of God. The historian of religion is expected to recognize the faith of Paul in the manifested Son of God *to be the factual result of his encounter with the crucified and exalted Jesus of Nazareth*. If he does not do so, if he fails to recognize *the objective content of this encounter*, then he can only stupidly fail to understand an event which made history; which, according to the Christian faith, is itself saving history.[13]

This is thoroughly confused. Unless Schoeps is using the German words *gegenständlich* and *Gegenständlichkeit* in a sense that the English 'objective' and 'objectivity' will not bear, the claims he is making go far beyond what most 'impartial' historians of religion would be prepared to concede. Paul's encounter with the risen Christ was not a historical event of the same order as Caesar's crossing of the Rubicon. The historical 'fact', if that is what it is, relates to the impact this experience (as neutral a word as I can find) had upon Paul. The rest is speculation. And speculation ranges far and wide....

(b) Here is an example of an author who favours the hypothesis of what Baur called an *external* (objective?) reality:

About noon, when Saul's party were enjoying their after-dinner siesta by the roadside not far from Damascus, he heard himself suddenly addressed by name and threatened ... 'Saul, Saul, why do you persecute me?' (Acts 9:4). Saul's illegal raid into 'strange' territory (Acts 26:11) was [probably] made with the sole object of arresting Jesus, news of whose re-appearance in Damascus had reached Jerusalem. He was accompanied by a party of armed Levites, whose task was to follow and waylay Jesus, but the plan

---

12. This is apparently an allusion to something that Karl Barth says in the preface to the second edition of his *Romans*. One does not have to have read Gadamer to recognize the absurdity of such a claim.

13. *Paul*, 54–5. (My italics.)

miscarried because Jesus had boldly taken the initiative. Saul roused himself when he heard his name called and, though dazzled by the glare of the midday sun on Jesus' white robes, peered at the stigmata in his outstretched hands and recognized him. In terror that Jesus had come with an armed following to take his life, he closed his eyes, bowed low, trembled, and begged for mercy.[14]

To the question how this was possible, the answer is that Jesus had survived both the crucifixion and thirty hours in the tomb, 'having remained in complete anaesthesia both when he was wounded in the side, and when the nails were drawn out'.[15] After emerging he put in a number of appearances to his disciples, but eventually saw that he could not remain in hiding indefinitely without exposing his friends to the charge of harbouring a criminal. Branded with the mark of Cain (the scars of the crucifixion), he decided that, like Cain, he would have to become 'a fugitive and a vagabond', and seek refuge 'in the Land of Nod to the East of Eden' (Gen 4:14–16), namely in the trans-Euphratean province of Susiana, where he spent the remainder of his life preaching repentance to his co-religionists.

Though we may be unconvinced by the picture of Jesus skulking in the background, watching his disciples from a safe distance as they told a succession of lies about his resurrection, it cannot be ruled out as an absolute impossibility – unlike the story of an actual physical resurrection, in any of its versions.

14. Robert Graves and Joshua Podro, *The Nazarene Gospel Restored* , 804–5. (This quotation is slightly modified and abbreviated.)
15. Ibid., 739. Graves backs up his theory of Jesus' survival with a story of his own experience in the First World War, when, after having his lung pierced by a shell-splinter, he was left for dead on the battlefield of the Somme, and with only a stretcher to shield his body from the bare earth managed to conserve his vital heat for very nearly thirty hours. 'The physical resistance of Oriental saints', he concludes, 'is notoriously greater than that of European sinners.' Graves is by no means the first to come up with the idea that Jesus survived the crucifixion. It was put forward as early as the end of the 18th century by a certain Karl Friedrich Bahrdt (not to be confused with the 20th-century Swiss theologian Karl Barth), of whom Albert Schweitzer tells us that he had an undisciplined sensuous nature and that after holding a chair for some years at the University of Halle, he 'died in disrepute in 1792' (*Quest*, 39).

(c) Before continuing, it is worth pausing for a moment over Baur's question (was the Damascus road incident an interior or an exterior reality?) and to take a last look at the primary evidence in Galatians and Acts. Paul's own answer to this question, I believe, is clear: 'God revealed his son *in* me.'[16] He experienced the revelation, then, as happening somehow inside himself.

If that is so, did it come to him as something *heard* or as something *seen*? Again, Paul's answer is clear, though it is given in another letter, addressed to a different community: 'Am I not an apostle? Have I not seen Jesus the Lord?' (1 Cor 9:1).

On the face of it this question might be taken to allude to an exterior seeing, but Paul's fuller account in chapter 15 gives no effective support to this interpretation, in spite of his repeated use of the verb 'to see'. For the Greek ὤφθη (vv. 6,7,8,9: 'was seen'), like the Hebrew נראה (or וירא) that it regularly translates, is frequently employed in the Bible of the appearance of angels or divine beings in dreams or visions (e.g. Gen 12:7; 35:1; 48:3; Judges 6:12; 13:3; cf. Matt 17:3||; Luke 1:11; 22:43); so any inference of physical vision in 1 Corinthians 15 is unjustified.

Is this the answer then: an interior vision and nothing more? Not quite. For Paul also interpreted the event as a call, and a call implies hearing. So Luke's third version in Acts 26 ('I saw a light…. I heard a voice') is not after all too hard to reconcile with the testimony of Paul himself.[17]

What Paul saw (the nature of his visionary experience) and what he heard (the content of his apostolic calling) present the interpreter with two distinct problems, whether vision and vocation occurred

16. I defer until the final chapter any discussion of the generally preferred alternative ('*to* me'), which demands a lot of strenuous philological wriggling if it is to be made to look respectable.

17. Luke nowhere states that Paul actually *saw* Jesus, which may have something to do with his sense that to have *seen* the risen Jesus was an indispensable condition of true apostleship: for Luke (barring Acts 14:4, 6) there were only twelve apostles, and Paul was not one of them. (Paul agreed with Luke about this condition, but insisted that he had seen Jesus – though not necessarily physically.) 'Ample evidence from the religious literature', remarks Betz, 'shows that the visionary experience and the verbal revelation do not exclude each other'; and he points in particular to the pseudo-Clementine Homilies (17.19.4) where we are told that Christ stayed with Paul for an hour, giving him instructions. 'This information', remarks Betz, 'tries to explain away the conflict, but it thereby shows also that this conflict is artificial to the ancient mind' (*Galatians*, 64).

together, as Paul appears to imply, or separately – which is what we would naturally conclude on the basis of the first two of Luke's three accounts. The questions arising from the call will be dealt with in the third and final section of this chapter. For the present we may concentrate upon the puzzle of what Paul saw on the Damascus road.

The answer to this question, perhaps surprisingly, is to be found neither in Galatians nor in Acts, but in a passage from another of Paul's letters, 2 Corinthians. Speaking of people from whom the truth of the gospel has been veiled, he says that their minds have been blinded by 'the god of this world' (a puzzling enough expression in itself)

> to keep them from seeing (εἰς τὸ μὴ αὐγάσαι) the light of the gospel of the glory of Christ (τῆς δόξης τοῦ Χριστοῦ), who is the image of God (ὅς ἐστιν εἰκὼν τοῦ θεοῦ). For what we preach is not ourselves, but Jesus Christ as Lord, with ourselves as your servants for Jesus' sake. For it is the God who said, 'Light will shine out of darkness ('Εκ σκότους φῶς λάμψει)', who shone (ἔλαμψεν) in our hearts to give the light of the knowledge of the glory of God in the face of Christ (τῆς γνώσεως τῆς δόξης τοῦ θεοῦ ἐν προσώπῳ Χριστοῦ).   2 Cor 4:4–6

In her commentary on this passage, Margaret Thrall remarks upon several features which suggest that Paul 'is referring to his own experience of Christophany. The aorist [past definite] tense of ἔλαμψεν points to one specific moment in the past, the shining of heavenly light was a characteristic of his experience according to the narratives in Acts ... and the glory is seen on the face of Christ (ἐν προσώπῳ Χριστοῦ) in a personal encounter, that is, in which Christ himself appeared. Hence, there is substantial support for the view that Paul alludes to the event of his own conversion and call to apostleship.'[18]

Thrall names a number of scholars who have advocated this view, the earliest being A. Klöpper (1874); but by far the most persuasive advocate in recent years has been Seyoon Kim. The arguments he advances in support of his thesis sprawl over hundreds of pages, but the essence of the thesis itself is stated quite succinctly. Paul's

18. M. E. Thrall, *Corinthians*, i , 316.

conception of Christ as the εἰκὼν τοῦ θεοῦ (image of God) 'is rooted', Kim submits, 'in the Damascus event: *Paul saw the exalted Christ in glory as the εἰκὼν τοῦ θεοῦ on the road to Damascus'*.[19]

The core of Kim's argument, in the course of which he comments on a wide variety of texts, is that Paul's experience was an instance of what has come to be called *merkabah mysticism*. (The meaning of this term will be explained in the excursus that follows this chapter.) Starting from the great vision of the throne of God at the beginning of the book of Ezekiel, there are numerous instances of God appearing to Jewish prophets and seers 'in the likeness of a man'. Ezekiel himself sums up his vision: 'Such was the appearance of the likeness of the glory of the Lord': (הוּא מַרְאֵה דְּמוּת כְּבוֹד־יהוה: ἡ ὅρασις ὁμοιώματος δόξης κυρίου). 'Glory' in the Bible is virtually a theophanic term in itself: it is always used in contexts where God, either explicitly or implicitly, is said to be manifesting himself. So when Paul speaks of 'the glory of God in the face of Christ' just after he has spoken of Christ as the *image* of God, it is reasonable to infer that his vision was basically of the same order as those of Ezekiel and other seers whose experiences followed a similar pattern.[20]

Kim goes on to assert that 'Ezekiel sees God not directly but as reflected in a mirror, that is the (mirror) image of God'.[21] This is an attractive, if speculative (!) suggestion, but though it would certainly reinforce his hypothesis, it is probably not an essential part of it. We can agree with Thrall's conclusion that when Paul speaks of the glory

---

19. *The Origin of Paul's Gospel*, 193.

20. See Christopher Rowland's *The Open Heaven*, especially pp. 78–123; 214–47 (although in the section on Paul (pp. 374–86) there is no mention of 2 Cor 4:4–6). This book appeared too late for Kim to make use of it; but he does draw extensively on the Cambridge doctoral thesis in which Rowland's ideas were first adumbrated: 'The Influence of the First Chapter of Ezekiel on Judaism and Early Christianity'. The necessary conditions of mystical experience in general will be discussed in the next chapter.

21. *Origin*, 207. Kim interprets the phrase כְּעֵין הַחַשְׁמַל (RSV 'as it were gleaming bronze') as if the חַשְׁמַל (more commonly understood to be a gleaming alloy of gold and silver – though see Rowland, op. cit., 487, n. 13) acted as a mirror – a meaning inferred from the use of the word עֵין ('eye', 'appearance') in its construct form. (The verse Kim actually cites is Ez 1:4, but if his argument is to work it must proceed from the other occurrence of the phrase כְּעֵין הַחַשְׁמַל, in 1:27.) This interpretation is supported by A. F. Segal, *Paul the Convert*, 323, n. 94.

of God revealed on the face of Christ, 'the Corinthians would surely understand this as an allusion to Paul's vision of the risen Christ (1 Cor 9.1; cf. 15.8) and would be intended so to understand it'.[22]

Further support for this approach is to be found in a book called *Paul the Convert* by a Jewish scholar, Alan Segal, written without reference to Kim's study. Segal's account of Paul's conversion (for as the title of his book suggests, he is a stout defender of this particular theory) comes in the second chapter, 'Paul's Ecstasy'. Not surprisingly, Segal discusses many of the same texts as Kim (and Rowland). He has a tendency to confuse Paul's actual conversion experience with the story of a later heavenly journey in 2 Corinthians 12 (to be discussed in the next chapter); but his wide-ranging discussion gives further support to the thesis that has just been outlined.[23]

The advantage of understanding 2 Cor 4:4–6 as an allusion to Paul's conversion is that it gives it both a context and a content that would otherwise be lacking. Yet even if we accept the suggestion that Paul believed himself to have had a vision of Christ on the Damascus road there is one aspect of the puzzle that is still to be resolved. Having considered what Paul *saw* we must now turn to what he *heard*. We shall see that the search for a satisfactory explanation of Paul's apostolic calling is in some ways even more problematic.

Early unrest? Instant call? Dawning recognition?

How are we to explain Paul's transformation from zealous Jew into apostle of the Gentiles? To appreciate the difficulty of this question we have to start quite a long way back. One of the questions that most exercised Paul and Luke is this: did God change his mind about the Jews and the Gentiles? Neither of them of course would have put it quite like that. God is frequently enough portrayed in the Bible as disappointed or angry with his people, even to the extent, in Isaiah, of determining to reduce them to a rump or a remnant (Isa 7:3; 10:20–21 etc.). But were God to reject Israel completely, then

22. *Commentary*, 317.
23. Segal, *Paul the Convert*, 34–71.

his very essence would have changed. When Hosea's wife Gomer bore him a third son Yahweh said, 'Call his name Not-my-people, for you are not my people and I am not your God' (Hos 1:9). This sounds harsh in English: the Hebrew is even bleaker: אָנֹכִי לֹא־אֶהְיֶה לָכֶם: '*I am* – not – yours'. With this stark declaration God is withdrawing the gift of his name to his people on Mount Sinai: 'I am who am': אֶהְיֶה אֲשֶׁר אֶהְיֶה, (Exod 3:14).[24] If Israel is no longer his people, her God no longer has a name. It is simply inconceivable that he should abandon Israel for another nation, or for all the other nations in the world, the *goyim*, the Gentiles. Naturally Jews were curious (how could they not be?) about God's plans for the Gentiles. We shall see that Judaism has a variety of strategies for dealing with this problem. But it simply could not contain the kind of answers given by Luke and Paul.

Scholars are now agreed that Jesus never intended to carry his message of the kingdom beyond the confines of Israel. Yet shortly after his death the idea of the Gentile mission had come to be accepted by a significant number of his followers, and this was the policy that was to prevail, with Paul as its most eloquent and vehement spokesman. How did this change come about?

Let us start with the Book of Acts. Right at the beginning of the book, just before his ascension, Jesus gives his apostles explicit instructions to be his 'witnesses' first in Jerusalem and all Judaea, then in Samaria, and then to the end of the earth: ἕως ἐσχάτου τῆς γῆς (Acts 1:8). On the face of it this could simply mean that they were to carry the gospel to the many *Jewish* communities scattered around the world (the diaspora). But the term 'end of the earth' turns out to be an allusion to a verse from Isaiah referring to the *Gentiles*: 'I have given you as a light to the Gentiles, for you to bring salvation to the end of the earth' (Isa 49:6 LXX). We can be sure of this because Paul quotes this very verse at the end of his speech to the Jews of Pisidian Antioch in order to justify his radical change of direction: 'Since you thrust away [the word of God] ... behold, we

---

24. The name *Yahweh* is probably the 3rd person singular of an ancient form of the verb 'to be' (*hawah*). Often referred to as 'the tetragrammaton' (four-letter word!), it is not pronounced by pious Jews, who use the name *Adonai*, 'my Lord', instead. The substitution of the vowels of *Adonai* for those of *Yahweh* resulted in the old-fashioned name *Jehovah*. (The opening vowel of 'Adonai' would have been pronounced like the a in 'amuse'.)

turn to the Gentiles' (Acts 13:46–47). So in making Jesus allude to this verse in the opening paragraph of Acts, Luke is setting out the plan of his book, which will concern the step-by-step progress of the gospel, right up to the end of the earth.

Had the requirement to carry the gospel to the Gentiles been clear to the apostles from the outset, then Luke's elaborate account of the conversion of the Roman centurion Cornelius (Acts 10–11) would make no sense. He describes in great detail how Peter found himself confronted with the agonizing decision of whether to allow Cornelius full rights within the new sect. The trouble was that Cornelius did not keep the Jewish food laws, and Peter, good Jew that he was, found this offensive. After being shown in a vision 'all kinds of animals and reptiles and birds', he was told to 'kill and eat'. Horrified, he replied, 'No Lord, for I have never eaten anything common or unclean.' He received the same command three times, and to emphasize the point Luke lets him tell the whole story again himself in the following chapter. In fact Luke gives more space to the account of this one man's conversion than to any other single episode in the book – including the thrice-repeated story of Paul's visionary call. The conclusion reached by all present, after hearing the Gentiles speaking in tongues and extolling God (proof positive that they had received the Holy Spirit), is that 'to the Gentiles also God has granted repentance and life' (11:18).

When the apostles and elders met in council some time later (the so-called Council of Jerusalem) the point at issue was not kashrut but circumcision. But the fundamental choice facing the assembled elders was the same: should Gentiles be admitted to full membership of the new community or not? Circumcision was not mentioned in the final decree, and the omission was significant: it was *not* to be a requirement. In all likelihood it never had been: this was a retro-spective ratification of what had been standard practice. Only when 'some believers who belonged to the sect of the Pharisees' made an issue of it were the leaders of the community forced to decide one way or the other. The decision they reached was surely one of the most momentous in the history of Christianity. (Paul's subsequent troubles with the Galatians show that the issue could still prove contentious, but in principle it had already been settled.)

In the course of the debate Peter stood up and said: 'Brethren, you know that from days of old God made choice among you, that by my mouth the Gentiles should hear the word of the gospel and believe' (15:7). 'From days of old' (ἀφ᾽ ἡμερῶν ἀρχαίων) is odd, because only a few chapters earlier the readers of Acts had had impressed upon them Peter's evident reluctance to allow any contravention of the Jewish food laws. What is more (and this is an important point), his scruples were finally overcome only some time after Paul had received *his* vision, summoning him to preach to the Gentiles. It is odd too that what occupies centre stage in the Council of Jerusalem is not the spectacularly successful mission in Cyprus and Asia, from which Paul and Barnabas had just returned, but Peter's achievement in bringing in his solitary convert. The 'signs and wonders' reported by Paul and Barnabas (15:12) are completely ignored in the only speech actually reported by Luke, that of James. By contrast James waxes lyrical about Simeon, as he calls Peter, to whom he credits the fulfilment of a composite prophecy concerning the Gentiles (15:14–18).

It is clear that Luke at any rate was convinced that Paul's call *preceded* Peter's vision; and whether we believe him or not, we are not entitled simply to assume that Paul was summoned to join a missionary church.[25] The truth is that the people Paul persecuted had been preaching to their fellow Jews – as well as, almost necessarily, to the Gentile hangers-on (god-fearers) present in substantial numbers in a large number of towns in the Mediterranean basin (Cornelius was one of these). There is no reason why, following his conversion experience, Paul could not have begun by persuading his companions to stop trying to arrest the spread of the Jesus movement, and then taken a step further by urging them to join him in adopting the new faith. In that case the Jesus movement, at least for the time being, would have been largely contained within Judaism. So there is still no explanation of Paul's overwhelming conviction of

25. Heikki Räisänen, pointing out that Paul saw a connection between his call and his work among Gentiles, adds, 'Presumably the Christians persecuted by him were already engaged in such a mission, which was an important reason for Paul to persecute them': 'Paul's Conversion', p. 406. Räisänen's comment is an excellent illustration of Donaldson's point (quoted above, p. 75) concerning the erstwhile *axiomatic* nature of Paul's mission to the Gentiles. It is a comment that begs some important questions. Moreover, if the Gentile mission was already fully established at the time of Paul's conversion there is no way of accounting for his obvious sense of pride and privilege at having been singled out to be 'the apostle of the Gentiles'.

his missionary vocation, his sense of being called to carry the good news outside Judaism to the Gentile world. We are thus compelled to look elsewhere, either to something in Paul's life that followed his conversion or to something that preceded it. Had this something been obvious, of easy access, then it would already have been found. We must expect difficulties. First I want to consider the possibility that Paul's sense of his missionary vocation was not immediate but slow, coming months or even years after the revelation on the Damascus road.

(a) *Dawning recognition: after the event*

Let us look at what Paul himself has to say, starting with the opening of the letter to the Galatians: 'Paul, an apostle – not from men nor through man, but through Jesus Christ and God the Father, who raised him from the dead' (1:1). He labours the point: the gospel he preached 'was not man's gospel. For I did not receive it from man, nor was I taught it, but it came through a revelation of Jesus Christ' (1:12). This is how he describes the revelation: 'When he who had set me apart from my mother's womb,[26] and had called me through his grace, was pleased to reveal his Son in me, in order that I might preach him among the gentiles, I did not confer with flesh and blood, nor did I go up to Jerusalem to those who were apostles before me, but I went away into Arabia; and again I returned to Damascus' (Gal 1:15–16).

Nothing, seemingly, could be clearer. Paul's revelation was direct and unmediated. The third of Luke's versions supports the argument for an instantaneous call, and the other two versions do little to weaken it. It is true that in both of Luke's earlier versions a disciple named Ananias, absent from Paul's own account, acts as an intermediary. In the first, God tells him in a vision, after three days have elapsed, that Paul 'is a chosen instrument of mine to carry my name before Gentiles and kings and the sons of Israel' (9:15). In the second, Ananias tells Paul: 'The God of our fathers appointed you to know his will ... for you will be a witness for him to all men of what you have seen and heard' (22:14–15). Yet Paul, writing of what

---

26. The RSV translation, 'from before I was born', obscures an implicit claim to a prophetic mission. The allusion to the prophetic calling from the womb – either Jeremiah (1:4) or Isaiah (49:1) – is almost certainly deliberate.

happened just after his call, says, 'I did not confer with flesh and blood, nor did I go up to Jerusalem to those who were apostles before me' (Gal 1:16–17). Even if the fuller account in Luke were correct, it is clear that for Paul Ananias would have been no more than a supernumerary; his intervention is of little moment and the link between vision and call remains intact.

In any case the basic difficulty would still persist, not removed but displaced, shunted across from one man's vision to another's. For an identical problem arises with respect to Ananias. Still missing is any trace of an explanation of the dramatic shift from the Jewish to the Gentile mission. The question may have receded slightly, but it is still there.

But now, returning to Paul's own account, let us consider another possibility, the possibility that the purpose-chain ('was pleased to reveal his Son in me in order that …') is not as tightly knit as it looks. The purpose of the revelation, no doubt, is to further God's original purpose in singling Paul out from his very conception. We must remember that Paul's account as well as Luke's is an *interpretation*. Could it be that when they appear to imply that the missionary vocation followed consequentially upon the appearance of Jesus, the connecting link they are suggesting was forged only after years of reflection? God, who had picked Paul out while he was still in the womb, had already waited for him to reach manhood and join the persecutors of the new sect before making his move. Could it be that the revelation on the Damascus road was only the first step of an inferential process that would take years to complete? If this were so then Paul would have started, certainly, with the unassailable conviction that the Jesus whom he had been persecuting was truly the Jewish Messiah, indeed the Son of God, but have been quite slow to come to the conclusion that Jewish particularism could not contain this truth.

Commentators generally assume that most of the three years that passed before Paul's visit to Jerusalem were spent in quiet medita-tion in Arabia, but we do not really know.[27] The most we can say for sure is that before commencing the missionary career recorded in

27. He may have remained in Arabia no longer than a few months (much less and the visit would scarcely have been worth mentioning). He may even have begun his missionary activity there. See R. Riesner, *Frühzeit*, 208, citing M. Hengel, *Zur urchristlichen Geschichtsschreibung*, 73.

Acts he had plenty of time to reflect on the implications of his extraordinary experience on the Damascus road.

So far all we have come up with is a series of rhetorical questions. There is room for one more. Is there anything that could count as evidence that Paul might have conceived the idea of the Gentile mission and the part he was to play in it through pondering on this remarkable event? It is hard to say. He certainly interpreted this experience as a prophetic calling in the manner of Isaiah (or Second Isaiah, as scholars now call the author of Isaiah 40–55). That much can be gleaned from the way he speaks of his call in Galatians 1:15: (ἐκ κοιλίας μητρός μου – from my mother's womb) corresponding exactly to Isaiah 49:1 (ἐκ κοιλίας μητρός μου ἐκάλεσεν τὸ ὄνομά μου – from my mother's womb he called my name). When writing of his missionary calling elsewhere Paul alludes to the same prophet, always either quoting or alluding to texts from that part of the book of Isaiah that lays most stress on the part the Gentiles are to play in God's plan.[28]

One could elaborate the argument by considering how the two authors (Paul and Luke) skilfully exploit the imagery of light and darkness, applying it both to Paul's own blinding and recovery of sight and to the light dawning upon the Gentiles. So there is certainly something to be said for the suggestion that at some time during his life Paul was struck by the bearing of the scriptures upon his vocation.

Here, then, is one possible answer to our problem. The sources are all mistaken, or at best economical with the truth. Paul did not receive any direct call. That was something he deduced only after pondering deeply on the implications of his experience on the Damascus road. But when, much later, he had occasion to introduce an account of his marvellous experience in a letter to the Galatians, he recognized with hindsight that it had already contained embryonically much that was to follow, especially his apostolic vocation.

This could be the right answer: it is hard to see how one could exclude it. Yet I remain unconvinced – not because of any intrinsic implausibility but because it conflicts with the simplest and most

---

28. Rom 15:20–21=Isa 52:15; cf. 2 Cor 6:2 (= Isa 49:8, LXX). Luke, in Acts, picks up some of the same themes: compare Acts 13:47 with Isa 49:6 and Acts 26:16–18 with Isa 46:16.

natural interpretation of the two sources, the Book of Acts and the Letter to the Galatians, both of which seem to imply that Paul's apostolic calling was inseparably bound up with his revelatory experience. Since this is the most obvious reading, we must take a fresh look at the problem, asking if there is any other way of accounting for the Gentile mission.

Before doing so, however, there is one final suggestion to be considered, Francis Watson's theory, based on a tendentious reading of Romans 11, that only the failure of Paul's initial mission to the Jews forced him to reconsider his position and turn to the Gentiles instead.[29] Prima facie, this theory looks as if it might find some support in Luke. Just over a week after Paul's lengthy discourse in Pisidian Antioch, 'almost the whole city', Luke informs us, 'gathered together to hear the word of God', much to the chagrin of the Jews, who were consequently rebuked quite sharply by Paul and Barnabas: 'It was necessary that the word of God should be spoken first to you. Since you thrust it from you, and judge yourselves unworthy of eternal life, behold, we turn to the Gentiles' (Acts 13:44–46). This episode (which we have already glanced at) is merely the most explicit of the many passages in Acts in which Luke endeavours to persuade his readers that Paul turned to the Gentiles only after being rebuffed by the Jews. His consistent determination to do this, however, paradoxically confirms the reliability of his three versions of Paul's call, since all three agree with Paul's own testimony that the purpose of the revelation he received was to establish him in his mission. (This is an example of the against-the-grain argument explained in Excursus IV.)

(b) *Increasing unease: before the event*

We are now in a position to consider a very different suggestion, one that has had a long history. Could it be that the event on the Damascus road was *preceded* by a period of struggle and self-doubt? As we now turn to examine this ancient theory, we should remind ourselves that we are still looking for some way of accounting for the Gentile mission. Is there anything in Paul's experience *before* his conversion that might help to explain why, in the very act of abandoning the law, Paul discovered an apostolate?

29. *Paul, Judaism and the Gentiles*, 28–38.

First, something of a curiosity. Andrew Wilson, for whom the most startling feature of the Damascus road experience is Paul's sudden acceptance of Jesus, believes that this can best be accounted for on the supposition that Paul had already encountered Jesus when he was still alive: 'We find Paul, when he makes his appearance in Acts, in the hire of the high priest. It does not seem unreasonable to suppose that he was in the same position in the temple guard when Jesus was arrested.'[30] So 'might he not reasonably have been supposed to have taken part in the arrest and execution of Jesus, the Galilean trouble-maker? ... If readers of the New Testament choose to believe that Paul never set eyes on Jesus and that he had no psychological interest or compulsion to inspire him throughout the thirty years in which he preached Jesus Christ Crucified other than the testimony of the friends of Jesus, whom he had barely met, then that reader is entitled to his or her point of view.'[31] Clearly Wilson finds the suggestion that Paul first encountered Jesus in a post-resurrection appearance too preposterous to entertain for an instant. Yet this may surely be inferred from what Paul himself says about this meeting in 1 Corinthians 15, and Wilson's own suggestion, that Paul had taken part in Jesus' arrest, really accounts for very little. What is more, it totally bypasses the connection between the vision and the call upon which Paul places so much emphasis: 'Am I not an apostle? Have I not seen Jesus our Lord?' (1 Cor 9:1).

Ed Sanders takes a different line: 'It is by no means inconceivable that he had native sympathy for the Gentiles and chafed at the Jewish exclusivism which either ignored them or which relegated

---

30. *Paul*, 54. This follows on from an even bolder suggestion in an earlier book that Paul is perhaps to be identified with Malchus (the name, according to John 18:10, of the high priest's servant whose right ear was severed by Peter just as Jesus was about to be arrested). The name Malchus resembles the Hebrew for king (*melek*), and the name of Israel's first king was Saul (!). Wilson adds, tongue-in-cheek, 'If I had the chance to return in time and meet Paul, I should take a look at his ears': *Jesus* (London, 1992), 205.

31. Ibid., 55. Wilson is by no means the first to argue that Paul must have known Jesus 'in the flesh'. A similar theory had been put forward in the first decade of the century by the famous Johannes Weiss, *Paulus und Jesus* (Berlin, 1909), 22. Weiss retreated from this position the following year, voicing serious doubts whether Paul's early knowledge of Jesus was direct and personal. See *Jesus im Glauben des Urchristentums* (Tübingen, 1910), 42.

them to second place in God's plan.'[32] Sanders focuses on the second aspect of the event, the Gentile mission, freely admitting that this, 'like other attempts to penetrate Paul's pre-call thought, is entirely speculative'. But this suggestion, however plausible, is no more helpful as an *explanation* than Andrew Wilson's much more far-fetched theory of an encounter between Paul and Jesus in the latter's lifetime; for it is precisely Paul's impatience with Jewish exclusivism that requires to be explained.

Terence Donaldson, who has written perceptively (and at length) on this subject,[33] is, as we have seen, especially insistent on the need to account for Paul's call. If it is to make any sense, the assumption of an explicitly verbal call ('Paul, I want you as a Jew to bring the message of Christ to the Gentiles') would have to fit into a framework already containing each of the three elements, 'Jew, Gentile and God's message about Christ'. Without such a framework, and in particular without any previous notion of *mission*, it would be hard to see how such a call could be heard (or uttered), much less understood. If however the reflection preceded the experience, as Donaldson himself believes, then the effect of a revelation of the Son of God in him, which is how Paul himself sums up what he saw and heard, will have been to fuse the three elements together in the way that both Paul himself and Luke, slightly less directly, present them, that is to say as an overwhelming sense of the presence of Christ accompanied by a call to carry his message to the Gentiles.

One interesting suggestion that may meet these conditions is to be found in an article by John Bowker (with which Donaldson is evidently unacquainted) comparing the story of Paul's conversion with the well-known Jewish tradition of 'the four who entered *pardes* [i.e. *paradise*, a garden]'.[34] Bowker finds common ground between the two in the opening of the Book of Ezekiel that we have already glanced at in connection with 2 Corinthians 4:4–6. He pictures Paul journeying to Damascus and reflecting 'on the road', like the four rabbis, on Ezekiel's vision. Immediately after his extraordinary

---

32. *Paul, the Law, and the Jewish People*, 52–3.
33. *Paul and the Gentiles*.
34. In the original version of the story, argues Christopher Morray-Jones, 'the term *pardes* is used without explanation as a technical term for the Holy of Holies in the highest heaven, where the glory of God resides': 'Paradise Revisited', 268. I will give a brief explanation of this story in Excursus II, Merkabah Mysticism.

vision (ch. 1) the prophet distinctly heard the voice of the spirit telling him: 'Son of man, I send you to the people of Israel'(2:3). 'It seems to me perfectly possible', says Bowker, 'that Paul, in the perfectly ordinary [!] process of *merkabah* contemplation, reflected on the voice of commission to Ezekiel in ch. ii.'[35] In his own account Ezekiel stresses that those to whom he is sent are impudent, stubborn and rebellious (2:3–7), and Bowker points out that Paul too was in pursuit of '(in his own view) recalcitrant or transgressing *Jews*', and continues: 'At the very least what appears to have happened is that Ezek. ii reversed Paul's attitudes, and that Paul was dramatically convinced in the vision that at the worst the Christians were a part of a whole rebellious people, but also, conceivably, that it was not the *Christians* who were the rebellious people, but the Jews who had commissioned him – that the truth, in other words, lay with Jesus, and that henceforth the "word of God" should be for all men. The association of Ezekiel i and ii would thus provide a totally coherent context for Paul's dramatic conversion.'[36] This is a strikingly original suggestion. It presupposes, of course, that even before his conversion Paul was already well-practised in the art of merkabah contemplation; but an assumption of this kind is far from implausible. At some point in his life Paul began to experience the 'visions and revelations' of which he speaks in 2 Corinthians (12:1). There is no obvious reason why these should not have begun before his call. Yet it might be argued that even if we accept the suggestion that the mystical experience accompanying Paul's conversion might naturally be followed (as in Ezekiel) by a call or mission, the specific nature of that mission – to the Gentiles – still requires explanation.

Donaldson's own solution is elegant and, up to a point, appealing. Jewish thinkers allowed for the inclusion of Gentiles in God's providential plan for the world in three ways: first by the so-called Noachide covenant,[37] secondly by the expectation of some kind of

---

35. '"Merkabah" Visions', 157–73. This quote, p. 171. Alan Segal knows this important article (see *Paul the Convert*, 315, n. 18), and comes very close to Bowker's central argument in a later essay entitled 'Conversion and Messianism'.

36. Art. cit., 172.

37. Reflecting on God's covenant with Noah, ratified by the appearance of the first rainbow (Gen 9:8–17), the rabbis came up with the idea of a series of seven commandments obligatory on everyone, Gentile as well as Jew. Obedience to

influx of Gentile well-wishers 'in the last days', and thirdly by active proselytizing. The first two presuppose some positive action on the part of the Gentiles without any prompting from the Jews, and so fail to furnish any reason for a missionary move. Accordingly Donaldson makes the interesting suggestion that Paul, in his Jewish phase, had taken an active part in the instruction of Gentile proselytes. These may in the first place have taken the initiative in approaching Jewish friends or acquaintances, but differ in one crucial respect from those Gentiles whose way of life accorded with the universal precepts of the Jewish law (the Noachide commandments), and from those who (it was foreseen) would come streaming into Jerusalem in the last days to offer homage and worship to the one true God. In contrast to both these groups their conversion was actively sought by Jewish proselytizers or missionaries.

One piece of evidence Donaldson uses to buttress his suggestion is a line from Galatians to the effect that Paul had at one time 'preached circumcision' (Gal 5:11). Preaching to the converted is, as we know, a waste of effort, as proverbially futile as pushing at an open door. And there seems particularly little point, if one may put it so, in preaching circumcision to the circumcised.[38] So Donaldson proposes that during the period in which Paul was busily persecuting the Jesus movement he was also actively engaged in making converts to Judaism. If he had been, this would account for the way in which, as a practical corollary of his switch of allegiance to Christ, he felt impelled to urge the very people he had been preparing for

---

all of these would constitute you 'a righteous Gentile'. Infringement of any one of them would render you liable to death by decapitation (*b.Sanh.* 56–60). This quite rigorous interpretation is a model of liberalism compared with the much earlier version found in *Jubilees* 7:20–1. *Sibylline Oracles* 4:24–39 (probably 1st century AD) has yet another version. For a fuller discussion see A. F. Segal, *Paul the Convert*, 194–201, and M. Goodman, *Mission and Conversion*, 112–16.

38. John Muddiman has pointed out to me that this is not quite true. Paul could have shared the concern of the author of *Jubilees* that the Jews of the diaspora should retain their pride in their nationhood and refrain from concealing the obvious effects of circumcision by the curious operation Paul calls ἐπισπᾶσθαι (1 Cor 7:18). See *Jubilees* 15:25–34, where the angel of the presence speaks glowingly to Moses of the glory of circumcision, telling him, for instance, that God's angels were privileged to have been created with their foreskins already cut (a theologoumenon resembling the Catholic doctrine of the Immaculate Conception).

Judaism to accept instead the new gospel that he had just welcomed himself. Since his own Jewish practice already contained an element of proselytizing, it would have been easy for him to conclude that having exchanged the law for the gospel he must now begin to persuade his erstwhile Gentile converts to change direction also. Donaldson sums this up by saying that 'Paul's Gentile mission may be understood as the christological transformation of a proselytizing concern already present in his pre-conversion days'.[39]

For all its attractiveness, I remain unpersuaded by this suggestion. When Paul, in Galatians, speaks of himself as 'preaching circumcision' he may mean no more than that at one time he was an ardent champion of the Torah as a whole. Such a use of synechdoche is quite characteristic of his style: he does not hesitate to use the term 'foreskin', the obvious antithesis to circumcision, to refer to the Gentiles.[40] Earlier in the same letter, distinguishing his own mission from Peter's, he says that he has been entrusted with τὸ εὐαγγέλιον τῆς ἀκροβυστίας (2:7). We are compelled to translate this as 'the gospel as preached to the uncircumcised', but the literal meaning is 'the foreskin gospel'. What is more, the use of the term 'circumcision' in Gal 5:11 is easily explained from the context. Arguing against the so-called Judaizers, who insisted that even people newly converted from paganism should be circumcised, Paul uses the term simply as a way of referring back to his previous life as a good Jew. There is nothing mysterious in such a usage, and it is scarcely surprising that neither of his two most recent biographers (Wilson and Murphy-O'Connor) feels the need to expatiate upon the verse in question (though it must be confessed that this neglect is in itself no argument for its irrelevance). More telling is the argument that for Donaldson's case to be fully persuasive Paul would have to have been not just a catechist but an active proselytizer.[41] How far proselytism (involving compulsory circumcision for males) was actively encouraged at this period is still debated. Scot McKnight and Martin Goodman have argued strongly against the

---

39. 'Israelite, Convert, Apostle to the Gentiles', 81.
40. E.g. Rom 2:26; 3:20; 4:10.
41. He says that all he needs to prove his case is for Paul to have acted as a catechist. But the phrase on which he relies, εἰ περιτομὴν ἔτι κηρύσσω, if it is to be any use to him, must imply active preaching.

view that Judaism was a missionary religion,[42] and I find their arguments persuasive. Jesus' forthright denunciation of the proselytizing activities of the Pharisees in Matthew 23:15 furnishes perhaps the strongest argument for the opposite position; but Goodman has argued, rightly, I think, that this refers to the Pharisees' efforts to gain adherents among other *Jews*.[43]

For a more likely solution we must turn instead to one of the possibilities that Donaldson dismisses. The idea of the eventual ingathering of the Gentiles, the pleasing thought that as the end drew near they would finally see the light and turn to worship the true God, goes back as far as Isaiah. Here is Paula Fredriksen's summary: 'The nations will stream to Jerusalem and worship the God of Jacob together with Israel (Is 2:2–4//Mic 4:1ff.); on God's mountain (i.e. the Temple mount), they will eat together the feast that God has prepared for them (Is 25:6). As the Jews leave the lands of their dispersion, Gentiles will accompany them: "In those days ten men from the nations of every tongue shall take hold of the robe of a Jew, saying, 'Let us go with you for we have heard that God is with you'" (Zech 8:23). Or the nations carry the exiles back to Jerusalem themselves (*Ps. Sol.* 7:31–41). Burying their idols, "all people shall direct their sight to the path of uprightness" (*1 Enoch* 91:14).'[44] Fredriksen goes on to argue that these Gentiles are not proselytes, for once they have been circumcised Gentiles count as Jews. They are converts, certainly, because in turning to the God of Israel they will have abandoned the worship of idols. But 'Gentiles are saved as Gentiles: they do not, eschatologically, become Jews.'[45] This large-scale conversion of the Gentiles came to be regarded as an important part of God's plan for the last days. The passage most frequently cited in this connection speaks of 'the foreigner' (בֶּן־הַנֵּכָר, ὁ ἀλλογενής) who

---

42. S. McKnight, *A Light among the Gentiles*; M. Goodman, *Mission and Conversion*.

43. *Mission and Conversion*, 69–74. When Matthew's Jesus tells his disciples to 'make disciples of all nations' (Matt 28:19) he understands this to mean 'teaching them to observe all that I have commanded you', i.e. his own (authoritative) interpretation of the law, contained in the Sermon on the Mount and elsewhere. What he objects to in the proselytizing of the Pharisees is that they are purveying their own version of the law, not his. Contra Donaldson, *Paul and the Gentiles*, 321, n. 40.

44. 'Judaism', 545.

45. Ibid., 547.

has joined himself to the Lord' (Isa 56:3–8).[46] Neither in the Hebrew nor in the Greek text is there the slightest hint of an end-time mission to the Gentiles. So is Donaldson right to conclude that since according to this conception the impulse to worship the God of Israel was quite spontaneous, not merely unforced but unsolicited, it fails to provide the necessary connection with the Gentile mission? I do not think so.

As they continued Jesus' preaching of the kingdom, which is how the Jesus movement began, the disciples will also have seen themselves as hastening the day when the Gentiles too would abandon their worship of idols and come to worship alongside Jews. But there was now an important modification of Jesus' own message; for the head of this new messianic kingdom was to be none other than Jesus himself, recently risen from the dead, and soon to return in triumph.

Luke remarks, again and again, on the hostility aroused by the new message among Jewish communities in the diaspora.[47] In the finely conceived article I have already quoted, Fredriksen convincingly argues that they must have been frightened by its likely impact upon the whole population of these cities: 'The enthusiastic proclamation of a Messiah executed very recently by Rome as a political troublemaker – a *crucified* Messiah – combined with a vision of the approaching end *preached also to Gentiles* – this was dangerous.' The promise or prediction of *this* kind of messianic kingdom could seriously perturb the Roman authorities, which were all too often savagely repressive when they sensed a danger emanating from the Jewish communities in their region. 'The open dissemination of a Messianic message', Fredriksen concludes, 'put the entire Jewish community at risk.'[48]

We do not have to suppose that the leaders of the Jesus movement deliberately planned to extend it, right from the start, to the Gentiles. It is enough to assume first that the god-fearers belonging

---

46. For further texts, and a useful summary discussion, see E. P. Sanders, *Jesus and Judaism*, 212–21.
47. Acts 13:13–52 (Pisidian Antioch); 14:1–6 (Iconium); 17:1–9 (Thessalonica), 10–15 (Beroea); 18:1–7 (Corinth) etc.
48. 'Judaism', 556.

to the synagogues of the diaspora will have been particularly
attracted to a message that promised imminent salvation for all,
without being obliged to submit to the repellent rite of circumcision
that their Jewish friends had previously insisted upon if they were to
be fully integrated into the community,[49] and secondly that their
resulting enthusiasm rendered them more than usually receptive
towards what they will have seen as a welcome modification of a way
of life that they already admired. What is more, their enthusiasm
may well have extended to other friends of theirs who unlike them
were not yet sympathetic to the Jewish religion. This suggestion
is of course speculative, but we should remind ourselves of the
exuberant enthusiasm of the propagators of the new faith. These
were all, in the strongest sense of the word, Pentecostalists! It is all
too easy to dismiss Luke's account of the first Pentecost because of
its intrinsic implausibilities. But we should retain from it a sense of
the disciples' exultant conviction that they were already living in the
last days, when 'your young men shall see visions and your old men
shall dream dreams' (Acts 2:17). Here is how Luke's version of
Joel's famous prophecy ends:

> I will show wonders in the heaven above
> and signs on the earth beneath,
> blood, and fire, and vapour of smoke;
> the sun shall be turned into darkness
> and the moon into blood,
> before the day of the Lord comes,
> the great and manifest day.
> And it shall be that whoever calls
> on the name of the Lord shall be saved.   (2:19–21)

This sense of the imminent end of the world as we know it (a con-

---

49. In Rome only 7 out of 550 legible epitaphs in the Jewish catacombs belong to
proselytes. 'This suggests', comments Wilson, 'that when the chips were down,
a literal willingness to save their skins took the better of the Roman god-fearers'
(*Paul*, 105). A little further on (p.131) he gives an uncomfortably graphic
description of this bloody, painful ritual. It took the grisly spectacle of the severed head of Holofernes, brandished aloft by one of Judith's men, to persuade
Achior, the leader of the Ammonites (already a great admirer of Israel), to go
the whole hog and agree to be circumcised (Judith 14:6–10).

viction that Paul was soon to share) must have permeated the preaching of the new gospel, lending it an especial urgency. Before the Gentiles had been actively wooed by Christian missionaries the knowledge that they too could participate in 'the great and manifest day' could well have excited them in the way that Fredriksen's thesis demands. We do not have to suppose, as Donaldson does, that Paul, before his call, took an active part in Jewish proselytizing in order to account for his early awareness that the Gentiles were, however indirectly, targeted by the movement he was attacking.

Fredriksen's discovery of a *political* motive for the Jewish hostility to the new movement highlights the gratuitousness (and implausibility) of a *religious* rationale. The truth is that the expectation of a coming Messiah was not then (and never has been) at the forefront of the Jewish religious consciousness. Idolatry, the desecration of the temple, and any slighting of the law – these are the things that infuriated pious Jews. As we know from the story of Jesus, the purpose of the priestly authorities when they accused him of messianic claims was to alarm the Roman governor and to provoke him into imposing the death sentence. 'If we knew', remarks Ed Sanders, introducing his own interpretation of Jesus' end, 'whether or not there was a direct connection between the Roman execution of Jesus and the Jewish persecution of some of his followers, many of the puzzles about early Christianity and its relationship to Judaism would be solved.'[50] Of course we do not *know* this, but one of the great merits of Fredriksen's brilliantly argued thesis (one that she herself, incidentally, does not remark upon) is that it furnishes precisely the connection that Sanders is seeking. 'Ideas and ideology', Fredriksen concludes, 'do provide important motivations for human actions; but in real life they are grounded in

---

50. E. P. Sanders, *Jesus and Judaism*, 11.
51. 'Judaism', 558. Probably the commonest reason advanced for the persecution of the Jesus movement is the offence a good Jew would take at the notion of a crucified Messiah: 'Cursed be everyone who hangs upon a tree' (Deut 21:23). Fredriksen effectively disposes of this theory, showing that there is no evidence that Jews responded to crucifixion in this way, or that, legally speaking, they should have done so ('Judaism', 551–2). This includes Paul, whose tortuous exegesis of this verse, part of an elaborate argument to the Galatians (3:13), cannot credibly be attributed to him before his conversion. Yet the same discredited suggestion continues to be put forward, most recently by Martyn, *Galatians*, 162. Intrinsically much more likely is Jürgen Becker's proposal (*Paul*,

social fact.'[51]

If then the persecution of the Jesus movement – which no doubt involved the kind of discretionary flogging that Paul says he himself received five times at the hands of the Jews (2 Cor 11:24) – was prompted by a fear of the reaction its teaching might provoke among the Gentile majorities in the cities of the diaspora, then we have the explanation we have been seeking of the link between Paul's early zeal in persecuting the ekklesia and his otherwise puzzlingly sudden conviction of a call to preach to those very Gentiles, along with a readiness to endure the hardships that this would entail. He was henceforth persuaded that it was not enough for them to join in worshipping the God of Israel: they must accept the very message concerning the Crucified Messiah that was the cause of all the trouble.

As for the hope that the Gentiles eventually would turn and worship the true God, a hope that Paul presumably shared, by the time he came to write the Letter to the Romans he found himself able somehow to transfer it to the Jewish race as a whole, and to find in it a consolation for his otherwise desolating awareness of how few Jews had accepted his gospel, his sense of the 'hardening' that had come upon part of Israel: 'and so all Israel will be saved' (Rom 11:26).[52]

Conclusion

Although it seems to me highly likely that Paul's missionary vocation was somehow anticipated in the way I have outlined, we must surely accept what the sources tell us about the immediacy of that vocation

---

66–9) that in his zeal for the law Paul was shocked above all by the readiness of the Jesus movement (by this time fully established in the Damascus synagogue) to flout the law by admitting into its ranks Gentiles who had never submitted to the rite of circumcision, thereby erasing the boundary between Jew and Gentile that had always been central to the Jewish perception of God's election of Israel. A sense of outrage at the attempted demolition of one of the pillars of Judaism is unquestionably quite a plausible motive to attribute to an ardent Pharisee like Paul. But this suggestion can be accepted only if we are prepared to set aside the clear import of Luke's account (discussed above) that Paul's conversion *preceded* any decision to admit Gentiles into the community.

52. This topic will be treated more fully in Chapter 6.

when it came. Yet such a conclusion should not be taken to imply that from then on he gave the matter no thought. His letters provide abundant evidence that his new faith received constant nourishment from the traditions and beliefs in which he was nurtured, above all from the scriptures. So it turns out that the full explanation of his calling, sudden and overwhelming though it must have been, is to be sought in his whole career, before, during and after the event on the Damascus road.

EXCURSUS II
Merkabah Mysticism

Scholars are familiar with 'merkabah mysticism', but since this book is primarily directed to a non-academic readership, it may be helpful to include a slightly longer explanation of the term than could be compressed into a footnote.[1] There are two main strands in the Jewish mystical tradition. One of these, *Ma'aseh Bereshit*, concerns the work of creation. *Ma'aseh* means 'work' and *Bereshit*, the first word in the Bible, means 'in the beginning': this strand of the tradition originates in a meditation on the first chapter of Genesis. *Ma'aseh Merkabah*, the second strand, originates in a meditation on the first chapter of Ezekiel.[2] (The word *merkabah* means chariot – the chariot of God.)[3] Any summary account of this would be misleading, and I have not attempted to abridge it:

> As I looked, behold, a stormy wind came out of the north, and a great cloud, with brightness round about it, and fire flashing forth continually, and in the midst of the fire, as it were gleaming bronze. And from the midst of it came the likeness of four living creatures. And this was their appearance: they had the form of men, but each had four faces, and each of them had four wings. Their legs were straight, and the soles of their feet were like the sole of a calf's foot; and they sparkled like burnished bronze.

1. Since, however, not all the information in this excursus is available even in scholarly writings, I have included a number of remarks with an academic readership in mind.
2. Also on Isaiah 6 and Daniel 7.
3. Alternatively, *merkavah*. The Hebrew letter ב (bêth) is sometimes transliterated as a vee when it occurs between two vowels, because that is how it is pronounced; in the same position the letter פ (pê) is pronounced f.

Under their wings on their four sides they had human hands. And the four had their faces and their wings thus: their wings touched one another; they went every one straight forward, without turning as they went. As for the likeness of their faces, each had the face of a man in front; the four had the face of a lion on the right side, the four had the face of an ox on the left side, and the four had the face of an eagle at the back. Such were their faces. And their wings were spread out above; each creature had two wings, each of which touched the wing of another, while two covered their bodies. And each went straight forward; wherever the spirit would go, they went, without turning as they went. In the midst of the living creatures there was something that looked like burning coals of fire, like torches moving to and fro among the living creatures; and the fire was bright, and out of the fire went forth lightning. And the living creatures darted to and fro, like a flash of lightning.

Now as I looked at the living creatures, I saw a wheel upon the earth beside the living creatures, one for each of the four of them. As for the appearance of the wheels and their construction: their appearance was like the gleaming of a chrysolite; and the four had the same likeness, their construction being as it were a wheel within a wheel. When they went, they went in any of their four directions without turning as they went. The four wheels had rims and they had spokes; and their rims were full of eyes round about. And when the living creatures went, the wheels went beside them; and when the living creatures rose from the earth, the wheels rose. Wherever the spirit would go, they went, and the wheels rose along with them; for the spirit of the living creatures was in the wheels. When those went, these went; and when those stood, these stood; and when those rose from the earth, the wheels rose along with them; for the spirit of the living creatures was in the wheels.

Over the heads of the living creatures there was the likeness of a firmament, shining like crystal, spread out above their heads. And under the firmament their wings were stretched out straight, one toward another; and each creature had two wings covering its body. And when they went, I heard the sound of their wings like the sound of many waters, like the thunder of the Almighty, a sound of tumult like the sound of a host; when they stood still, they let down their wings. And there came a voice from above the firmament over their heads; when they stood still, they let down their wings. And above the firmament over their heads there was the likeness of a throne, in appearance like sapphire; and seated above the likeness of a throne was a likeness as it were of a human form. And upward from what had the appearance of his loins I saw as it were gleaming bronze, like the appearance of fire enclosed round about; and downward from what had the appearance of his loins I saw as it were the appearance of fire, and there was brightness round about him. Like the appearance of the bow that is in the cloud on the day of rain, so was the appearance of the brightness round about.

Such was the appearance of the likeness of the glory of the LORD. And when I saw it, I fell upon my face, and I heard the voice of one speaking.

I have divided this passage into three paragraphs plus a brief conclusion, which introduces the divine command discussed by John Bowker in the article I commented on in Chapter 3. Ezekiel's vision resembles traditional theophanies (appearances of God) in that it opens with a storm. Before the storm has cleared he catches sight of what look like four living creatures, three animals and a man. (These reappear in the Book of Revelation, and will eventually become the symbols of the four evangelists.) In the second paragraph the wheels appear: wheels within wheels, with curiously ornamented rims. Finally, above all these (for the firmament was conceived as a kind of carapace over the earth separating it from heaven), the prophet has a vision of a divine throne: there is no doubt that the figure with the likeness of a human form is conceived as a representation of God.

Not only is the word 'chariot' missing but it is clear that the vision of the divine throne *followed* the vision of the wheels. So why does Gershon Scholem, in one of the great classics on Jewish mysticism, speak of 'the first chapter of Ezekiel, *the vision of God's throne-chariot* (the "Merkabah")', as a favourite subject of discussion and interpretation in esoteric circles during the second temple era (i.e. up to the destruction of the temple by the Romans in AD 70)?[4] What

4. *Major Trends*, 42.

accounts for the conflation of the progressive elements of the prophet's vision? Part of the answer to this question is to be found in other visions later in the book, where the living creatures, now identified as cherubim (10:15), act, along with their wheels, as a kind of throne for 'the glory of the Lord'. And some time in the second century BC Ben Sira, in the long section of his book known as 'the praise of famous men', said of Ezekiel that 'he recounted the kinds (?) of the chariot' (ויגד זני מרכבה).[5] In the instructions he gave to his son Solomon concerning the construction of the temple David included 'his plan for the golden chariot (מרכבה) of the cherubim that spread their wings and covered the ark of the covenant of the Lord' (1 Chr 28:18). Like Greek centaurs and Norse mermaids the cherubim were therianthropes, half-animal, half-human winged figures that Israel had borrowed from her neighbours (either the Babylonians or the Phoenicians) and used for a variety of functions, most especially to protect the lid (propitiatory or 'mercy seat': כַּפֹּרֶת, ἱλαστήριον) of the ark of the covenant (Exod 25:17–22): 'the cherubim shall spread out their wings above, overshadowing the mercy seat with their wings, their faces one to another'). It seems that the Chronicler had read Ezekiel and drawn the natural conclusion that the wheels he claims to have seen in a number of visions formed part of a chariot.

At some point Ezekiel's wheels (אוֹפַנִּים, *'ōpannim*) were transformed into angels. (The cherubim of course were too.) This hypostasization seems to have already occurred in the so-called *Songs of the Sabbath Sacrifice*, an important grouping of parchment fragments from the Dead Sea (in this case, Masada),[6] and in the

---

5. Sirach (= Ecclesiasticus) was transmitted in Greek, not in its original Hebrew, and even now there are some bits missing, though many significant fragments of the Hebrew text have turned up in various places, most importantly in the so-called Cairo Genizah (= treasury), at the end of the 19th century, and most recently at Masada in 1963. The verse that concerns us here (49:8) comes from a manuscript in the Bodleian Library in Oxford, first published by Cowley and Neubauer in 1897. The meaning of the word זני (tr. 'kinds'), which also occurs in 2 Chr 16:14, is uncertain. The Greek text has: 'It was Ezekiel who saw the vision of glory (ὅρασις δόξης) which God showed him on [Hebr. 'above'] the chariot of the cherubim (ἐπὶ ἅρματος χερουβείμ)'. This summary fits ch. 10 better than it does ch. 1.

6. In Carol Newsom's critical edition (Harvard, 1985) the line in question (4Q403 1.ii.15) reads: והללו יחד מרכבות דבירו וברכו פלא כרוביהם ואופניה. Geza Vermes omits this passage from his edition of *The Complete Dead Sea*

'Similitudes' section of *1 Enoch*, which says of a heavenly structure of fiery crystals that 'seraphim, cherubim, and ophanim – the sleepless ones who guard the throne of [God's] glory – also encircle it' (71:7, tr. Isaac). This switch of roles is typical of this kind of literature, in which sudden transformations are no less common than in ordinary dreams. Visions resemble dreams, and are sometimes scarcely distinguishable from them.

Merkabah mysticism was flourishing well before the Christian era. There are examples in the *Songs of the Sabbath Sacrifice*, already mentioned, in *The Testament of Levi*, and earliest of all in Ethiopic Enoch, where the seer, although evidently more interested in the construction and materials of the heavenly palace itself, does speak of the wheels of the divine throne (*1 Enoch* 14:18).

There are three further points to be made. The first is that while there are a number of features shared by all the accounts associated with the Merkabah tradition there is also a great variety. What they have in common is their starting-point in the prophecy of Ezekiel and the theme of mystical ascent for the purpose of discovering secrets inaccessible to ordinary mortals. The secrets however vary, ranging from, say, the divisions of the calendar, the composition of the divine throne or of the halls of heaven to the way the world will end (eschatology), and the dimensions of God (the *Ši'ur Qomah*).

Secondly, a word should be said about the tradition of the four individuals who 'entered *pardes*' (garden, orchard, paradise), three of them coming to grief and only one, the Rabbi Aqiba, surviving unscathed.[7] Although the origins of the story are disputed it came to be interpreted as an account of a mystical ascent in which three of the would-be seers were punished for inappropriate behaviour, whereas the success of the fourth proved that visionary experience of the kind implied was, though rare and difficult of access, not

---

Scrolls in English (London, 1997) – presumably on the grounds of obscurity – but F. G. Martinez translates: 'And the chariots of his *debir* praise together, and his cherubim and *ofanim* bless wonderfully': *The Dead Sea Scrolls Translated* (Leiden, 1994). Since in this song the various appurtenances of the temple, including the *debir* – the innermost chamber – all participate in the hymn of praise, we should not be surprised to find the chariots (note the plural!) and their wheels joining in too.

7. For the four different versions of this story in rabbinical writings see Rowland, *Open Heaven*, 309–12.

impossible. The fact that Paul too speaks of an ascent into Paradise suggests a link between this story and his own mystical experience as recorded in 2 Corinthians 12 (see Chapter 4, *infra*). Christopher Morray-Jones argues that the original version of this story 'refers unambiguously to an ascent to the heavenly temple in the face of fierce opposition on the part of the demonic "angels of Destruction" (*mal'akei-habbalah*)'.[8] It may well be that this was precisely the function of the 'angel of Satan' of which Paul speaks in the context of his own mystical ascent (2 Cor 12:7).

Lastly, a word about the later Jewish tradition, the *Hekhalot* (literally 'palaces'). These offer detailed instructions concerning the techniques to be practised by the would-be visionary if he wants to be sure of a successful rapture. Ithamar Gruenwald says of this corpus of works that 'it might be defined as technical guides, or manuals, for mystics. A lot of the material contained therein is introduced by technical questions.... These technical details, the "praxis" of the mystical experience, generally consist of special prayers or incantations, of prolonged fasts and special diets, of the utterance of magical names and the use of magical seals, and of the ritual of cleansing the body.'[9] Here, in another tradition, and under another name, we find something closely resembling the shamanic techniques of ecstasy of which Eliade speaks in his classic study.[10]

The parallels between shamanism and the Jewish mystical tradition, both biblical and post-biblical, are well brought out in an arresting article by Susan Niditch entitled 'The Visionary', in which she argues that 'the heavenly ascent visions lead not only to comparison with Ezekiel but to a much broader comparison with non-Israelite visionaries – the shamans, ecstatics, and mystics discussed by Eliade, Lewis, and Scholem'.[11] I will end this excursus by extracting from her article a few remarks of particular interest.

---

8. 'Paradise Revisited', 268.
9. *Apocalyptic*, 99.
10. Segal, in the context of merkabah mysticism, speaks of 'the magic use of shamanic techniques to stimulate ... out-of-body experiences' (*Paul the Convert*, 54).
11. 'Visionary', 154. Coming across this article long after I had begun my own work, I was pleased to find so much in it to confirm and complement my basic thesis.

1. Following their initiation shamans are often appealed to by their communities in a variety of crisis situations: drought, famine, illness, unexplained death. The personage Niditch calls 'the pseudepigraphic seer' also 'suffers acutely from the crisis of his community and sees visions in response to shared crisis situations'. She names Baruch, Ezra, and finally Enoch, commissioned by the Watchers (fallen angels) to petition God for forgiveness: 'Enoch accepts this typically shamanistic charge to mediate between God and the Watchers and then undergoes a vision experience (*1 Enoch* 12–13).'

2. Niditch underlines the parallels between the Eskimo shaman's initiation ceremony as described by Mircea Eliade (see Chapter 4) and the preparations for visionary experiences of Jewish seers such as Daniel, Baruch and Enoch.

3. Just as the shamans interviewed by Eliade described sensations 'of flying through the sky, of being carried through the sky', so Enoch speaks of the storm-wind or whirlwind that carries him up from the earth: 'my spirit was carried off, and it went into the heavens' (*1 Enoch* 71:1). (Cf. 2 Cor 12:2–3.)

4. Apropos of various paraphernalia associated with merkabah mysticism (the fiery surroundings, the cherubim, the throne image, the wheels) Niditch says that the author of Enoch 'has not necessarily copied earlier Israelite or Jewish materials or artificially included the throne scene as something which "he should have seen". Rather as Eliade says of shamans he has "interiorized" a certain mythology or cosmology; features of this mythology then become "the itinerary for [his] ecstatic journeys"' (*Shamanism*, 266).

5. 'Yet certain features of the tour itinerary and of non-traveling visions point to an almost archetypal set of notions and images about encounters with the other world: The existence of various heavens or levels of heaven, images of fire and other natural phenomena, such as trees, mountains, rivers, and of natural phenomena in turmoil or a state contrary to their normal condition in nature (i.e. blood waters [*sic*], earth rocking, waters whirling) are common.'

6. 'The visionary experiences described for the Rabbis, like those

applied to the pseudepigraphic seers, are reminiscent of experiences of the shaman: the state of altered consciousness is emphasized: a special state of ritual purity is necessary to receive visions; the seers are guided by angelic figures, visit seven heavens, and so on.'[12]

It is surely unnecessary to spell out in detail the relevance of many of these parallels to the general comparison undertaken in this book between Paul's experiences and those of the typical shaman.

12. 'Visionary', 158–62; 168.

4

Paul the Mystic

I have had a dream, past the wit of man to say what dream it was.
Man is but an ass, if he go about t' expound this dream.
Methought I was – there is no man can tell what. Methought I
was, and methought I had – but man is but a patch'd fool, if he
will offer to say what methought I had. The eye of man hath not
heard, the ear of man hath not seen, man's hand is not able to
taste, his tongue to conceive, nor his heart to report, what my
dream was.

(*A Midsummer Night's Dream*, Act 4, Scene 1)

There is irony as well as humour in Bottom's waking speech. Paul
had adapted a verse from Isaiah (64:4) to declare his own inability
to express 'what God has prepared for those who love him' (1 Cor
2:9) and Bottom's stammering parody is – or can be – very funny.
But it will not be lost on the audience of an actual performance of
A Midsummer Night's Dream that they have just been watching,
even to the extent of 'seeing with their ears', what Bottom is now
asserting to be indescribable.

Nevertheless, what Bottom says about his dream is not wrong.
To say of the ineffable that it cannot be put into words is more
than a truism: it is a tautology. 'If I have spoken of it,' warns
Meister Eckhart, 'I have not spoken of it, for it is ineffable.'[1] The
mystical is a looking-glass world, or rather mansion, with a paradox
in every room, where the door to wisdom may be the sound of one
hand clapping, and where darkness may be a source of light: *nox*

---

1. Quoted by James M. Clark, *Meister Eckhart*, 83.

illuminatio mea. Putting the ineffable into words is only the most salient of its many contradictions. At the beginning of the chapter on mysticism in his *Varieties of Religious Experience* William James says that the first important characteristic of mystical experience is negative: 'The subject of it immediately says that it defies expression, that no adequate report of its contents can be given in words.'[2] There follows page after page of detailed reports from a multitude of mystics, some of a mind-boggling banality and the majority paradoxically verbose.

No one could accuse Paul of verbosity, at any rate not on this topic. Not only theologians but also anyone interested in his religion would wish that he had been somewhat more forthcoming on his mystical experiences. We have already seen that he would have been rather puzzled to hear himself called a convert: to be called a mystic would have embarrassed him.

In the passage where we have to begin, 2 Corinthians 12:1–10, Paul uses a stock term: ἄρρητα ῥήματα. The Greek conveys more strongly than the English ('things that cannot be told') the unavoidable paradox of things that cannot be spoken of without falsi-fying them yet have no reality until they are put into words.

Dreams and visions (or, from the outsider's viewpoint, hallucinations) that are properly qualified as mystical not only defy description but transcend, almost by definition, ordinary human experience. To try and make sense of them (a task that Bottom shied away from) the mystic has to find conceptual structures to slot them into, categories of thought familiar to his hearers or listeners that will enable them to go just so far in penetrating the impenetrable. The only words he has (and this is equally true of theology in general) are human words, words drawn from a particular language and demanding a particular context if they are to make sense.

Steven Katz goes even further: 'mystical reports do not merely indicate the post-experiential description of an unreportable experience in the language closest at hand. Rather, the experiences themselves are inescapably shaped by prior linguistic influences such that the lived experience conforms to a preexistent pattern

2. (London, 1960), 367.

that has been learned, then intended, and then actualized in the experiential reality of the mystic.'[3] This must be right.

We observed in the first chapter that after watching Paul and Barnabas heal a cripple, the people of Lystra instinctively identified Paul and Barnabas with Zeus and Hermes. This can hardly be called a mystical experience, but involves a similar application of what Katz calls a preexistent pattern. The fourteen-year-old French peasant-girl Bernadette Soubirous, when recounting her vision of a beautiful lady somewhere in the Pyrenees, reported her as saying, 'I am the Immaculate Conception.'[4] She must have learnt this at school or in church, for she had this vision in 1858, four years after Pope Pius IX had infallibly proclaimed to the Catholic world the truth of the doctrine of the Immaculate Conception. It may make little sense to us, but it made sense to Bernadette. Francis of Assisi, the first and best-known of dozens of Christian mystics to develop the marks on his body called the stigmata, would never have done so without having reflected on Paul's claim to carry in his body the marks of Jesus (Gal 6:17): *stigmata* is the Greek word, found nowhere else in the New Testament.

There are plenty of other examples. Teresa of Avila, clever and well-read, along with her fellow-mystic John of the Cross, wrote of their experiences in language partly derived from theological textbooks. All Christian mystics had plenty to draw upon. Like St Patrick centuries earlier, Ignatius of Loyola, the founder of the Jesuits, had an extraordinary vision of the Trinity – though he did not seek to explain it with the help of a shamrock. To Hindu and Sufi mystics (about whom I know distressingly little) the Trinity is obviously unavailable as a category of interpretation; but they too have plenty of religious traditions to guide them.[5]

Paul, evidently enough, can be no exception to this rule. But he presents the student of religion with a particular problem. His own religious traditions were unequivocally Jewish and all that he says about his mystical experience, little enough in all conscience, bears

---

3. 'Mystical Speech', 5. Cf. 'The "Conservative" Character of Mystical Experience' in *Mysticism and Religious Traditions*, ed. S. T. Katz (New York, 1982), 3–60.

4. In good Pyrenean patois: 'Que soy era Immaculada Councepciou'.

5. The exception, evidently, is Mohammed, who, like Paul, emerged from a distinct religious background but, again like Paul, is more famous for what he founded than for what he found.

this out.[6] Yet it would be odd indeed if the visions and revelations of which he claims to have had an abundance (2 Cor 12:1, 7) were all totally unaffected by the event on the Damascus road (also a revelation, as we saw in the last chapter) and indeed by all that happened to him since. Segal, in fact, simply assumes that his mystical experiences, for all their Jewishness, were nevertheless fundamentally those of a Christian convert.[7] But this needs to be shown, and the purpose of this chapter is to argue that it was indeed Paul's Damascus road experience, perceived as a transformation of all his previous values, that coloured the whole of his subsequent life. Up to this point in this book I have made use of Paul's own writings rather sparingly. Now, however, I want to focus directly on a number of passages from four of his letters which, though very different from one another, will go towards building up what I hope will look like a coherent argument. These are (1) 2 Corinthians 12:1–10; (2) Philippians 3:7–11; (3) 1 Corinthians 15; (4) Romans 6:1–11; (5) 2 Corinthians 3:18; 4:16–17; (6) Romans 8:23–30.

Paul's Greek is difficult, difficult to understand and even more difficult to translate satisfactorily (or even adequately). Partly in order to illustrate the difficulty, partly in order to justify my own interpretation, I have chosen mostly to set out what is still on the whole the most reliable English translation available, the RSV, in parallel columns with my own, enclosing in brackets a few crucial Greek phrases for the sake of readers with some knowledge of that language.

2 Corinthians 12:1–10

RSV	JA
1 I must boast; there is nothing to be gained by it, but I will go on to visions and revelations of the Lord. 2 I know a	1 Boasting is required: though there is no advantage in it, I will go into visions and revelations (εἰς ὀπτασίας καὶ

---

6. 'Those who labour to explain him on the basis of Hellenism', Albert Schweitzer rightly remarks, 'are like a man carrying water in leaky watering-cans for the purpose of sprinkling it on a garden lying beside a stream' (*Mysticism*, 141: translation modified).
7. The chapter on ecstasy in *Paul the Convert* (pp. 34–71), though packed with information about the Jewish mystical tradition, is carelessly assembled, with no obvious guiding thread.

man in Christ who fourteen years ago was caught up to the third heaven – whether in the body or out of the body I do not know, God knows. 3 And I know that this man was caught up into Paradise – whether in the body or out of the body I do not know, God knows – 4 and he heard things that cannot be told, which man may not utter. 5 On behalf of this man I will boast, but on my own behalf I will not boast, except of my weaknesses. 6 Though if I wish to boast, I shall not be a fool, for I shall be speaking the truth. But I refrain from it, so that no one may think more of me than he sees in me or hears from me. 7 And to keep me from being too elated by the abundance of revelations, a thorn was given me in the flesh, a messenger of Satan, to harass me, to keep me from being too elated. 8 Three times I besought the Lord about this, that it should leave me; 9 but he said to me, 'My grace is sufficient for you, for my power is made perfect in weakness.' I will all the more gladly boast of my weaknesses, that the power of Christ may rest upon me. 10 For the sake of Christ, then, I am content with weaknesses, insults, hardships, persecutions, and calamities; for when I am weak, then I am strong.

ἀποκαλύψεις) of the Lord. 2 I know a man in Christ, fourteen years ago, whether in the body or out of the body I do not know, God knows, snatched up, this man, as far as the third heaven (ἁρπαγέντα τὸν τοιοῦτον ἕως τρίτου οὐρανοῦ). 3 And I know that this man – whether in the body or out of the body I do not know, God knows – 4 was snatched up into Paradise (ὅτι ἡρπάγη εἰς τὸν παράδεισον) and he heard things ineffable (ἄρρητα ῥήματα) that humans cannot utter. 5 About this man I will boast: about myself I will not boast, unless it be in adversities (ὑπὲρ δὲ ἐμαυτοῦ οὐ καυχήσομαι εἰ μὴ ἐν ταῖς ἀσθενείαις). 6 For if I do choose to boast I will not be without sense, for I shall be telling the truth. But I refrain, lest anyone reckon in my regard something beyond what he sees in me or hears from me. 7 Therefore, to prevent me from being raised too high by the abundance of revelations (καὶ τῇ ὑπερβολῇ τῶν ἀποκαλύψεων ἵνα μὴ ὑπεραίρωμαι) a thorn was given me in the flesh, an angel of Satan, to buffet me, to prevent me from being raised too high (ἵνα μὴ ὑπεραίρωμαι). 8 Three times I entreated the Lord about this, that it should leave me. 9 And he said to me: 'My grace is enough for you, for [my] power is fulfilled in adversity' … .

Our starting-point is the only passage in Paul's letters, apart from the description of his vocation in Galatians, to refer explicitly and unmistakably to a mystical experience. It comes in the middle of a long tirade that occupies the last four chapters of 2 Corinthians, and in all probability was originally sent as a separate letter. In it Paul urges the Corinthians not to listen to a group of people that he calls, ironically, super-apostles, but to accept wholeheartedly his own apostolic credentials. Paradoxically (for the passage is full of paradox), instead of appealing to his strengths he lays stress on his weaknesses and adversities, starting with a disparaging comment about his own physical appearance: 'For they say, "His letters are weighty and strong, but his bodily presence is weak, and his speech of no account"' (10:10). The whole passage is characterized by a determination on Paul's part to restrict what he calls his boasting to aspects of his life and work that any normal person would take to be serious handicaps in his chosen career – or rather the career for which he had been chosen. The Greek word he employs throughout (καυχᾶσθαι), generally translated as 'boast', often bears the sense, elsewhere in his letters, of 'rely upon' or 'have confidence in'. It is one of those words for which no single translation will suffice. Another word that is very difficult to translate satisfactorily is ἀσθένεια. The usual rendering, 'weakness', does not really work in the context, where the word appears to imply *anything at all that saps the strength*. (This is close to the literal meaning of *absence of strength*.) Paul is probably thinking most of the time of physical illness, but I have opted for the more general term 'adversity'.[8] What Paul boasts of are his *adversities*, and he appeals to them not just as a justification for his own confidence, but also as an argument likely to impress his readers. This is how the present passage ends: 'For the sake of Christ, then, I am content with adversities', and he spells them out: 'insults, hardships, persecutions, and calamities; for when I am weak [when I suffer setbacks], then I am strong' (12:10).

Although he tells us nothing whatsoever about *what* he saw on the occasion of this experience (perhaps he saw nothing at all), Paul dangles one tantalizingly precise piece of information in front of his readers. It took place, he says, 'fourteen years ago'. Not a few commentators have eagerly clutched at this straw and made it the centrepiece of some elaborately thatched arguments designed to prove that Paul's trance (for it was certainly that) took place in such-and-such a year, or even on such-and-such an occasion.[9] If we

8. The noun ἀσθένεια is found 5 times in this letter, the verb 6 times and the adjective once. Robert Butterworth has suggested to me that 'what saps your strength', 'what undermines you', 'a set-back' are all renderings that catch Paul's thought better than the standard 'weakness'. I hope I have benefited from this insight. Cf. Jacob Jervell, 'Der schwache Charismatiker', 191–3.

9. One especially elaborate suggestion comes from Christopher Morray-Jones, 'Paradise Revisited'. [References to earlier studies arguing to a connection between Paul's mystical experiences and the merkabah tradition are easily accessible in Morray-Jones's footnotes, from Bousset (1901), Windisch (1924), Bietenhard (1951), Scholem (1960), Morton Smith (1963), Bowker (1971), Rowland (1982), through to Segal (1990) and many others.] Morray-Jones argues that Paul's rapture is to be identified with the vision in the temple

accept, as I think we must, that 'this man' or 'the man in question' (ὁ τοιοῦτος) was Paul himself,[10] then by far the most important question is whether Paul is referring to his original conversion experience. For Paul's first readers, who knew him far better than we do, the 'fourteen years' may have been all the clue they needed. But it must be confessed that the evidence is too slim to warrant certainty in this matter.

In a recent doctoral thesis Paula Gooder has argued that what Paul says about his mystical experience here, contrary to received wisdom, fits in very well with the general message of boasting in weakness.[11] Paul was not snatched up *into* but only up as far as (ἕως) the third heaven and, by implication, left outside it. And, to pursue the argument a little further, the purpose of the thorn in the flesh was not to keep him from being too elated, but from being carried up too far into the heavenly realm (μὴ ὑπεραίρωμαι).[12] Visions and revelations were his in abundance, but in a league table of Jewish mystics Paul would not rate himself very high.[13]

This is a novel and attractive thesis. Although not all scholars agree that the passage describes two stages of a single experience, this is certainly one possible way of reading it. Against Gooder's interpretation, however, is the intrinsic improbability that a narrator

---

recorded in Acts 22, which 'corresponds precisely to the point at which the rapture to paradise occurs in the narrative sequence of 2 Corinthians 11–12, in which Paul's account of his escape from Damascus is followed immediately by his vision' (288–9). This ingenious suggestion ignores the likelihood that in this, his second account of Paul's call and conversion, Luke is offering his own redaction (designed to suit Paul's Jewish audience) of the first account in Acts 9.

10. *Contra* M. D. Goulder, 'Visionaries'. For a persuasive refutation of Goulder's argument that the man in question was a friend of Paul see Morray-Jones, 'Paradise Revisited', 272–3. Segal points out that if the rabbinic rule forbidding public discussion of mystic phenomena goes back to the first century this 'would explain why Paul could not divulge his experience *in his own name*' (*Paul the Convert*, 58).

11. Paula Gooder, *Only the Third Heaven?*.

12. The meaning of the little word ἕως, 'up to' or 'as far as', is concealed by RSV's 'to'; and the verb ὑπεραίρεσθαι though it can bear a middle sense ('be too elated'), is equally well understood as a passive ('be carried up too far'). This seems preferable to Gooder's 'lest I raise myself higher', though she may well be right in suggesting a deliberate ambiguity: 'Therefore, lest I exalt myself, a thorn of the flesh was given me, an angel of Satan to trouble me, lest I raise myself higher (i.e. into another heaven)' (p. 248).

13. *Contra* James D. Tabor, *Things Unutterable*.

telling of a single experience involving two stages would describe the second stage first. Why, having recounted his failure to reach the third heaven, would Paul continue by saying that he was nevertheless taken (snatched) up into paradise (located on this conception *below* the third heaven)? Yet her thesis needs only a slight modification to be made to work. What if Paul is talking of two different occasions, the first in which he got as far as the threshold of the third heaven and a second occasion on which he did reach paradise (but no further), in each case being prevented from rising too high?[14] In that case we may begin to see how Paul's conception of his own mystical experience is reconcilable with a sense of satisfaction, almost of pride, in his own frailty. Having pleaded with the Lord (three times) to remove the one obstacle standing in the way of a further elevation – the thorn in the flesh, the angel of Satan, however this is conceived – he receives the reply, 'My grace is sufficient for you, for power is fulfilled in adversity' (12:9).

It is here then that we have to seek the explanation of Paul's bizarre boasting. We might well wonder what kind of man it is who relies upon his frailty (or setbacks) rather than his strengths. Is Paul being very clever, selecting just the right arrows from a full quiver of rhetorical tricks – 'I come to bury Caesar, not to praise him' – that sort of thing? Surely not. All the indications are that he means what he says. Otherwise what would be the point of going through one by one, as he does a little earlier in the letter (11:23–27), that remarkable (truly awesome!) catalogue of dangers and disasters, including physical hardships of every kind, hunger, thirst, sleeplessness, and freezing cold? That Paul was fully aware how odd his whole approach must have seemed we can see from the way he prefaces this brief snatch of autobiography: 'Are they servants of Christ?' he asks of his rivals, 'I am a better one – I am talking like a madman – with far greater labours, far more imprisonments, with countless beatings, and often near death' (11:23). And so on.

Now if this were all, we might put it down to a kind of perverse masochism. Apart from the fact that Paul did not actually seek out all these miseries, he could almost figure as the first of a long line of Christian ascetics (the best-known being the 'pillar people' [στυλῖται]), who set themselves to perform feats of endurance that

---

14. I owe this suggestion to Christopher Rowland.

would excite the admiration of all who saw them. But so far as we can judge, Paul was not like that. The deeper reason for this strange boasting emerges towards the end of his long tirade, as he responds to a request for proof that, as he puts it, 'Christ is speaking in me'. What proof does he offer? 'He is not frail in dealing with you, but is powerful in you. For he was crucified in frailty [his crucifixion was a setback?], but he lives by the power of God. For we are frail in him, but in dealing with you we shall live with him by the power of God' (13:3–4). Here we see his wholehearted acceptance of 'the Lord's' refusal to remove what he saw as the obstacle to his further advancement in the path of mystical perfection.

This is a typical example of the kind of passage in Paul's writings that many scholars regard as a proof of his *theological* acumen. And this is a perfectly comprehensible reaction. For right at the beginning of the first of Paul's letters to these same Corinthians he had summed up his gospel in a single trenchant phrase: Christ crucified. That is what he preached, this is what he taught, and this is what he seems to be reflecting upon here. Nevertheless – and this cannot be stressed too strongly – Paul's eagerness to endure so many hardships and so much pain cannot have issued smoothly and consequentially from a day, or a night, or a month, of theological rumination. His catalogue of adversities, however impressive, is far from unique. Men and women in all ages and in all societies have performed feats of endurance that more than match those on Paul's list. What puts him in a different category from almost all the others is not his courage but the extraordinary satisfaction that he takes in what he calls his frailties or adversities. This is not just a matter of stoical resignation or an understandable pride in his pertinacity in confronting pain. The conviction that his sickness and setbacks are really a source of strength is not one he arrived at simply by thinking. Throughout this passage, beginning, middle and end, what he has been talking about is not reflection but experience, not theology but religion.

So the question arises: what kind of experience? And the answer is, almost in so many words, a sort of dying and rising. And so a further question arises: how can this be? How could Paul have *experienced* a dying and rising analogous to that of Christ? And the answer to *this* question is to be found on the Damascus road. Paul's radical change of mind and heart, so much more than a new idea or a revised opinion, coincided with his call and conversion. It was then that he died to his old life and then that the risen Christ began to live in him. No doubt this is not exactly how he describes his own experience. Frustratingly, he nowhere spells out the content of any of the abundant revelations that he claims to have been granted in the text we have been considering. But to explain what happened we have to postulate something like the shaman's traumatic sense of being torn apart and reconstituted as a new person at the time he was established in his calling. Having once been a man (with the form of a slave, as Paul puts it elsewhere), Paul's spirit guide and familiar attained a new kind of spiritual existence with a spiritual rather than an ordinary natural body by dying on a cross and (so Paul believed) rising from the dead.

At this point I want to commence an argument (to be pursued in the following section) justifying an appeal to the very widespread (some might say universal) human experience of death and resurrection as a condition of initiation into a new form of existence. There is a rabbinical tradition concerning the death and resurrection of the people of Israel (!) at Mount Sinai. Although this tradition is relatively late (third century) it illustrates the rich potential of the Sinai story. God's voice (not just his visible appearance in a theophany) is thought to be lethal. Here is the the most important passage:

> R. Joshua b.Levi said: At each and every word which comes forth from the mouth of the Holy One (blessed be He) the soul of Israel expired [literally, 'went out' (יצאה)] when he spoke, as it is said, 'My soul failed me [literally 'went out'] when he spoke' (Song of Songs 5:6). But since their soul expired after the first commandment, how did they receive the second commandment? He brought down the dew which will resurrect the dead in the future and He resurrected them, as it is said, 'A bounteous rain you did pour down, O God' (Ps 68:10).
>
> *b.Shabbat* 88b

Ira Chernus sums up the basic themes as follows: 'the direct vision of God conceived in an ecstatic context, the fire phenomenon related to revelation, the need to accept death as a means for special access to the knowledge of the Torah, and the dew as the agent of resurrection'.[15] He goes on to ask why R. Joshua did not deny the possibility of such revelatory experiences in the first place: he could simply have said – in accordance with the biblical text – that Israel did not receive *any* commandment directly from the mouth of God. Chernus thinks that there is only one possible answer: 'He believed, in fact, that such experiences were possible and that mystics in his own time or earlier did have them.' At the height of this experience the mystic 'dies', overwhelmed by the sheer force of God's revelation. Yet at the same time 'the mystic who accepts this self-annihilation will be resurrected by the dew of life which God will pour down upon him'.[16]

Chernus goes on to compare this experience with the initiatory death discussed by Mircea Eliade that is seen as a repetition of the death of the primordial being thought to have founded the original ritual: 'By dying ritually, the initiate shares in the supernatural condition of the founder of the mystery … . Initiatory death becomes the *sine qua non* for all spiritual regeneration.'[17]

Remembering that Paul's evocation of his own revelatory experience on the Damascus road (2 Cor 4:4–6) follows immediately after an extended reflection, amounting almost to a midrash, upon the inability of the Israelites to look on Moses's shining face as he descended from Mount Sinai (2 Cor 3:7–18), we may view with less scepticism the suggestion that he too, like the Israelites in the rabbinic tradition discussed by Chernus, underwent an initiatory death-and-resurrection experience. The appeal to Eliade's repeated insistence upon the universal relevance of 'rites of passage' is as valid for Paul as it is for the third-century rabbis discussed by Chernus.

Philippians 3:7–11

RSV	JA
7 But whatever gain I had, I counted as loss for the sake of Christ. 8 Indeed I count everything as loss because of the surpassing worth of knowing Christ Jesus	7 Whatever used to be gain to me *I have come to think of* (ἥγημαι) as loss for the sake of Christ. 8 But at any rate the point is that I now think of everything (πάντα)

15. *Mysticism in Rabbinic Judaism*, 34–5. The relevant chapter is entitled 'Revelation and Initiatory Death in Third Century Midrash'.
16. Ibid., 40.
17. *Rites and Symbols*, 131. Some of the examples adduced by Eliade in his *Shamanism* will be quoted in the next section.

my Lord. For his sake I have suffered the loss of all things, and count them as refuse, in order that I may gain Christ 9 and be found in him, not having a righteousness of my own, based on law, but that which is through faith in Christ, the righteousness from God that depends on faith; 10 that I may know him and the power of his resurrection, and may share his sufferings, becoming like him in his death, 11 that if possible I may attain the resurrection from the dead.

as a dead loss because it has all been surpassed by the knowledge (διὰ τὸ ὑπερέχον τῆς γνώσεως) of Christ Jesus my Lord, for whose sake *I suffered the loss of the whole world* (τὰ πάντα ἐζημιώθην) and now think of it as ordure (σκύβαλα) in order to gain Christ 9 and be found in him with a righteousness (δικαιοσύνη) not of my own, from the law, but one that comes from faith in Christ, the righteousness from God, based on the faith 10 that consists in knowing him (ἐπὶ τῇ πίστει τοῦ γνῶναι αὐτόν), the power of his resurrection, and the communion of his sufferings, being [continuously] transformed by his death (συμμορφιζόμενος τῷ θανάτῳ αὐτοῦ), 11 in the hope of attaining the resurrection from the dead.

The second passage we have to consider, more polemical in tone, is in some respects more puzzling too. Some of Paul's language here is mystical, especially the use of the substantival form of the infinitive 'to know', τὸ γνῶναι, found nowhere else in his writings, preceded by the word γνῶσις (*gnosis*, 'knowledge') and both applied to Christ;[18] but the emphasis on considered reflection ('I have come to think', v.7; 'I continue to think', v.8, *bis*) suggests that the views Paul espouses here have been reached only after lengthy lucubrations; in other words, that we have to do here with theology rather than religion. Indeed, if we had to rely upon linguistic evidence alone that is what we would be forced to conclude.

18. Dibelius asserts that the word is used in the technical sense it bears in Hellenistic mysticism: 'not of a knowledge related to the intellect but of the penetration (*Innewerden*) of the divinity into the vision and behaviour of the seer' (*Philipper*, 89),. But it also corresponds to the Hebrew דעת, a key concept at Qumran, especially in the Community Rule (e.g. 1QS 2.3; 4.4, 22; 8.9; 10.12, 25; 11.3, 11) and in the Thanksgiving Hymns (1QH 9.19; 10.18; 12.11, 18 ['vision of knowledge']; 20.13, 29). Also 1QpHab 11.1: 'And knowledge shall be revealed to them abundantly, like the waters of the sea', and Dan 2:21: 'He gives wisdom to the wise and knowledge (מנדעא [=דעת]) to those who know understanding'. See further Morray-Jones, 'Paradise Revisited', 187, and the literature he cites in n. 31.

Such a conclusion, in my view, would be mistaken, for four reasons. The first is that, like most of what Paul writes, the passage is part of an attempt to persuade. He is encouraging the Philippians to stand firm against Jews or Judaizers. So in stressing that he was right to abandon his own Jewish ways and Jewish values and adopt a totally new set of values, Paul is not just giving a history of his own change of heart. He is emphasizing how firmly he holds to his new set of values and implying that any reasonable person would do the same – hardly, when one looks at the substance of what he is saying, a very plausible position; but no doubt that is why he is concerned to underline it.

The second reason for thinking that Paul is appealing to experience as well as expressing conviction is the extremity, amounting almost to absurdity, of the position he is advocating: '. . . the knowledge of Christ Jesus my lord, for whose sake I suffered the loss of the whole world (τὰ πάντα)[19] and yet now regard it as ordure[20] so that I may gain Christ' (v.8). The last phrase is a strong, compressed and rather clumsy way of saying that if Christ is to be the recompense, the whole world is a price worth paying. This of course is what a *mystic* would say, but how many *theologians* would say it and mean it?

In the third place there is the movement of the argument, which starts off as a piece of spiritual autobiography. As this proceeds, Paul talks of himself as a persecutor of the church, and in the very next verse of gaining Christ. This dramatic change took place on the Damascus road. The allusion to his call/conversion experience may be indirect, and easy to miss, but it is there none the less.

Finally, and most importantly, there is the nature of the change. It is violent, uncompromising, and extreme, swinging from total acceptance of Judaism (circumcision, the law, zealous persecution

19. This is what τὰ πάντα generally means in Paul (Rom 11:36; 1 Cor 8:6; 15:28; Gal 3:22; Phil 3:31) and indeed elsewhere in the Greek Bible. 1 Cor 15:28 is particularly instructive, for after quoting Ps 8:6, one of the very rare cases in the LXX in which the anarthrous form refers to the whole universe, Paul himself adds the article when he comes to comment on it, as does the author of Hebrews in Heb 2:8. For a full exposition of the evidence relating to a felt difference between the two forms (apropos of John 1:3) see J. Ashton, *Studying John*, 20, n. 37.
20. The Greek word σκύβαλα really means dung or excrement, but is usually bowdlerized by the translations into an odourless 'refuse'.

of the church, everything he can think of) to a complete rejection of it all (perhaps this is what Paul meant when he said 'the whole world') for the sake of achieving one thing only, and that is Christ. A change of this magnitude, despite the measured introduction ('I have come to think'), amounts to a truly Nietzschean reversal of all values, in which absolutely everything is turned upside down.[21] Such a change does not come about from hard thinking. No doubt Paul pondered long and hard on the implications of his Damascus road experience. But the substitution of the law by Christ and, implicitly, grace (Rom 6:14) was inextricably bound up with, part and parcel of, the experience itself.

This, however, was not the end of the matter, as the conclusion of the passage shows: there remained the continuous transformation (into Christ, or by the instrumentality of his death) that gave Paul grounds for hope in an eventual resurrection. Writing from prison, he identifies his own sufferings with those of Christ more plainly than anywhere else in his writings. And the sufferings involve a participation in the death.

To sum up, this is not theology but the best way Paul can find of expressing what he now believes: it is the outcome of a raw and *unsystematic* reflection on the most important *religious* experience of his life. But what kind of experience? A sort of dying and rising. But how can this be? The answer, once again, is to be found on the Damascus road. Paul's reversal of all his values, his radical change of mind and heart, *coincided* with his call and conversion. It was at that very moment that he died to his old life and Christ began to live in him. What he endured at that time was, though he nowhere describes it in this way, the equivalent of the shaman's traumatic sense of being torn apart and reconstituted at the moment of his vocation. But Paul's new spirit guide was different. Christ had attained his own new status, through an actual death and, so Paul believed, an actual rising from the dead. He had lost for ever his old, natural body, but his new, spiritual body freed him from all physical restraints, so that Paul could now think of him in a fresh way, and no longer 'according to the flesh' (2 Cor 5:16).

---

21. *Versuch einer Umwerthung aller Werthe* was the subtitle of the first (post-humous) edition of *Wille zur Macht* (1911). See *Werke*, ed. Karl Schlechta, vi (Munich/Vienna, 1980), 930.

Here, continuing the argument begun in the preceding section, I want to quote what Eliade says of the initiatory experiences of Siberian and other North Asian shamans in the second chapter of his famous book. From among his many examples I will simply quote his introduction, some of his summaries, and his final conclusion:

> We shall soon see that all the ecstatic experiences that determine the future shaman's vocation involve the traditional schema of an initiation ceremony: suffering, death, resurrection.
>
> For example, a Yakut shaman … states that as a rule the shaman 'dies' and lies in the yurt for three days without eating or drinking…. Another shaman … gives further details. The candidate's limbs are removed with an iron hook; the bones are cleaned, the flesh scraped, the body fluids thrown away, and the eyes torn from their sockets.
>
> In all these examples we find the central theme of an initiation ceremony: dismemberment of the neophyte's body and renewal of his organs; ritual death followed by resurrection.
>
> Each of these elements in the initiatory story is consistent and has its place in a symbolic or ritual system well known to the history of religions…. Taken together they represent a well-organized variant of the universal theme of the death and mystical resurrection of the candidate by means of a descent to the underworld and an ascent to the sky.
>
> We must not forget the immense role played by the inner light in Christian mysticism and theology. All this invites us to a more understanding judgment of the Eskimo shaman's experiences; there is reason to believe that such mystical experiences were in some manner accessible to archaic humanity from the most distant ages.
>
> We have several times observed the *initiatory* essence of the candidate's 'death' followed by his 'resurrection' in whatever form this takes place – ecstatic dreams, unusual events, or ritual proper.[22]

22. *Shamanism*, 33, 36, 38, 43, 45, 61–2, 64.

It may well be that Eliade is using the essentially *Christian* language of death and resurrection to sum up all these initiatory experiences without being fully aware of the significance of this. In many of the examples he cites, *resuscitation* would in fact be a more appropriate term than resurrection. Paul, on the other hand, was brought up as a Pharisee to believe in the resurrection of the dead, and so thought of (and experienced) his vision of Christ not just as of a man somehow restored to life, but as of someone who had emerged from the land of the dead (Sheol). The next two passages from his writings are selected for the light they throw on his own understanding of death and resurrection, first (1 Corintians 15) in reference to Christ himself, and secondly (Romans 6) in reference to the experience of all Christians.

1 Corinthians 15: 3–8

For I delivered to you as of first importance what I also received, that Christ died for our sins in accordance with the scriptures, that he was buried, that he was raised on the third day in accordance with the scriptures, and that he appeared to Cephas, then to the twelve. Then he appeared to more than five hundred brethren at one time, most of whom are still alive, though some have fallen asleep. Then he appeared to James, then to all the apostles. Last of all, as to one untimely born, he appeared also to me.

For I handed down to you principally what I myself received, that Christ died for our sins in accordance with the scriptures, and that he was buried and that he was raised on the third day in accordance with the scriptures, and that he appeared to Cephas, and then to the twelve. Subsequently he made a single appearance to more than five hundred of the brethren: most of these are alive to this day, though some have gone to their rest. Subsequently he appeared to James, and then to all the apostles. Last of all, as if by an abnormal birth, he also appeared to me (ὡσπερεὶ τῷ ἐκτρώματι ὤφθη κἀμοί).

The death and resurrection of Christ is *the* foundation myth of Christianity. It is at the very heart of what is among the earliest of Christian creeds, passed down to Paul in a formula that stresses the element of tradition (vv. 3–4). The creed is followed by a list of the appearances of the Risen Christ, concluding with the appearance to Paul himself (vv. 5–8). Although ἔκτρωμα really means a miscarriage, it seems likely that Paul thought of his apostolic calling as a kind of premature birth, premature insofar as, unlike the other apostles, he did not have to qualify for it by a long period of spiritual growth. Then comes the famous defence of the truth of the resurrection (vv. 12–19). Then this: 'Christ has truly been raised from the dead (ἐκ νεκρῶν), the first fruits of those who have fallen asleep. For as by a man came death, by a man has come also the resurrection of the dead. For as in Adam all die, so also in Christ shall all be made alive' (vv. 20–22).

The expression 'first fruits of those who have gone to their rest' (ἀπαρχὴ τῶν κεκοιμημένων) gives us the clue to the way Paul experienced his vision of Christ. We have just noted that having been brought up as a Pharisee, he believed in the general resurrection of the dead.[23] We might be tempted to conclude that it was this belief that allowed him to interpret his experience as a vision of the Risen Christ; but it would be more accurate to say that it ensured that he actually *had* a vision of the Risen Christ. Like all religious seers, as we have already insisted, the style of his vision was predetermined by his own traditions. These included in his case a conviction that people are not properly dead until they are buried. The real horror of Jezebel's death as recorded in 2 Kings 9:30–37 was not just that her body was eaten by dogs but that at the end of it all no one could say 'This is Jezebel'. Christ, on the contrary, was really dead and when his body was placed in the tomb he entered *the realm of the dead*, the νεκροί. This Greek word means 'corpses', but as Paul uses the term it means those dead people who, having been buried, inhabit Sheol. When the witch of Endor summoned up the spirit of Samuel from Sheol (1 Sam 28) he did not appear as a risen body but as a ghost: paradoxically his appearance was not a proof that he was risen but a confirmation that he was dead. In order to overcome death Christ had to emerge out of the realm of the dead *in bodily form*: otherwise he would have lost the battle with death. Paul uses the term σῶμα πνευματικόν, spiritual body: 'It is sown a natural body [σῶμα ψυχικόν, a body informed by a *psyche* or soul], it is raised a spiritual body [a body informed by a *pneuma*]. If there is a natural body, there is also a spiritual body. Thus it is written,

---

23. See Paul's speech before Felix, where he cleverly appeals to the beliefs of 'the Jews' who have charged him with sedition and profanation of the temple: '... having a hope which these themselves accept, that there will be a resurrection of both the just and the unjust' (Acts 24:15).

"The first man Adam became a living soul [ψυχὴ ζῶσα]"; the last Adam became a life-giving spirit [πνεῦμα ζῳοποιοῦν]' (1 Cor 15:44–45).

None of this is easy. Paul did not have a nice neat theological language ready to hand: he had to fashion one for himself. We may find it puzzling that in the same breath he calls Christ both a spiritual *body* and a life-giving *spirit*, but he needed both terms to express – what? His new faith, his altered perception, yes; but also, I think, his experience.

He does not expect his own converts to repeat his experience in quite the same way, but he does expect them to believe his account of it: 'if you confess with your lips that Jesus is Lord, and believe with your heart that God raised him from the dead, you will be saved' (Rom 10:9).

Romans 6:1–11

RSV	JA
1 What shall we say then? Are we to continue in sin that grace may abound? 2 By no means! How can we who died to sin still live in it? 3 Do you not know that all of us who have been baptized into Christ Jesus were baptized into his death? 4 We were buried therefore with him by baptism into death, so that as Christ was raised from the dead by the glory of the Father, we too might walk in newness of life. 5 For if we have been united with him in a death like his, we shall certainly be united with him in a resurrection like his. 6 We know that our old self was crucified with him so that the sinful body might be destroyed, and we might no longer be enslaved to sin. 7 For he who has died is freed from sin. 8 But if we have died with Christ, we believe that we shall also live with him. 9 For we know that Christ being raised from the dead will never die again; death no longer has dominion over him. 10 The death he died he died to sin, once for all, but the life he lives he lives to God. 11 So you also must consider yourselves dead to sin and alive to God in Christ Jesus.	4 We were buried therefore with him by baptism into death, so that as Christ was raised from the dead by the glory of the Father, we too might conduct ourselves (περιπατήσωμεν) in newness of life. 5 For if we have been joined together by the likeness of his death, we shall certainly be joined by the likeness of his resurrection (εἰ γὰρ σύμφυτοι γεγόναμεν τῷ ὁμοιώματι τοῦ θανάτου αὐτοῦ, ἀλλὰ καὶ τῆς ἀναστάσεως ἐσόμεθα) 6 in the knowledge of this truth, that our old self was crucified with him so that the body of sin (τὸ σῶμα τῆς ἁμαρτίας) might be done away with, and we might no longer be enslaved to Sin. 7 For whoever has died has been freed from Sin into a right relationship [with God] (ὁ γὰρ ἀποθανὼν δεδικαίωται ἀπὸ τῆς ἁμαρτίας). 8 And if we have died with Christ, we believe that we shall also live with him, 9 knowing as we do that having been raised from the dead Christ will never die again; death no longer has dominion over him. 10 In his dying (ὁ γὰρ ἀπέθανεν) he died to sin once for all; in his living (ὁ δὲ ζῇ) he lives to God …

So far I have been arguing that the decisive mystical experience of Paul's life was his vision of the crucified and risen Christ on the Damascus road, which he interpreted not just as a missionary vocation but as a death to his old life as a follower of the law and the beginning of a new life under Christ. God, he says, revealed his Son 'in me', and part of the meaning of this is that God had reproduced in Paul a pattern of dying and rising.

Paul was both a mystic and a charismatic, but we do not know if the same can be said of any of his converts. Paul undoubtedly thought that in some sense they all participated in the death and resurrection of Christ; but if not through the same intense mystical experience as himself, then how? The passage in Romans that we are about to consider gives the answer.

Not that the answer is unambiguous. The Greek is difficult, posing many teasing little problems for the translator, and there are other uncertainties too, above all the role assigned to baptism. For although the passage is generally assumed to be *about* baptism, it is far from certain that baptism figures in this passage as anything more than a simile. I shall argue that *this does not matter*, since the central message is none other than the appropriation by individual Christians of the victory over sin accomplished by Christ through his own death and resurrection.

Romans 5 is a pronouncement on an epic scale of the victory of grace over sin and death. The scope is cosmic, the genre myth. With chapter 6 the scope shrinks from the cosmic to the microcosmic: the forum of the human heart. The mythological conclusion of chapter 5 prompts a practical question. The defeat of Sin, after an epic struggle, took place on the world stage. This was Sin as a cosmic force (Sin with a capital S). Witnessing her defeat, the spectators are moved to ask, Should we then persist in sin (sin with a small s)? The reasoning behind their question, evidently, is this: if Sin has been defeated, then why should our small sins count? The two chapters are linked together by the common theme of dominion. Whereas before the coming of Christ, 'Sin reigned in death' (5:20), after Christ's resurrection 'death no longer has dominion over him' (6:9). And again: 'Sin will no longer have any dominion over you, since you are not under the law but under grace' (6:14). It is true that the perspective has shifted from the universal to the individual, but in this, the second wing of the diptych, Paul is responding to the question with which the chapter opens (should we then persist in sin?) and urging upon each and every individual the need to appropriate the victory over sin and death in their own lives. His argument is built round a metaphor, which, as we can now see, emerged in his own consciousness through his experience on the Damascus road. This is the metaphor of death to sin.

One difficulty that frequently crops up when reading Paul is that his metaphors have lost their shine: overuse has left them worn and lustreless: they are dead metaphors. (This is true of grace and, as we shall see in the next chapter, of salvation.) Death to sin is another dead metaphor. Douglas Templeton brings it to life. In the context of Romans 6, he says, 'being dead … is the metaphorical equivalent of being alive and not to be a Christian is best re-described as being "dead" and becoming dead is also the metaphorical equivalent of giving up the way of life that is equivalent to being "dead".[24] "Death", that is, has a double reference: (1) to a way of life that should be given up, and (2) to the giving up of that way of life. Paul is an economical writer: why use two terms where one will do?'[25]

Templeton succeeds in bringing out the paradoxical ambivalence of a term which on the one hand retains some of the literal sense of lifeless inertia, seeing life under Sin as no proper life at all but rather death, dull, purposeless and empty; and yet on the other hand takes on a positive meaning by, with an almost Hegelian resonance, negating the negation; for death to sin is a death to death, and is therefore life.

Here is how Templeton concludes his discussion: 'There is a plain historical sense of being dead. This plain sense supplies the material for live metaphors: a metaphor for not *really* being alive before you are dead, and a metaphor for making the transition from not *really* being alive to something better, to pre-mortem "life". Simultaneously, the plain, historical sense of being dead remains, but being dead in the plain historical sense is succeeded by being "alive"

---

24. Cicero says something similar in the dream of Scipio: those who have escaped from the prison-house of the body are really alive, whereas 'your so-called life is really death' (*De republica* 6.14). There is a similar play on the different meanings of death, moral and physical, in the first few chapters of the Book of Wisdom.

25. *Re-exploring Paul's Imagination*, 15.74.

in a sense that is neither plain nor historical. Only a well-honed machete can take us through this undergrowth of language.'[26]

Behind the double negative, and lending it force and significance, is the extraordinarily powerful concept of resurrection, whose meaning we have just been considering in relation to 1 Corinthians 15. For Paul resurrection is an interruption of death in much the same way that death is an interruption of life. Above all, it is important to see that both imply *movement*, a change of place. As well as a state, life is a place, the land of the living; so is death – the realm of the dead. The Hebrew name for this place, as we have seen, is Sheol, the Greek is Hades. The Jewish Paul and the Greek Homer both have the same idea of a gloomy underworld peopled by shivering shades. This is the world that Christ moved out of when, like Orpheus, he ascended ἐκ νεκρῶν – from among the dead.

This is a digression, but not a pointless one, for it is important to grasp both the strangeness of Paul's concept of resurrection and its central significance in his thought: resurrection transforms the metaphor of death.

So far I have said nothing about baptism. If, which is certainly the case, baptism is not what this passage is about, then what is it doing here, what is its function? 'To be baptized into Christ Jesus' is an odd expression. Elsewhere Paul speaks of the Israelites being baptized into Moses in the cloud and in the sea (1 Cor 10:2). Since he is prepared to use the term metaphorically there, then perhaps he is using it metaphorically here too.

The word βαπτίζειν literally means to dip, but is employed by the Jesus of Mark's gospel (in what is very likely to be an authentic saying) in a context where it plainly refers to his death: 'Are you able', he says to the disciples, 'to drink the cup that I drink or to be baptized with the baptism with which I am to be baptized?' (Mark 10:38; Luke 12:50). If you dip a cloth into water it will not emerge dyed; and if you dip a man into water he will not emerge dead unless you have held him under for a long time.[27] And even if he does emerge dead he is certainly not buried – which means that by pursuing the metaphor you get no closer to

26. Ibid., 15.76.
27. G. R. Beasley-Murray informs us that as early as 1614, some twenty years before Baptists can be shown to have adopted the practice of total immersion, the assertion that to be baptized is to be 'dipped for dead in the water' is found in

Paul's meaning; in fact since what he is looking for in baptism is not death but burial you are really veering away from it. Moreover, since the full Christian symbolism of baptism suggests a rising out of the water to a new life, we are rather left groping at this point.

If we are content to leave some problems unsolved, especially the knotty little puzzle of how to translate v. 5,[28] then it is fairly safe to say that the passage concerns the appropriation by individual believers of the benefits of Christ's saving death and resurrection as they join the community and assume new responsibilities. These are seen as a sort of dying to their previous existence and starting a new life.

There is something more here than the assimilation by the Christian community of one man's mystical experience. Whether baptism is introduced here simply as a metaphor or, as most people think, Paul is commenting on the significance of an already established practice, we are looking at an example of what, following a coinage of van Gennep, has come to be known as a 'rite of passage'.[29] In accordance with our programme of *comparative* religion, I want to conclude this discussion with some remarks based on a paragraph in *La Pensée sauvage*. One of Lévi-Strauss's constant preoccupations was the revalorization of the conceptual processes lying behind what Henry Wilde called 'the lower religions of mankind'. Towards the end of his book he remarks upon the striking similarity of initiation rites all over the world, Africa, America, Australia, Melanesia. The novices are first taken from their parents and symbolically killed, then hidden away in the bush or the forest to undergo the ordeals of the other world ('les épreuves de l'au-delà'). Then, reborn as full-fledged members of their society, they are restored to their parents,

---

a book called '*Religions Peace: A Plea for liberty of conscience*. Long since presented to King James and the High Court of Parliament then sitting by Leonard Busher'. See *Baptism*, 133, n. 3.

28. Many scholars follow the RSV in supplying the pronoun αὐτῷ, This allows the translation: 'united *with him*'. But what Paul actually writes is this: 'if we have been united by/with the likeness of his death'. I wonder whether the σύμφυτοι (knit together) might be taken to imply the unity of believers within one body, leaving the translator free to take τῷ ὁμοιώματι as an instrumental dative: 'if we have been knit together by the equivalent of Christ's death', i.e. the spiritual death involved in renouncing sin and committing oneself to a new life.

29. A. van Gennep, *Les rites de passage*. The French word *passage* in this title really means 'change' or 'transition'; so 'rites of passage' is really a mistranslation. But of course it has come to stay, and may reasonably be called a borrowing (like 'garage').

who patiently undertake the task of teaching them all over again how to feed and dress themselves. It would be tempting, says Lévi-Strauss, to interpret all this as a proof that thought is here wholly entangled in praxis ('toute entière engluée dans la *praxis*'). On the contrary, he objects, it is our own scientific *praxis* that has effectively evacuated the notions of birth and death of everything except their purely physiological connotations and rendered them incapable of being used to mean anything else. He sees this as a radical impoverishment of thought and language: societies still able to transcend the distinction between the real and the imaginary have the edge over our own, reduced as we are to a simple play on words. They really mean what they say when they speak of birth and death, whereas in what he calls comparable circumstances 'il ne s'agit pour nous que de "jeux" de mots': for us it's a mere 'play' on words.[30]

The Christian sacrament of baptism, even where it involves total immersion, is clearly no more than a token gesture when placed beside the lengthy 'rites of passage' practised in other societies. We cannot even be sure whether in the passage from Romans we have just been considering Paul was drawing upon an already existing symbolism, or whether subsequent practice was inspired by a symbolism that had somehow germinated in his own fertile imagination. However that may be, the church came to see baptism as a rite of entry into the Christian community that entailed an explicit renunciation of sin ('the devil and all his pomps') and a promise of the kind of new life urged by Paul. If I am right, then the starting-point of this whole process will have been Paul's experience of a shamanist type of initiation: death and resurrection on the Damascus road.

2 Corinthians 3:18; 4:16–17

3:18 And we all, with unveiled face, beholding the glory of the Lord, are being changed into his likeness from one degree of glory to another; for this comes from the Lord who is the Spirit.	3:18 And all of us, with unveiled face, beholding as in a mirror (κατοπτριζόμενοι) the glory of the Lord, are being transformed into the same image (τὴν αὐτὴν εἰκόνα μεταμορφούμεθα) from one degree of glory to another (ἀπὸ δόξης εἰς δόξαν) as is to be expected from the Spirit of the Lord (καθάπερ ἀπὸ κυρίου πνεύματος).

30. *Pensée sauvage*, 350–1; (ET: London, 1972), 264–5.

4:16 Though our outer nature is wasting away, our inner nature is being renewed every day. 17 For this slight momentary affliction is preparing for us an eternal weight of glory beyond all comparison, 18 because we look not to the things that are seen but to the things that are unseen; for the things that are seen are transient, but the things that are unseen are eternal.

4:16 But even though our outward self (ὁ ἔξω ἡμῶν ἄνθρωπος) is being destroyed, our inner self (ὁ ἔσω ἡμῶν) is being renewed day by day. 17 For our temporary slight affliction is producing for us an eternal and quite exceptional weight of glory (τὸ γὰρ παραυτίκα ἐλαφρὸν τῆς θλίψεως ἡμῶν καθ' ὑπερβολὴν εἰς ὑπερβολὴν αἰώνιον βάρος δόξης κατεργάζεται ἡμῖν).

The section of 2 Corinthians from which these verses are taken (2:14–7:4) presents the would-be commentator with quite exceptional difficulties, both in translation and in interpretation. In style, tone and content it is totally different from the section that gave us our first passage (chs 10–13), which originally, as we have seen, was probably sent as a separate letter. There he was talking about himself, and apologizing for having to write an apologia. Here he is focusing primarily on the condition in which the Corinthians find themselves, endeavouring to understand how each one of them, 'in Christ', as he says, 'a new creation' (5:17), may be thought to be assimilating the benefits of the gospel. The language he uses is different from that of the preceding passage, taken from Romans 6, and here he is laying much more stress on the transformation that is being effected in the lives of the converts he is addressing. Although he is not attempting in either passage to organize his thought systematically, it is hard to deny that these are the reflections of a theologian, anxious to express as faithfully as possible the *religious* consequences of this 'new creation'.

At the heart of these chapters is Paul's sense of transformation and renewal. Many of the verbs he uses are in the first person plural. Sometimes he is clearly speaking of himself, sometimes of his converts; at other times the reference is uncertain. He is trying to articulate his conviction that the Corinthians (like the Romans whom he is addressing in Romans 6) must in their own way be experiencing the new life that will ensue once their old selves (ὁ ἔξω ἡμῶν ἄνθρωπος) have been successfully eradicated.

Paul himself, having *seen* the Lord (1 Cor 9:1), uses the language of a theophany (the *glory* of the Lord) when speaking of what 'we all', i.e. all Christians, now behold – though he qualifies this vision (in a way that most translations fail to acknowledge) by the use of the verb κατοπτρίζεσθαι, implying the use of a mirror (κάτοπτρον). Since ancient mirrors give an imperfect reflection, qualified by Paul in another context by the term 'riddling' (ἐν αἰνίγματι), we get the impression that Paul here, as often, is holding something back. Yet he does speak quite definitely of *being transformed into that same image*, using the word that Mark applies to Jesus' transfiguration (9:2); and though the change on that occasion was immediate and complete we should not underrate the significance of the fact that whether we employ the language of transfiguration or of transformation when translating this term, there is in both cases an allusion to some kind of mystical experience. The image in 2 Cor 3:16 (ignored by the RSV) is evidently *the image of the glory of God as seen in a mirror*, and since a little later (4:4) Christ is said to be the image (once again, εἰκών) of God then we can say with some confidence that the mould or pattern to which the Corinthians must now conform is, however difficult it may be for us to conceive this, Christ himself : 'for while we live we are always being given up to death for Jesus' sake, so that the life of Jesus may be manifested in our mortal flesh' (4:11).

Speaking of the same transformation in another letter, Paul uses the future tense. But there is no contradiction here, since he nowhere suggests that the transformation will be complete in the course of the Christian's earthly existence: 'we await a saviour, the Lord Jesus, who will change (μετασχηματίσει) our lowly body in conformity with (σύμμορφον) his glorious body (τῷ σώματι τῆς δόξης αὐτοῦ) by the power which enables him to subject the whole world (τὰ πάντα) to himself' (Phil 3:20–21; cf. Rom 8:29).

When thinking of the Christian's transformation, Paul never forgets the *death* of Christ (see the conclusion of Phil 3:7–11). Preaching Christ crucified, and having undergone the same death on the occasion of his own conversion, Paul bears the marks of Christ on his own body (Gal 6:17). The death of Christ, then, can be thought of as instrumental in the transformation of the Christian, and his risen body as the exemplar of what will eventually belong to his followers too: 'Just as we have borne the image of the man of dust [Adam], we shall also bear the image of the man of heaven [Christ]' (1 Cor 15:49).[31]

If the death of Christ is the *instrument* of transformation, and his resurrection what prefigures the Christian's future state, the *agent* is the Spirit. 'Spirit of the Lord' is probably the best translation of the ambiguous κυρίου πνεύματος in 3:18,[32] but 'the Lord who is the Spirit' is also possible: Paul clearly thinks of Christ as a kind of spiritual presence.

Most of this is, strictly speaking, nonsense. It is hard enough to empathize with Paul when he is doing his best to say something intelligible about an experience that he himself admits to be inexpressible (2 Corinthians 12); it is even harder once he starts arguing about it. But this is what the interpreter has to do. That it *can* be done, even by someone who does not share Paul's faith, may be seen from the work of the Jewish scholar Alan Segal, whose discussion of what he calls 'Paul's use of mystical vocabulary' is one of the best things in his book.[33] At one point Paul expresses the hope that no one will think him crazy (ἄφρων: 2 Cor 11:16), but it is evident that he rather expects that some people will. Yet even when he talks nonsense his intelligence and sincerity shine through.

Romans 8:23–30

23 And not only the creation, but we ourselves, who have the first fruits of the Spirit, groan inwardly as we wait for adoption as sons, the redemption of our bodies. 24 For in this hope we were saved. Now hope that is seen is not hope. For who hopes for what he sees? 25 But if we hope for what we do not see, we wait for it with patience.	What is more, we ourselves, who already have the first fruits of the Spirit, sigh inwardly as we await our adoption as sons (υἱοθεσία), the redemption of our bodies. For as far as hope goes we have been saved (τῇ γὰρ ἐλπίδι ἐσώθημεν). But a visible hope is no hope at all. For who hopes for what he can see? But if we hope for what we cannot see, we await it

31. In 1 Cor 15:40–49 Paul discusses the nature of the risen body, which, unlike that of Adam (and the rest of mankind), will be infused with a spirit rather than a soul (ψυχή). Had he argued that Christ's natural body (σῶμα ψυχικόν) had risen 'from among the dead' (ἐκ νεκρῶν) then he could be fairly described as defending a physical resurrection; but he does not: he is quite clear that the risen body is *spiritual* (πνευματικόν). It is also, like the sun, the moon and the stars (v. 41), radiant and enduring.

32. As is argued by Margaret Thrall in her commentary, ad loc. She gives a full and fair discussion of all the alternatives.

33. *Paul the Convert*, 58–71.

26 Likewise the Spirit helps us in our weakness; for we do not know how to pray as we ought, but the Spirit himself intercedes for us with sighs too deep for words. 27 And he who searches the hearts of men knows what is the mind of the Spirit, because the Spirit intercedes for the saints according to the will of God. 28 We know that in everything God works for good with those who love him, who are called according to his purpose. 29 For those whom he foreknew he also predestined to be conformed to the image of his Son, in order that he might be the first-born among many brethren. 30 And those whom he predestined he also called; and those whom he called he also justified; and those whom he justified he also glorified.

patiently. Similarly the Spirit comes to the assistance of our weakness; for we do not know what we should rightly be praying for; but the Spirit himself intercedes on our behalf with sighs beyond all words. And the searcher of hearts knows the mind of the Spirit, because the Spirit, in harmony with God, intercedes for the saints. We know that he ensures that everything works for the good ($\pi\acute{\alpha}\nu\tau\alpha$ $\sigma\upsilon\nu\epsilon\rho\gamma\epsilon\hat{\iota}$ $\epsilon\grave{\iota}\varsigma$ $\grave{\alpha}\gamma\alpha\theta\acute{o}\nu$) of those who love God, who are called according to his purpose ($\tauο\hat{\iota}\varsigma$ $\kappa\alpha\tau\grave{\alpha}$ $\pi\rho\acute{o}\theta\epsilon\sigma\iota\nu$ $\kappa\lambda\eta\tauο\hat{\iota}\varsigma$). For those whom he foreknew he also predestined to be conformed to the image of his Son ($\pi\rho\omicron\acute{\omega}\rho\iota\sigma\epsilon\nu$ $\sigma\upsilon\mu\mu\acute{o}\rho\phi\omicron\upsilon\varsigma$ $\tau\hat{\eta}\varsigma$ $\epsilon\grave{\iota}\kappa\acute{o}\nu\omicron\varsigma$ $\upsilon\grave{\iota}\omicron\hat{\upsilon}$ $\alpha\grave{\upsilon}\tauο\hat{\upsilon}$), in order that he might be the first-born among many brethren. And those whom he predestined he also called; and those whom he called he also justified ($\grave{\epsilon}\delta\iota\kappa\alpha\acute{\iota}\omega\sigma\epsilon\nu$); and those whom he justified he also glorified ($\grave{\epsilon}\delta\acute{o}\xi\alpha\sigma\epsilon\nu$).

This passage is the start of the climactic conclusion to a long argument (chapters 5–8) that began several pages earlier. It would be foolish to pretend that this strongly articulated statement is no more than an instinctive, gut reaction response on Paul's part to reports that have reached him concerning the situation of the Roman church. If anything in his writing is entitled to be called theology it is a carefully composed paragraph such as this, obviously the fruit of long reflection. Yet behind and beneath these finely composed sentences (about to be followed by a passionate expression of Paul's own hope) lies the same *religious experience* from which all his amazing spiritual energy has flowed.

To comment briefly on this passage is not easy. Let us start by observing that *salvation* is disposed of right at the start. This is the only time that Paul uses the verb $\sigma\acute{\omega}\zeta\epsilon\iota\nu$ (to deliver) in the past tense, and he hastens to qualify it by 'in hope'. Future hope overrides a grammatical past. Salvation (or deliverance) is excluded from the string of aorist (past definite) verbs that is about to follow, an exclusion that cannot but be significant. For Paul salvation has not been experienced (except inchoately), still less 'seen', but is confidently awaited in the future.[34]

---

34. I shall be commenting more fully on this important concept in the next chapter.

The Spirit lies at the heart of this passage, and indeed of the whole of Romans 8, but since his role and nature will receive extensive discussion later in this book, I will make no comment here except to point out that the translation reflects my view that it is the Spirit – not God (RSV) nor, as many commentators would have it, 'everything' – which is the driving force that eventually guarantees a blissful destiny for those who are 'called' according to God's purpose.[35]

The last sentence in the paragraph is technically what rhetoricians call a sorites (from the Greek σωρός, heap), a progressive series of five verbs piled one on top of another. There are only two occurrences of each of the first two of these ('foreknow' and 'predestine') in Paul's authentic letters. 'Foreknow' is also used in Rom 11:2 to refer to God's choice of Israel. 'Predestine' (a word with a fateful future!) is used in 1 Cor 2:7 of God's secret plan for the world (in which Israel was to play a key role): 'But we speak of a mysterious and hidden wisdom of God, which God predestined before the ages for our glory' (ἀλλὰ λαλοῦμεν θεοῦ σοφίαν ἐν μυστηρίῳ τὴν ἀποκεκρυμμένην, ἣν προώρισεν ὁ θεὸς πρὸ τῶν αἰώνων εἰς δόξαν ἡμῶν). This divine wisdom is clearly central among those mysteries of which Paul declares himself, in the same context, the servant (ὑπηρέται) and the steward (οἰκόνομοι) (1 Cor 4:1: both nouns in the plural).[36]

So for Paul God's final purpose is neither salvation nor justification (righteousness),[37] but *glory* or *glorification*, a concept we have already seen in 2 Corinthians and which comes at the conclusion of the passage under discussion here. As we know, this glorification has already commenced, but we should note that for Paul it is not just one essential element but rather the last triumphant fulfilment of

---

35. In strict grammar there are three possible subjects for the verb συνεργεῖ: (1) God, who has just been mentioned; (2) the Spirit, the subject of the preceding sentence; (3) all things (πάντα): in classical and Koine Greek verbs with neuter plural subjects are put in the singular.

36. It is worth noting that Eliade numbers the 'revelation of secret doctrines' among what he calls 'the chief elements of the shamanic tradition' (*Shamanism*, 314).

37. I am inclined to agree with Albert Schweitzer that 'the doctrine of righteousness by faith is … a subsidiary crater, which has formed within the rim of the main crater – the mystical doctrine of redemption through the being-in-Christ' (*Mysticism*, 225); though I should formulate the alternative differently: the mystical sense of glorification through transformation in Christ. There will be no further mention of righteousness (or justification) in the present book.

God's overarching design. But where did he get the idea in the first place? *From a personal revelation.*

The theme of glory in this passage of Romans may remind us (as no doubt it did Paul) of his vision of glory on the face of Christ on the Damascus road. In the preceding chapter I expressed my agreement with Seyoon Kim's suggestion that this is the best way of understanding Paul's reference to 'the light of the knowledge of the glory of God in the face of Christ' in 2 Cor 4:6. No *theological* interpretation of this passage has anything remotely approaching the explanatory power of Kim's thesis. Alan Segal, though apparently unacquainted with Kim's work, pursues a similar argument in the densely packed and highly suggestive second chapter of *Paul the Convert*.[38]

Segal builds up his thesis cumulatively, and much of its force derives from the sheer abundance of the texts he relies upon. Here I can only quote the one that seems to me the most important, taken from the so-called *Parables* or *Similitudes of Enoch* (*1 Enoch* 37–71). On Segal's reading the last chapter of this document

> gives us the experience of an adept undergoing the astral trans-formation prophesied in Dan. 12:2, albeit in the name of a pseudepigraphical hero. If this is true, then Paul gives us the actual, confessional experience of the same spiritual event, with Christ substituting for the son of man. In both cases, the believer is subsumed into the body of heavenly savior and becomes a kind of star or celestial immortal.… 'And it happened after this that his living name was raised up before that son of man and to the Lord from among those who dwell upon the earth' (70:1) [the super-scription to chs 70–71]. The journey is taken by Enoch's name, not precisely his soul.… It may be that the transformation motif is particularly important because the notion of the soul had not deeply penetrated this level of Jewish society.…

Whatever the intention of the author of 1 Enoch, the relationship to Paul's experience is important. Like Enoch, Paul claims to have gazed on the Glory, whom Paul identifies as Christ; Paul understands that he has been transformed into a

---

38. 'Paul's Ecstasy': *Paul the Convert*, 34–71. See too J. D. Tabor, *Things Unutterable*, 9–19; S. Kim, *Origin*, 193–257.

divine state, which will be fully realized after his death; Paul claims that his vision and transformation is somehow a mystical identification; and Paul claims to have received a calling, his special status as intermediary. Paul specifies the meaning of this calling for all believers, a concept absent in the Enochic texts, although it may have been assumed within the original community.[39]

In the concluding section of the same chapter, headed 'Paul's Use of Mystical Vocabulary', Segal goes on to discuss a number of passages from Paul's letters.[40] It is perhaps worth adding one final quotation, the last mention of mystery in 1 Corinthians, where Paul speaks of the consummation of the process of transformation: 'I tell you this, brethren: flesh and blood cannot inherit the kingdom of God, nor does the perishable inherit the imperishable. Lo! I tell you a mystery. We shall not all sleep, but we shall all be changed, in a moment, in the twinkling of an eye, at the last trumpet. For the trumpet will sound, and the dead will be raised imperishable, and we shall be changed ($\dot{\alpha}\lambda\lambda\alpha\gamma\eta\sigma\acute{o}\mu\epsilon\theta\alpha$). For this perishable nature must put on the imperishable, and this mortal nature must put on immortality' (1 Cor 15:50–53). This mystery too belongs to the original revelation of glory.

---

39. *Paul the Convert*, 47
40. Including some that I have chosen to omit, especially 2 Cor 5:15–6:1; Phil 2:5–11; 3:20–21; Gal 4:19.

Schweitzer's Mysticism[1]

Since Albert Schweitzer's *The Mysticism of Paul the Apostle* has some claim to be regarded as the best book on Paul published in the twentieth century (it is certainly among the front-runners) one might well ask why it has never received the acclaim it deserves. There are, I think, two reasons. The first is that in taking on the whole of the Protestant establishment by denying outright that the doctrine of righteousness by faith lies at the heart of Paul's theology, Schweitzer was entering a fight that he could not win. In the second place, his use of the term mysticism was calculated to arouse the anger of precisely the same people. By the time his book was published (1930) the history of religions school had long fallen out of favour, largely, as we have seen, because of the powerful opposition of Karl Barth some ten years earlier.

The odd thing is that the title of Schweitzer's book, *Die Mystik des Apostels Paulus*, is a misnomer. For in truth his book is not about mysticism at all: its real subject is Paul's theology. On the first page we meet the distinction between 'primitive' and 'developed' mysticism. 'Primitive' mysticism involves entering into communion with a divine being and sharing his supernatural mode of existence:

---

1. Albert Schweitzer (1875–1965) is known worldwide as a medical missionary who spent most of his career running a hospital in the West African country of Gabon (and in fact he wrote the prefatory note to *Die Mystik des Apostels Paulus* on the Ogowe steamer on the way to Lambaréné). But he was also an accomplished organist, an expert on the works of Bach, and the author of one of the undisputed masterpieces of New Testament scholarship, *The Quest of the Historical Jesus*. In 1952 he was awarded the Nobel Peace Prize. In 1932 he was awarded an honorary Doctorate in Divinity by the University of Oxford. Elsewhere he received honorary doctorates in Music and Letters and he would have been an equally worthy recipient of a similar degree in Medicine.

'In the cults of Attis, Osiris, and Mithras, as well as in the Eleusinian Mysteries in their later more profound form, the believer attains, by means of an initiation, union with the divinity, and thereby comes to share in the immortality for which he yearns.' So far, so good. 'But', says Schweitzer, 'when the conception of the universal is reached and human nature reflects upon its relation to the totality of being and to Being in itself, the resultant mysticism becomes widened, deepened, and purified.' Small wonder that when, on the following page, he comes to name the protagonists of 'developed' or 'intellectual' mysticism, he includes philosophers like Spinoza, Schopenhauer, and Hegel. No doubt he also mentions some genuine mystics – people like Meister Eckhart, Suso and Tauler, who write of their own experiences of trance or ecstasy – but he over-emphasizes the intellectual side of the mystical tradition and makes thinking rather than experience its salient feature.

Turning to Paul, he places his mysticism *between* the 'primitive' and the 'intellectual'. His reason for doing so is that Paul stops short of a 'God-mysticism' and stays, uniquely according to Schweitzer, in a 'Christ-mysticism'. But although he sums this up accurately enough as 'being-in-Christ', he insists that its origins were in thought and reflection. Much later in his book he states that 'Paul never set out the *problems* which demand his mysticism, or the *general conception* on which it is based. He does not even explain how the elements of his teaching on being-in-Christ are connected.'[2] For all that (a page or so further on), 'how totally wrong are those who refuse to admit that Paul was a logical thinker, and proclaim his lack of system as the supreme wisdom! He is a logical thinker and his mysticism is a complete system.'

So it is not surprising that Ed Sanders, who admires Schweitzer, and has gone some way in his own work on Paul towards restoring (or perhaps establishing) his reputation, feels justified in jettisoning the term mysticism altogether: '"Mysticism" has generated so much misunderstanding ... that perhaps it is better to drop it than to hedge it by repeated definitions.'[3]

2. *Mystik*, 138; ET, 138 (my italics). Since the published English translation is unreliable, and at times positively misleading, I use the German original throughout, adding page references to the standard translation for the convenience of those who know no German.
3. *Paul and Palestinian Judaism*, 435, n. 19.

Defending his own starting-point, the eschatological expectation of the early church, Schweitzer dismisses some alternative approaches: 'in attempting to understand Paul some took his anthropology as their starting-point, others his psychology, others his manner of thinking in his pre-Christian period (as though we knew anything about that!), others his personality, others his attitude to the Law, and others the experience on the Damascus road. Grasping the first thread that came to hand they tangled the skein before they had even started, and condemned themselves to having to pass off as Paul's teaching an inexplicable chaos of thought.'[4]

The purpose of this excursus is to watch how Schweitzer tugs his own favoured thread loose from the tangled skein of Paul's theological thinking and exposes what he regards as the ultimate mystery.[5]

'The only practical procedure', he declares, 'is to begin with the one simple thing (*mit dem Einfachen*) that Paul fully and completely shares with the early church, and to see how his teaching grows out of this.'[6] The one simple thing is a shared eschatological expectation, and this, accordingly, is Schweitzer's chosen thread.

Coming first into view is 'the community of the holy' (the communion of saints) – the preordained union of those chosen or 'elected' ('the elect' is one of Schweitzer's favourite expressions) to be united with the Messiah in his kingdom. This concept is present in a large number of Jewish texts, both in and out of the canon.[7]

The next step is the *anticipatory realization* of this concept through the unexpectedly early arrival of the Messiah (Jesus), resulting in what Schweitzer calls a 'Christ-mysticism', something he finds both in the preaching of Jesus and in the writings of Paul. But if both Jesus and Paul preach a 'Christ-mysticism' they do so in different ways. What makes the difference (and this is crucial) is the

4. *Mystik*, 41; ET, 40.
5. *The Mysticism of Paul the Apostle* is a long book (some 400 pages), and it would be impossible to do it full justice in a short excursus. Chapter 6, 'The Mystical Doctrine of the Dying and Rising again with Christ', is undoubtedly the heart of the book, and what follows is mostly an analysis, with some unavoidable gaps, of the argument of this chapter.
6. Ibid.
7. Schweitzer cites or mentions Isa 4:3; Dan 7:27; 12:1; Mal 3:16–17; Ps 59:29; *1 Enoch* 38:1–5; 62:7–8, 14–15; 103:2; 104:1; 108:3; *Ps. Sol.* 15:4–6.

resurrection of Christ. 'In spite of a whole mass of facts that tell against it' (*sämtlichen entgegenstehenden Tatsachen zum Trotz*), Paul asserts that 'the solidarity (*Zusammengehörigkeit*) of the Elect with Christ was already working itself out in the period between his resurrection and the second coming'.[8] Other Christians already believed that this would happen in the future (at the end of time). Paul alone saw it happening in the here and now.

'By understanding and explaining the eschatological concept of the predestined solidarity of the Elect with one another and with the Messiah as something in the real world'[9] Paul succeeds in solving three problems all at once: (1) the preliminary participation in Christ's resurrection of those who die before the Second Coming; (2) the immediate entry into the resurrection state of those still alive when Christ comes again; (3) the fact that Christ's resurrection sets in train the gradual transformation of the 'elect' and ensures, through his victory over death, the eventual resurrection from the dead of all mankind.

'With ruthless reasoning, Paul's eschatological Christ-mysticism hurls itself against the course of events',[10] determined to settle once and for all the first and most immediate problem of Christian belief, which is the temporal gap between the resurrection of Christ and his Second Coming. The resurrection of Christ, his manifestation as Messiah, and the commencement of the messianic kingdom (which comprises both the resurrection and the transformation of the elect) factually coincide (*gehören zeitlich und sachlich zusammen*). This means that the elect, whilst preserving the appearance of ordinary men, are already 'resurrected along with Christ' (*Mitauferstandene Christi*), 'the first-fruits of those that have fallen asleep' (1 Cor 15:20).

---

8. *Mystik*, 110; ET, 109.
9. *Mystik*, 112; ET, 110–11. The published translation renders the word *naturhaft* (translated here as 'something in the real world' and elsewhere simply by 'real') as 'quasi-physical' or (elsewhere in the same chapter) simply 'physical' or (once) 'actual'. But despite his use of the word *physisch* in a similar context in his earlier book I do not believe that Schweitzer thought of 'the mystical body of Christ' in physical terms. He would have been crazy to do so. Volker Rabens expresses a preference for 'ontic' over 'real'; but whatever extra precision this may add would certainly be lost on most English readers.
10. 'In gewalttätigem Denken wirft sich die eschatologische Christus-mystik Pauli dem Laufe der Ereignisse entgegen' (*Mystik*, 112; ET, 111).

'In a tremendous paradox Paul replaces the reality perceived by the senses with one that is true only for those with a clear understanding of the point in time the world has now reached (*das Denken, das sich über die Stunde der Weltzeit im klaren ist*).'[11] This observation is followed by a wonderful image in which the Risen Christ is seen as the first visible peak of a larger island that is gradually emerging, by a series of volcanic upheavals, from the ocean of transience and perishability, until with the resurrection of the dead at the end of time 'the whole land-mass of what is imperishable' (*das ganze Festland der Unvergänglichkeit*) will have become visible. 'At that point the end has arrived when all things are eternally in God and God is all in all.'[12]

The resurrection of the dead at the end of time, then, is the culmination of a long process that, for Paul, began with the resurrection of Christ and continued with the gradual transformation of Christian believers (the elect) into their new supernatural condition. And 'since this mysticism is simply one possible way of expressing the general idea of redemption, Paul is entitled to regard it as something that should be immediately obvious to early Christian belief'.[13]

Schweitzer thinks that Paul and Jesus shared the same eschatological beliefs, the only difference being that since Jesus' death and resurrection time has moved on, and it is now already possible for the elect to enter into the resurrection mode of existence.

At this crucial point of his argument Schweitzer contests the widespread conviction that the doctrine of the mystical body arose simply out of faith in Christ. First belief in Christ, so runs the common view, leading to belief in 'being-in-Christ', and thence to belief in the mystical body. Quite the reverse, says Schweitzer: it is the concept of the mystical body that is responsible for the Christian conviction of 'being-in-Christ', and *that* concept arises directly out of eschatological beliefs. Christians are united with Christ. This union is conceived as a *bodily* union, and the elect as participating in the same bodily reality (*Leiblichkeit*) as Christ himself, that is to say as belonging to *the body of Christ* – the mystical body.

11. *Mystik*, 113; ET, 112.
12. *Mystik*, 113; ET, 112.
13. *Mystik*, 114; ET, 113.

Now since as far as Christ is concerned the process of transformation is already complete and since the elect are conceived as really belonging to his 'body', they too are now conceived to be participating in that transformation. Once begun, this process is thought of as a continuous one: 'Thus out of the original conception arises the derivative and simplified conception that the elect are assumed into the body of Christ. Taken in isolation, this is unintelligible. It only makes sense when considered in the light of the original starting-point.'[14] Paul's mysticism, says Schweitzer on the following page, 'marks the last stage of the battle fought by the idea of resurrection to establish its place in eschatology'.

Accordingly the phrase 'being-in-Christ' is simply a shorthand way of affirming belief in the mystical body, but because, taken in isolation, it *may* refer to an individual rather than a corporate participation there is a risk of its being misunderstood. Nevertheless, 'the original conception, that is to say the participation of Christ and the elect alike in the same bodily reality, is constantly breaking through'.[15] The mystical body of Christ, Schweitzer concludes, 'is not an image (*Bild*), nor a concept arrived at by means of symbolic and ethical reflections, but a real entity (*eine naturhafte Größe*)'.[16] 'That in Paul's mysticism it is a matter of a real union (*eine ganz naturhafte Gemeinschaft*) between Christ and the elect rests on the fact that the term "being-in-Christ" corresponds to and replaces the natural term "being in the flesh".'[17]

For Schweitzer, then, eschatology is the key that enables us to see Paul as 'a thinker of elemental power, the only man of his time to recognize the special character of the period between Jesus' resurrection and his second coming, and the first to look for a solution to the problem of the delay of his return'.

---

14. *Mystik*, 119; ET, 118.
15. *Mystik*, 126; ET, 125.
16. *Mystik*, 127; ET, 127.
17. *Mystik*, 128; ET, 127. Even though Schweitzer certainly denies that we are dealing with a (mere) image, the published English translation, which speaks at this point of 'an actual physical union', distorts Schweitzer's much less emphatic way of putting the matter. (See n. 3.) The sort of confusion to which the concept of the mystical body can give rise is well illustrated by John Robinson's warning that 'one must be chary of speaking of the "metaphor" of the Body of Christ' because Christians 'are in literal fact the risen organism of Christ's person in all its concrete reality': *The Body*, 51. In literal fact? Concrete reality?

'Just as a spider's web is an admirably simple structure', he concludes, 'as long as it remains stretched between the threads that hold it in position, but becomes a hopeless tangle once it is loosed from them, so Paul's mysticism is admirably simple just as long as it remains stretched in the sustaining frame of eschatology, but once cut loose from this it too becomes a hopeless tangle.'[18]

I have four comments to make.

1. First, in the emphasis he places throughout his book on Paul's reasoning processes, in his determination to follow these step by step, starting with the first link in the logical chain, and above all in his insistence that Paul is a master of systematic thought, Schweitzer gives the picture of a rational thinker who is anything but a genuine mystic, groping for ways of expressing the ineffable.

2. Secondly, there are numerous points at which, on Schweitzer's own showing, Paul's reasoning is faulty. There is no logical progression from the belief that Christ is risen to the assertion that Christian believers too participate in the resurrection mode of existence. (Schweitzer admits that no one else in the early church held this view.) Here is where Schweitzer speaks of Paul's thought-processes as ruthless (or even brutal: *gewalttätig*), flying in the face of 'the course of events'. Was it really reasoned logic, however powerful, that led him to this conclusion? Schweitzer is the first to acknowledge that a massive array of facts tells against it. There is something slightly perverse, it seems to me, in speaking of the tremendously paradoxical nature of Paul's reasoning on one page and extolling him as a systematic thinker on the next.

3. In the third place, the conclusions to which, according to Schweitzer, Paul is driven by the sheer force of his own logic are far from being clear or precise theological statements. 'Mystical Body', 'being-in-Christ', 'dying and rising': these are all, surely, characteristically fumbling attempts of the genuine mystic to give expression to the ineffable. 'Mystical Body', the theologoumenon of a later age, is not of course a Pauline coinage, and it is arguably better applied to the author of Ephesians than to the authentic Paul, who uses the term 'body of Christ' of *local* churches, as in 1 Cor 12:27 and Rom 12:5 ('the one body in Christ'); see too Gal 2:28 ('all one in Christ Jesus'). Schweitzer, however, accepts the term, and it may be that

18. *Mystik*, 140; ET, 140.

the more general conception of Ephesians is integral to his own vision. However that may be, I would contend that one of the threads of the tangled skein that Schweitzer picked up and then discarded, the vision on the Damascus road, offers an easier and more plausible explanation of these mysterious expressions than the eschatological thread he himself chose to follow.

4. Lastly, there is a much simpler and better explanation ready to hand for those who share Schweitzer's estimate of what constitutes the core of Paul's theological thinking. Ed Sanders, after a long discussion of Paul's theology which shows him, despite various nuances and demurrers, to be in basic agreement with Schweitzer, concludes that 'the participationist language bring [*sic*] us closer than the juristic to the heart of Paul's thought and reveals the depth of it'.[19] But while this term accurately sums up his (and Schweitzer's) views, it does nothing to clarify the root meaning of Paul's own words. To be fair, Sanders is well aware of this. Here is his (slightly fuller) response to Rudolf Bultmann's existentializing interpretation of Paul: 'It seems to me best to understand Paul as saying what he meant and meaning what he said: Christians really are one body and Spirit with Christ, the form of the present world really is passing away, Christians really are being changed from one stage of glory to another, the end really will come and those who are in Christ will really be transformed.'

And here is his comment: 'But what does this mean? How are we to understand it? We seem to lack a concept of 'reality' – real participation in Christ, real possession of the Spirit – which lies between naïve cosmological speculation and belief in magical transference on the one hand and a revised self-understanding on the other. I must confess that I do not have a new category of perception to propose here.'[20]

Whilst I do not wish to lay claim to 'a new category of perception' I suggest that many of the problems that arise out of Schweitzer's discussion and have been well spotted by Sanders cease to be problematic as soon as we see Paul's understanding of the characteristically Christian mode of existence as 'being-in-Christ' to be a matter of visionary insight rather than of logical thought. If

19. *Paul and Palestinian Judaism*, 520.
20. Ibid., 522–3.

Schweitzer had portrayed Paul as a real mystic instead of simply applying the language of mysticism to what, on the evidence of his own language, he actually conceived to be rational thinking, then he would have had no trouble in meeting the most serious criticisms that can be made of his fascinating book.

5

Paul the Apostle

Ay, but to die, and go we know not where;
To lie in cold obstruction, and to rot;
This sensible warm motion to become
A kneaded clod; and the delighted spirit
To bathe in fiery floods, or to reside
In thrilling region of thick-ribbed ice;
To be imprison'd in the viewless winds
And blown with restless violence round about
The pendant world; or to be worse than worst
Of those that lawless and incertain thought
Imagine howling – 'tis too horrible!
The weariest and most loathed worldly life
That age, ache, penury, and imprisonment
Can lay on nature is a paradise
To what we fear of death.

Measure for Measure, Act 3, Scene 1

Claudio's Christian upbringing – for we must assume he had one –
was not strong enough to overcome his terror at the prospect of
imminent death, very different from Paul, who (in prison, like
Claudio) longed 'to depart and be with Christ' (Phil 1:23). How
likely is it that Paul's own faith in personal survival was one of his
selling-points as he began to preach his new gospel in Greece and
Asia? This is one of the questions that must be included in the much
larger question that is the subject of this chapter: how to account for
Paul's phenomenal success as a Christian missionary.

Of all the titles I have given Paul in this book 'apostle' is probably the only one that would meet with his wholehearted approval.

Apostle, a man with a mission, is how he saw himself and what he called himself. Of course he was not alone. But on the evidence of the Book of Acts it was he who spearheaded the missionary drive in the Eastern Mediterranean, and on the evidence of his own letters he had already reached the Balkans (Illyricum: Rom 15:19) and had plans to push as far west as Spain (Rom 15:24, 28).[1] So how did he manage to win so many converts, and how did this strange new gospel come to stick? For stick it certainly did. By the year AD 112, as we know from a famous letter of the younger Pliny, Christians were to be found in the coastal region of Pontus (by the Black Sea) among people of 'every rank, age and sex'.[2] Paul himself did not get as far as Pontus (though three churches in the Lycus valley, Colossae, Laodicea and Hierapolis, had certainly fallen within his orbit of influence)[3] and he had been personally active in only one of the seven churches addressed in the Book of Revelation, namely Ephesus. Three of the others had had time, by the last decade of the century,[4] to grow slack, one of them, Laodicea, neither hot nor cold but nauseatingly tepid (Rev 3:16). In Asia Minor and Greece, then, Christianity was well established by the end of the first century, and in Rome too. Not long afterwards there were flourishing communities in Africa and Gaul.

The question of perseverance is outside the scope of this book. Here we are concerned with the problem of Paul's initial success.[5] I suspect that even nowadays the majority of Christians would accept unhesitatingly Origen's verdict, that 'God was preparing the nations for his teaching by submitting them all to a single Roman Emperor (*Contra Celsum* 2.30). Origen's pupil Eusebius plumps this explanation out a little, but still leaves it very thin.[6] The new religion would

---

1. Clement of Rome, writing towards the end of the century, claims that Paul did not die before he had 'instructed the whole world in righteousness' and 'reached the farthest bounds of the West' (ἐπὶ τὸ τέρμα τῆς δύσεως): *1 Clem* 5.
2. *Ep.* 10.96.9.
3. See W. A. Meeks, *First Urban Christians*, 41–2.
4. The persecution alluded to in Revelation is probably (though this is disputed) the one that raged towards the end of the reign of Domitian (AD 81–96).
5. Harnack (*Mission*, vol. i, p. 84) says that he writes 'with the object of explaining the amazing success of Christianity'. But he fails to distinguish between the beginnings (Paul) and the continuance (Paul and others).
6. 'It was not by mere human accident that the greater part of the nations of the world were never before under the one nation of Rome, but only from the time of Jesus. And no one could deny that the synchronizing of this with the

certainly have not made nearly as much headway as it did without the ease of movement afforded by the *pax Romana,* not to mention the remarkable travelling facilities in the Eastern Mediterranean in the first century, plus, of course, the widespread knowledge of Greek, a legacy not of Augustus but of Alexander. But if we are looking for the factors that permitted and enabled the spread of the new religion, the most interesting (and the one that concerns us here) is the human factor: the social and religious circumstances prevailing in Anatolia and Greece at the time Paul was conducting his mission.

Much work has been done recently on the closely related question of the *expansion* of Christianity, from the second century onwards.[7] E. R. Dodds concludes a much-praised earlier study, *Pagans and Christians in an Age of Anxiety*, by mentioning 'some of the psychological conditions which favoured the growth of Christianity and contributed to its victory'.[8] But these for the most part have to do with the attractiveness to outsiders of established churches or communities, factors like the affection displayed by the members of these communities towards one another – what Paul, in what most take to be the earliest of his letters, 1 Thessalonians, calls brotherly love, φιλαδελφία (1 Thess 4:9). The only one of Dodds's psychological conditions that was present from the outset in Paul's own preaching was the conditional promise he held out to the disinherited of 'a better inheritance in another world'.[9] It is to this we now turn.

Arnoldo Momigliano, after criticizing certain alternative explanations (of Scheid, Wardman, Leibschuetz and MacMullen), prefers

---

beginning of the teaching about our Saviour is of God's arrangement, if he considered the difficulty of the disciples' taking their journey, had the nations been at variance with one another, and not uniting together because of varieties of government' (*Demonstratio Evangelica* 3.7.140). And further on, referring to the *pax Romana* and the prophecy that nation should not take sword against nation: 'As this state of things was never achieved at any other time but during the Roman Empire, from our Saviour's birth until now, I consider the proof irrefutable that the prophet refers to the time of our Saviour's coming among men' (8.3.47).

7. The title of Ramsay MacMullen's book, *Christianizing the Roman Empire,* AD *100–400*, spells it out; see also R. Lane Fox, *Pagans and Christians*; Stephen Mitchell, *Anatolia*.

8. E. R. Dodds, *Pagans and Christians*, 133.

9. Ibid., 135.

'the old-fashioned notion that the message of St. Paul was not founded on social premises but on universal [!] expectations of immortality, salvation, and resurrection'.[10] If we leave aside immortality, which was never part of Paul's message, we are left with the double promise of salvation and resurrection. It is far from obvious, to say the least, why first-century pagans would give such promises an enthusiastic welcome. Modern pagans, after all, hear promises of salvation quite frequently at street-corners, but I for one have not observed many stopping to listen. And we are told by Luke that the only time Paul tried resurrection out on a pagan audience he was greeted with derision (Acts 17:32). Yet he did succeed, somehow, in impressing audiences in many towns in both Anatolia and Greece. The problem remains: how?

If we are to make any progress in our enquiry we must start by asking what it was about the society of the time that might have allowed entrance and purchase to what looks on the face of it to be one of those extravagant promises that are far easier to utter than to fulfil. If we think of Christian evangelists in general as climbing a steep mountain with the aid of ropes and pitons carefully and advantageously placed during many previous ascents, then how are we to picture Paul, Paul the mountaineer, tackling a climb that no one had attempted before him? Without the assistance of footholds and handholds, he must surely have remained stuck at the foot of the cliff – as he did, seemingly, at Athens, and maybe in other places too.

We have to ask, then, where he found a grip. What appeal can his message have had to pagans in Anatolia and Greece? The question can be asked in relation first to resurrection and then to salvation.

Resurrection

'The two most persistent themes of village epigraphy in Asia Minor', comments Stephen Mitchell, 'are burial and religion.' 'The most numerous inscriptions found at any village site in Anatolia', he continues, 'are the tombstones; next come votive dedications to the

10. *On Pagans, Jews, and Christians*, 164; cf. Ramsay MacMullen, 'Two types of conversion', esp. p. 182.

gods; other types of document are altogether rare.' And he remarks too that 'a villager who looked around him for visible symbols of permanence in his family and community would turn to the cemetery and the family tombs'.[11]

All the evidence suggests, then, that here and elsewhere people encountered frequent reminders of their ancestral dead. Many of the inscriptions are curses invoked upon violators, as in Shakespeare's tomb: 'cursed be he that moves my bones' – that sort of thing. Constant concern for one's own dead, in any age or society, must prompt at least an occasional wry reflection on the certainty of death and the likelihood of extinction. So it is not inconceivable that the promise of resurrection might come as a welcome relief from the prospect of lying forever in a cold tomb, however sumptuously adorned. The people who are said to have scoffed at Paul for speaking of resurrection were, after all, sophisticated Athenians. Yet we know that the most urgent anxiety of one of Paul's first churches was the fear that deceased members of the community might be deprived of a share in the glory of the Second Coming. The Thessalonians, perhaps unsurprisingly, had not fully grasped what Paul had taught them about this bizarre new doctrine. The return of Christ in glory, the parousia, yes; the resurrection of their family dead, no. So Paul was forced to spell it out for them: 'the dead in Christ will rise first; then we who are alive, who are left, shall be caught up together with them in the clouds to meet the Lord in the air; and so we shall always be with the Lord' (1 Thess 4:16–17).

The Corinthians too, as we know, had problems – at any rate some of them did. Paul professed himself unable to understand: 'how can some of you say that there is no resurrection of the dead?' (1 Cor 15:12). What we do not know is how the doubters reacted to his reply: 'if there is no resurrection of the dead, then Christ has not been raised; if Christ has not been raised, then our preaching is vain and your faith is vain' (1 Cor 15:13–14). Even if some doubters remained unconvinced by what looks on the face of it a decidedly shaky argument, this strange new doctrine was certainly accepted by future generations. Despite its extraordinary improbability it established itself as a fundamental part of the church's teaching and came to figure in all its creeds.

11. *Anatolia*, i, 189.

A distinction should be drawn, however, between these future generations, instructed from childhood to accept the literal truth of this fantastic promise, and people hearing it for the first time. John Donne may envisage a grave-digger opening his grave and spying 'a bracelet of bright hair about the bone' without drawing the obvious conclusion; but surely most uninstructed people must share the fears of Shakespeare's Claudio.[12] Attractive as the prospect of a future resurrection might have seemed – to some – it is hard to believe that it was one of Paul's original selling-points. Experience is overwhelmingly against it; and the Homeric and earlier Jewish alternatives, Hades and Sheol, homes of witless ghosts, were a sight easier to believe. If the teaching of the Pharisees concerning the resurrection had penetrated as far as Asia Minor and Greece, and had been passed on to their pagan friends (the people Luke calls god-fearers), then conceivably he might have found there a more sympathetic hearing than he got in Athens. But as far as I know there is no evidence for this.

Even more uncertain is the extent to which there was any expectation of life after death in the regions through which Paul passed. Socrates, in Plato's *Phaedo*, argues strongly and, given his predicament, piquantly, for the immortality of the soul; and Jacques Dupont has pointed out that θαρρεῖν, the Greek word he uses to express his courageous confidence, is precisely the same as the one chosen by Paul in a comparable context (2 Corinthians 5:6).[13] But one suspects that few of Plato's readers, who must in any case have been confined to the intelligentsia, gave his arguments more than a notional assent.

Possibly more telling is the evidence from a child's tomb in Philippi, Paul's first stop in mainland Greece. A charming epigraph in Latin verse pictures the boy living happily in the Elysian fields,

---

12. In 'The Situation of Death', 290, n. 4, Godfrey Lienhardt records a brief conversation he had with 'a witty, elderly Anuak' in the early 1950s (Anuakuland lies on the southern borders of the Sudan and Ethiopia):
    Didimo: What do you think happens after you have died?
    (I gave a brief account of Christian belief.)
    Didimo: All lies! Nobody knows where the dead are, they have not seen them.
    I: But you believe England exists and you have not seen it.
    Didimo: No, but I have seen people who come from there, and I have never seen even my dead mother again.
13. *ΣΥΝ ΧΡΙΣΤΩΙ*, 158–60.

and adds that this was his reward for deserving well by the supreme deity.[14] Winfried Elliger, in a book about Paul's journeys in Greece, is persuaded that a genuine hope is being expressed here. The widespread cult of certain Thracian deities at this time in Macedonia (both the so-called Thracian rider and the goddess Bendis, possibly a Thracian counterpart of the goddess Cybele) points, he thinks, in the same direction. In her left hand Bendis is portrayed as carrying a branch known to signify either immortality or else protection against the powers of death. 'Whichever of these aspects is selected for individual representations [of the goddess],' he concludes, 'the common denominator is a belief in life after death that was strongly rooted throughout Thrace.'[15] But to be protected *whilst alive* against the powers of death is not the same as, and is no guarantee of, life *after death*. Elliger's argument looks rather threadbare at this point.

On the whole, then, it seems wisest to side with Ramsay MacMullen here. After acknowledging that among the felt wants of these ancient pagans, 'the modern observer expects to find none sharper than the need for life, promised for ever', he goes on to remark that 'assurances of immortality prove unexpectedly hard to find in the evidence. Even the longing for it is not much attested.'[16]

Salvation

If the sheer abundance of Anatolian tombstones does not permit us to draw any conclusions concerning the likely impact of Paul's message of resurrection, what may be said of the other main epigraphic source, the votive offerings to the gods? Do not these at least suggest that his message of salvation, chiming in with the local sense of the salvific powers of their own gods, could have found a ready hearing?

'Salvation', like 'grace', is a word that has had all the blood drained out of it by theology. The religious concept of salvation is –

14. … et reparatus item vivis in Elysiis.
       Sic placitum est divis aeterna vivere forma
       qui bene de supero numine sit meritus.
15. *Paulus in Griechenland*, 65.
16. *Paganism*, 53. Wayne Meeks, however, disagrees: *First Urban Christians*, 181–2 and n. 44.

can only be – a metaphor. There is some advantage then, if we want to appreciate its force, in using another word instead. What I suggest is 'deliverance'.

In the Hebrew Bible, notably in the Psalms, deliverance is sought and expected of God. Psalm 107 is a good example. The psalmist paints four frightening scenarios, recalling how one group after another of terrified people 'cried to the Lord in their trouble and he delivered them from their distress': some were lost in the desert, 'and found no city to dwell in'; others 'sat in darkness and in gloom, prisoners in affliction and in irons'; still others, who were sick and had drawn near to the gates of death, were similarly delivered from destruction. Most striking of all is the escape of a crew of sailors: the writer clearly admires the courage of those who, in the words of the Authorized Version, 'go down to the sea in ships, that do business in great waters'. A storm blows up, and they find themselves tossed around on the deck: 'they reel and stagger like a drunken man, and are at their wits' end'; but they too cried to the Lord in their trouble and he delivered them from their distress: 'he maketh the storm a calm, and the waves thereof are still'.

None of the inscriptions recording prayers to the saviour gods of Anatolia and Greece is as brilliantly evocative as this wonderful psalm. But they are varied and widespread enough to show that Paul's promises of deliverance will have struck a chord with most of his hearers. Most of them will have witnessed death and disease; some may have experienced imprisonment or the terror prompted by those violent storms that blow up so suddenly in the Eastern Mediterranean. Paul tells the Corinthians of three shipwrecks in which he himself had been involved (2 Cor 11:15), and there was one more to come, off the coast of Malta, as he was sailing under guard to Rome (Acts 27). Sir William Ramsay, in his book on the historical reliability of the New Testament, goes so far as to say that 'the world wished and was praying for something like the "Salvation" that Paul announced to all'.[17] And he adduces some fascinating epigraphical evidence in support of this contention.[18]

Of the various distressing situations depicted in the psalm we have just been considering, the most relevant to our general theme

17. *Recent Discovery*, 174.
18. Ibid., 183–90.

is that of disease and imminent death. It should not be forgotten that Paul's word for 'deliver' or 'save' (σώζειν) is the same as that commonly employed of healing miracles in the gospels;[19] whilst in Acts the cripple whom Paul healed at Lystra 'had faith to be made well'. Though correct, the translation obscures the nature of the cripple's confidence in Paul's powers: it was a confidence of being saved or delivered (σωθῆναι). Thus he was responding to Paul exactly as many sick people responded to Jesus in the gospels.

An identical power was regularly ascribed to the pagan gods, and numerous votive inscriptions testify to people's belief that their god (Zeus, Apollo, Men, etc.) could, if he so chose, ward off disease from them, their families and their crops. These are examples of the second great fund of epigraphical evidence of which Mitchell speaks in his book on Anatolia, proof enough, one might suppose, that these people would not be entirely deaf to Paul's own message of deliverance.[20]

Here, though, we must tread carefully. When Paul used the word I have translated as 'deliver' (σώζειν), it was always, if we can rely upon the evidence of his own letters, in its metaphorical or religious sense. Moreover, when we enquire what precisely he promises deliverance from, we might be surprised to find that it is from the wrath of God.[21] (In Paul's writings the words 'deliver' and 'deliverance' are properly eschatological terms: they allude to the last judgement.) There is another side to deliverance, the obverse of what, until we have turned it over, is an exceptionally attractive coin. Ranged opposite those whom Paul categorizes as οἱ σωζόμενοι, those on the way to salvation, are οἱ ἀπολλύμενοι, those on the way to perdition (1 Cor 1:18; 2 Cor 2:16; 4:3). The promise of

19. Mark 5:23, 28, 34; 6:56; 10:52, etc.
20. Alan Segal also suggests a link (in my opinion rather far-fetched) with the perceived advantages of international trade: this resembles the awareness of salvation in the sense that 'they both involved perceptions of human significance beyond the local level' (*Paul the Convert*, 109). See too (ibid.) a comparison with Apuleius's *Golden Ass*.
21. 1 Thess 1:10; 2:16; 5:9; Rom 5:9. Cf. Rom 1:18; 2:5, 8; 3:5; 4:15; 9:22; 12:19; 13:4–5. We should question the assumption, widespread among Pauline scholars, that 'salvation' or 'God's saving work in Christ' is an adequate summary of Paul's gospel. In a vague and somewhat portentous allusion to an escape from physical death somewhere in Asia (2 Cor 1:8–10) Paul uses a different verb, ῥύεσθαι ('deliver').

deliverance is accompanied by a threat of destruction. Although there is little evidence that Paul took much over from the preaching of Jesus, we should recall that this included threats of eternal punishment – the undying worm and the unquenchable fire (Mark 9:48). 'The flames of hell', remarks MacMullen, 'illuminated Christianity quite as much as the light of grace.'[22] MacMullen is at pains to point out how different the Jewish and Christian God is from the pagan gods, to whom 'prayers went up seeking benefits only not to avert their wrath. We do not find in the non-Christian world much evidence even of punishment by the gods for wicked behaviour.'[23] If he were right, and the pagan world was for the most part comfortable with its gods, then it is hard to see the appeal of Paul's vengeful deity – unless perhaps the response was less to the promise than to the threat. But there are two reasons for hesitation here. In the first place, the tone of Paul's message is predominantly positive and consolatory rather than threatening.[24] In the second place, MacMullen's habitual impartiality deserts him at this point. Much of the evidence adduced in *Paganism in the Roman Empire*, where the point he makes is basically the same, comes from intellectuals like Plutarch and Lucian, who are pleading a cause. There *were* vengeful deities around: Nemesis, Hecate and 'the all-seeing sun' (πανόπτης ἥλιος); and Stephen Mitchell is surely right to argue that as many votive offerings were made to placate the gods as to thank them: 'If there was an overriding motive that caused men to pray, it was not gratitude for services rendered, but awe and fear of what the gods might do if their cult was overlooked.'[25]

This means that there were real similarities between the pagan gods and the Jewish God worshipped by Paul. Even his evocation of another figure, half human, half divine – the son of God – may have struck a chord and found a hearing. Concluding his rapid survey of the religions of Asia Minor in the late Roman Empire, Mitchell observes a marked similarity between the deities of all three, pagan,

22. 'Two Types of Conversion', 181.
23. Ibid., 176.
24. Moreover if E. P. Sanders is right in his contention that for Paul 'the solution preceded the plight' (*Paul and Palestinian Judaism*, 442–3), then the calamitous scenario he sketches in the first chapter of Romans shows him in his reflective, theological mood, and will not have been included in his original preaching.
25. *Anatolia*, ii, 12.

Jewish and Christian: 'God was an awesome, remote, and abstract figure to be reached through the agency of divine intermediaries, such as angels, or human ones, such as prophets.'[26]

These then are the features of Paul's original message which, in the judgement of many, were most likely to catch the attention of the pagans of Greece and Asia Minor whom he was addressing. They correspond, however indirectly, to the evidence of the multifarious votive and funerary inscriptions which, more clearly than any literary source, give us some inkling of how religion worked. But are they enough? Do the similarities we have found give us what we are looking for, a roughness of surface that would afford Paul enough grip upon his hearers' minds and hearts to make them stop and listen to a gospel which, in spite of certain superficial resemblances, was, deep down, strange and disturbing? I do not believe that they do: the features of Paul's message singled out by Momigliano, immortality, salvation and resurrection, cannot, even in combination, account for his success.

The Book of Acts

One reason for my reluctance, up to this point, to make no more than a few cursory references to the Acts of the Apostles is that its author, Luke, has no interest in the question that so intrigues us. The book is dominated throughout by Luke's sense of the providence of God, and in particular by his conviction that the action of the story he is telling was driven by God's determination to see that the good news about Jesus rejected by the Jews was passed on to the Gentiles (see Acts 13:46). For those with eyes to see it, the outlines of this plan could be descried in scripture, which is why Paul spent so much time demonstrating that Jesus was the long-promised and long-awaited Messiah.[27] Luke's evident interest in portraying a Paul eager to use the scriptures for proving the truth of the gospel is part and parcel of his overall theological project. The truth is, however,

26. *Anatolia*, ii, 48.
27. In this he had a forerunner in Jesus himself, who, 'beginning with Moses and all the prophets ... interpreted to them [the disciples on the road to Emmaus] in all the scriptures the things concerning himself' (Luke 24:27). Cf. Acts 9:20, 22; 17:3; 18:5, 28.

that people are not turned into converts by theological arguments, certainly not by arguments hurled precipitately at them by a stranger from abroad. If we are to learn anything from Acts we must pierce beneath Luke's theological agenda.

Paul

First, however, we must turn at last to our key witness, Paul himself. In a crucially important passage (crucially both literally and metaphorically) at the beginning of his First Letter to the Corinthians, he says this: 'When I came to you, brethren, I did not come proclaiming to you the testimony of God in lofty words or wisdom … and my speech and my message were not in plausible words of wisdom, but in demonstration of the spirit and power (ἐν ἀποδείξει πνεύματος καὶ δυνάμεως), that your faith might not rest in the wisdom of men but in the power of God' (1 Cor 2:1–5). There may be a touch of special pleading here, a hint that Paul was perfectly capable of employing alternative methods to get his message across. But there can be no doubt about the key phrase here: 'in demonstration of the spirit and power' or, reading it in the way I prefer, as a hendiadys, 'with a display of spiritual power'.

It should not surprise us that some such demonstration was required to lend conviction to Paul's preaching. He has just acknowledged that the burden of his message, the crucified Christ, was 'to Jews a stumbling-block, to Gentiles folly' (1:23). Maddeningly reticent about the nature of the spiritual power he has just manifested, he has for the most part persuaded his commentators to respect his reticence. But the historian is free both to investigate and to speculate.

The word δύναμις, like the English word generally used to translate it, 'power',[28] has many meanings. In the New Testament it is often associated with 'spirit' (πνεῦμα), especially by Luke and Paul. Luke speaks of Jesus as returning to Galilee 'in the power of the spirit' (Luke 4:14; cf. Acts 10:38), the very phrase Paul turns into a

28. This is true of the singular form. In the plural, although 'powers' is often enough the right translation, it is used more commonly in the gospels in the sense of miracles.

hendiadys in order to describe his own activity at Corinth. And on his return he began his career as a wonder-worker, performing what the gospels frequently refer to as δυνάμεις, which we can only translate as 'miracles'.[29] These are the means chosen by God to endorse his authority (Acts 2:22). If, provisionally, we stick with Luke, we see that he uses the same word, in the singular, when speaking of Jesus' healing powers (5:17; 6:19), as well as of his power over demons (4:36; 9:1). If we are ever to understand the activity of Jesus and his disciples, including Paul, who is portrayed in Acts as healing the sick and expelling demons just as Jesus did himself, it is essential for us to keep in mind this close association between the power itself and its manifestation in the form of visible miracles, exorcisms and cures. When he comes to catalogue the spiritual gifts or charismata in 1 Corinthians 12:28, Paul distinguishes the gift of miracles (δυνάμεις) from that of healing (ἰάματα), so there must have been some marvellous acts that were not simply works of healing. Luke actually tells us in a general way, summarizing the work Paul did at Ephesus, that 'God continued to perform extraordinary miracles with Paul as his instrument': Δυνάμεις τε οὐ τὰς τυχούσας ὁ θεὸς ἐποίει διὰ τῶν χειρῶν Παύλου (Acts 19:11).[30]

This passage continues: 'so that handkerchiefs or aprons were carried away from his body to the sick, and diseases left them and the evil spirits came out of them' (Acts 19:12). These, evidently, are miracles at a distance; and in any case ascribed by Luke to Paul's ministry at Ephesus, not to that at Corinth. In fact he says little about Paul's work at Corinth, confining himself to the simple observation that Paul 'argued in the synagogue every sabbath, and continued to persuade (ἔπειθεν) Jews and Greeks' (Acts 18:4).

What we have here, it should be noted, is something not far short of a formal contradiction of what Paul says himself. Paul had said that he did *not* use 'persuasive words of wisdom'[31] to get his message across to the Corinthians (1 Cor 2:4). Luke implies that he did. On

---

29. Matt 7:22; 11:20, 21, 23; 13:58; Mark 6:2, 5; Luke 10:13; cf. Acts 2:22; 8:13.
30. The RSV simply says 'God *did* extraordinary miracles by the hands of Paul'; but the imperfect often has the continuative force that I have given the word ἐποίει in my own translation.
31. The MS tradition is very confused here; but the word πειθός, which I have translated as 'persuasive', is cognate with the word Luke uses of Paul in Acts 18:4.

this point we have to side with Paul; but I believe that it is possible to take a step further by transferring what Luke tells us elsewhere about Paul's activities as a healer and exorcist to his preaching. If I am right, then the 'display of spiritual power (δύναμις)' must have been the performance of miracles (δυνάμεις). Luke tells in his gospel that Jesus conferred upon his disciples the same authority over the spiritual world that he enjoyed himself (Luke 10:19), and it is clear from Acts that Paul too had the same powers. In fact, as we saw in the last chapter, Paul announces to the Corinthians – in a passage where he is rather diffidently comparing himself to those whom he sardonically calls 'super-apostles' (ὑπερλίαν ἀπόστολοι) – that 'the signs of a true apostle were performed among you in all patience, with signs and wonders and mighty works' (2 Cor 12:12).[32]

Here, then, is the attention-grabber we have been looking for, the feature of Paul's preaching that will have made people stop and look, and convinced many to listen also. Even in the sceptical society of the late twentieth-century men and women who would no more than glance at, say, the devotees of Hare Krishna, with their castanets and their saffron robes, and who would shut their ears to the paradoxically gloomy-sounding message of salvation still peddled by innumerable street preachers – even today's passers-by, more sophisticated but often enough no less ignorant than their first-century predecessors, will stop and watch those modern miracle-workers, the sword-swallowers and the fire-eaters. The difference is, of course, that these particular marvels have no follow-up; whereas hard on the heels of Paul's 'display of spiritual power' came his startlingly discomforting good news.

Drawing on evidence relating primarily to the second and third centuries, but no doubt equally relevant to the first, Ramsay MacMullen paints a vivid picture of the religious fairs large and small which, he argues, were the chief means of introducing people to the religious lore of paganism:

---

32. Cf. E. Käsemann, 'Die Legitimität des Apostels', esp. pp. 61–3. Käsemann's real interest in this article lies elsewhere. But he admits that Paul included an appeal to his wonder-working powers when presenting his own credentials. The theme of signs and wonders was regularly associated with the activity of the spirit. (Cf. Acts 2:22; Rom 15:19; Gal 3:5; 2 Thess 2:9; Heb 2:4.)

Their senses were assaulted by messages directing their attention to religion; shouts and singing in public places, generally in the open air, not in any church, and to an accompaniment as loud as ancient instruments could sound; applause for highly ornate prose paeans before large audiences; enactment of scenes from the gods' stories performed in theaters and amphitheaters by expert actors, singers, and dancers, while the idols looked on from seats of honor; the god-possessed swirl of worshippers coming down the street to the noise of rattles and drums; and all of this without the onlooker's offering a pinch of incense or so much as glancing at a temple. So obtrusive upon the attention of the least interested was the world of the divine.[33]

If we have ever been curious about the idols abandoned by Paul's converts, this is where to look…. Included in the 'world of the divine' was the astonishingly widespread cult of Asclepius the healer-god. His best-known sanctuaries were at Epidaurus, near Corinth, at Pergamum, some miles to the north of Ephesus, and in the island of Cos; but it has been estimated that by the end of the third century AD there were more than two hundred shrines in his honour throughout the Greco-Roman world.[34] The magical cures attributed to his intercession will have prepared people's minds to accept the equally amazing cures of wandering miracle-workers like Apollonius of Tyana and Paul of Tarsus.

Once the seeds of the new faith had been sown and taken root, then no doubt other factors, including the promise of salvation and the fear of perdition, will have helped to ensure the survival of the springing shoots. As we have seen, some concept of salvation – or deliverance – was widespread throughout the early Roman Empire. Even the wildly improbable notion of resurrection had fully established itself by the end of the first century. But, to repeat, neither of these ideas is likely to have caught the attention of Paul's hearers as his magic cures and exorcisms surely must have done.

In a chapter on conversion later in his book MacMullen asks why such throngs of people were attracted to Christianity. His answer

---

33. *Paganism*, 27.
34. See David Aune, *Prophets and Prophecy*, 26, citing B. Kötting, *Peregrinatio Religiosa* (Münster, 1950), 13.

focuses on 'supernatural powers new in the world [which] it would be quite irrational to credit without proof of their efficacy before one's own eyes. *That*', he concludes, 'is what produces Christians. Nothing else is attested.'[35] One example (from among many) of such evident efficacy is drawn from Tertullian, who, addressing pagans on the subject of exorcisms, says that it is the witness of the pagan gods [visibly mastered and overcome] that produces Christians.[36] Another eminent historian of late antiquity, Peter Brown, agrees with MacMullen: 'However many sound social and cultural reasons the historian may find for the expansion of the Christian Church, the fact remains that in all Christian literature from the New Testament onwards, the Christian missionaries advanced principally by revealing the bankruptcy of men's invisible enemies, the demons, through exorcisms and miracles of healing.'[37] One example of the persuasive force of miracles that I find particularly telling, however, comes not from a Christian source but from the historian Josephus, in a paragraph recording the response of King Hezekiah to Isaiah's promise that he would live another fifteen years. The fact that this story is not in the Bible is a strong indication that even the relatively sophisticated Josephus had no trouble in believing in the miraculous powers of Israel's great prophets.

> When the prophet at God's command told him these things, he would not believe because of the severity of his illness and because the news brought to him surpassed belief, and so he asked Isaiah to perform some miraculous sign [σημεῖόν τι καὶ τεράστιον] in order that he might believe in him when he said these things, as in one who came from God. For he said, things that are beyond belief and surpass our hopes are made credible by acts of a like nature. When the prophet inquired what sign he wished to have performed, he asked him to cause the sun, which in declining had already cast a shadow of ten degrees in the house, to return to the same place and again cast one there. And,

---

35. Op. cit., 97.
36. *Contra haereses* 2.30.7 and 2.31.2.
37. *The World of Late Antiquity*, 55.

when the prophet exhorted God to show his sign to the king, he saw what he wished and was at once freed from his illness.

(A.J. 10.28–9, tr. Marcus)

Such evidence as we have, then, supports MacMullen and Brown in their contention that the strongest arguments for the truth of the Christian faith lay in the ability of its propagators to exorcise demons and dazzle their audiences with other prodigious feats. But if that is the case why is that their views have made so little impression on historians and New Testament scholars alike?

Let us take the historians first. The first answer is that they have not given the question much thought. Robin Lane Fox, for instance, dismisses the problem of the initial impact of the preacher's message. Understanding conversion, he says, is not a matter of understanding 'an unrecoverable first moment when a person decided to go along to church and give the sect a try. It is certainly not a process dominated, or largely explained, by sudden miracles.'[38] Picturing conversion as a *process*, he has no interest in the 'unrecoverable first moment'.

In the second place there is a risk of being swamped by our own scepticism. Unable ourselves to place any credence in the stories of magical cures, expulsions of demons, miraculous escapes from prison and the like, we may well move from seeing these stories in Acts as incredible to seeing them as, for that very reason, unimportant. It is not only the poet but the historian too who needs to engage in what Coleridge calls 'that willing suspension of disbelief'.[39] Edward Gibbon, who attributed the rapid growth of the Christian religion to, among other things, 'the miraculous powers attributed to the primitive church', saw this very clearly. 'Accustomed long since', he remarks, 'to observe and respect the invariable order of Nature, our reason, or at least our imagination, is not sufficiently prepared to sustain the visible action of the Deity.'[40] But he is clearly aware that imagination is required.

Since the vast majority of New Testament scholars are still Christian believers, many of them are likely to be influenced,

38. *Pagans and Christians*, 317.
39. *Biographia Literaria*, ch.14.
40. *Decline and Fall*, vol. i, ch.15.

perhaps unconsciously, by the views of Origen and Eusebius that I mentioned at the beginning of this chapter. They may of course point to the fact that Paul himself says very little about his manner of preaching. But Paul is notoriously coy whenever the topic of spiritual gifts is broached; and in any case, as I have argued, he says enough. But I suspect that there is often enough another factor contributing strongly to a widespread reluctance to take the stories of Acts seriously. To appreciate nineteenth-century grand opera, Charles Rosen remarks somewhere, one requires not only a suspension of disbelief, but also a suspension of distaste. Most thinking Christians of today follow the evangelist John in their horror of any dependence upon visible signs.

The burden of this chapter has been an argument that only if we succeed in combining a suspension of disbelief with a suspension of distaste will we be in a position to understand the remarkable success of Paul the Apostle. It seems appropriate to conclude, however, with a final glance at what Paul has to say on the subject of his apostolate in what many take to be the last of his letters to have been preserved:[41]

> I myself am satisfied about you, my brethren, that you yourselves are full of goodness, filled with all knowledge, and able to instruct one another. But on some points I have written to you very boldly by way of reminder, because of the grace given me by God to be a minister of Christ Jesus to the Gentiles in the priestly service of the gospel of God (εἰς τὸ εἶναί με λειτουργὸν Χριστοῦ Ἰησοῦ εἰς τὰ ἔθνη), so that the offering of the Gentiles may be acceptable, sanctified by the Holy Spirit. In Christ Jesus, then, I have reason to be proud of my work for God. For I will not venture to speak of anything except what Christ has wrought through me to win obedience from the Gentiles (εἰς ὑπακοὴν ἐθνῶν), by word and deed, by the power of signs and wonders (ἐν δυνάμει σημείων καὶ τεράτων), by the power of the Holy Spirit, with the result that from Jerusalem all round to Illyricum (καὶ κύκλῳ μέχρι τοῦ Ἰλλυρικοῦ) I have completed [the preaching of] the gospel of Christ (ὥστε με πεπληρωκέναι τὸ εὐαγγέλιον τοῦ

41. Some scholars believe that Philemon and Philippians (both sent from prison) date from Paul's incarceration in Rome.

Χριστοῦ), thus making it my ambition to preach the gospel, not where Christ has already been named, lest I build on another man's foundation, but as it is written, "They shall see who have never been told of him, and they shall understand who have never heard of him."

Rom 15:14–21

This is a remarkable statement. After an arduous preaching career that had already lasted some two decades, not merely undeterred but actually encouraged by innumerable sufferings and setbacks, Paul (already turned sixty if Murphy-O'Connor's calculations are correct)[42] is now planning to carry the gospel into Spain. His enthusiasm is undimmed, his determination unchecked. There have been other missionaries too, especially to Rome, the city he is anxious to visit on his journey westward, but Paul has a sense of having himself completed a circle extending from the Eastern Mediterranean to the Adriatic. The submissive obedience he has won from the Gentiles he sees as a kind of sacrifice offered to God. (The Greek word he uses gives us our term 'liturgy'.) His preaching has not been to the Jews: that task, in accordance with the agreement described in Gal 2:7–8, was left to Peter. From the moment of his dramatic conversion onwards he never lost the sense that his vocation was to carry the gospel to the *Gentiles*. And he had done this 'by word and deed': if 'the word' was Christ, 'the deed' was the signs and wonders performed in the power of the Spirit.

---

42. Murphy-O'Connor places Paul's birth in 6 BC (p. 8) and the letter to the Romans in AD 55–6 (p. 332).

EXCURSUS IV

The Historicity of Acts

The best advice for anyone about to wrestle with the problem of the historical reliability of Acts would be to start by clearing his or her head with a careful perusal of Loveday Alexander's paper 'Fact, Fiction and the Genre of Acts'.[1] It is a bracing draught. She begins with the observation that one very common approach to the question is indirect: What sort of book is it? What is its *genre*? She then conducts a subtle, thorough and penetrating survey of various styles of contemporary Greek and Roman writing that have some prima facie affinity with Acts. This leads her to the conclusion that 'we shall never solve the question of Acts' historicity by solving the genre question' (p. 394). The signals it sends out to its readers are simply too conflicting, some prompting a comparison with romances like Longus's *Daphnis and Chloe* or Chariton's *Chaereas and Callirhoë*, others suggesting that the proper place for Acts is on the same shelf as Herodotus's *History* or Plutarch's *Lives*.

Even if it were possible to answer the question of genre satisfactorily by concluding with Sir William Ramsay that the author of Acts deserves a place 'among historians of the first rank',[2] or alternatively by denying that the book is properly described as a history at all, we should not be out of the wood. For not all histories are free from invention and few fictions are altogether devoid of fact.

So we may prefer to leave aside the question of genre, and ask instead of Acts, as we would of any work of literature that happens to interest us, which bits are 'fact' or at least 'fact-like' (susceptible in principle of rational verification), and which are not. Alexander

1. *NTS* 44 (1998), 380–99.
2. W. M. Ramsay, *St Paul the Traveller*, 4.

points out that ancient writers have a variety of techniques at their disposal for indicating to their readers how to respond to their work at any given point, the simplest and commonest being the distinction between 'I saw' and 'I have heard but I do not believe'.[3]

Turning to the Book of Acts, however, we find that this author behaves very differently from other Greek historians. For at no point does he stand aside from his narrative or exhibit the slightest degree of detachment from it. Indeed at a certain point, when Paul is about to cross over from Greece to Asia (16:10, the first of the famous 'we'-passages), he quietly steps inside his own story, lending it the additional authority of what scholars call *autopsia*: 'I have seen with my own eyes'.

This would cause no problem if Luke's narrative, like that of the fastidious Thucydides, were simply of the 'fact-like' kind. But, as we know, this is not the case. Indeed, almost immediately after a cool, stylish introduction Luke invites his readers to join Jesus' remaining disciples in gazing upwards at their beloved master, now risen from the dead, as he is transported by a cloud out of their sight (1:9). And so it goes on: the miracle of tongues at Pentecost (really a miracle of ears) is followed by exorcisms, healings, blindings, marvellous escapes; even a raising from the dead.

Alexander concludes her essay by remarking how different Luke's 'committed' narrative is from most of Greek prose literature: 'Acts is a narrative which both implies and creates the presumption of a shared religious experience: and that is something difficult to accommodate within the standard fact/fiction grid of Greek literature' (p. 399). The truth-claim implicit in Luke's lack of detachment distinguishes him from other Greek historians in that they, mostly and most of the time, are rationalists, and look on strange and inexplicable happenings – especially when these have anything to do with religion – with mingled curiosity and scepticism, sometimes tempered by disgust.[4]

---

3. She instances Herodotus's comment on the phoenix: 'I have not seen a phoenix myself except in paintings, for it is very rare and only visits the country (or so they say in Heliopolis) at intervals of 500 years, at the death of the parent-bird.... But I do not believe it' (2.72).
4. The characteristic detachment of ancient historians prompts a sardonic reflection from the cynical Lucian: 'If a myth comes along you must tell it but not believe it entirely; no, make it known for your audience to make of it what they

Those modern critics who share the rationalist bent of the Greeks may greet these conclusions with a tranquillity unclouded by worry or regret: 'So what?' they might retort. (Others of course may protest that bent implies bias.) Similarly, many of Paul's biographers will be totally unfazed if they think that they are obliged to rely for their information first on Paul's own letters, secondly on what external data happen still to be available, and thirdly on the non-magical parts of Acts. But what of historians of religion, whose primary interest is focused directly on the very parts of Acts that have just been jettisoned by their colleagues for being clearly unreliable, if not downright false? Is there any way of salvaging these without abandoning all pretence of intellectual honesty?

Let us take as a test-case two passages from Acts and consider how they are handled in one major commentary and two recent biographies:

(1) Acts 16:11–18. (Here I simply summarize.)
Shortly after Paul had made the momentous decision to cross over from Asia into Greece (16:9–10), he found himself in Philippi, 'which is the leading city of the district of Macedonia, and a Roman colony' (16:12). Luke follows up this information by telling an engaging little story about a slave-girl with a spirit of divination (πνεῦμα πύθωνα: she used to be called the Pythoness),[5] who trailed after Paul and his companions ('us') for days, proclaiming over and over again, 'These men are servants of the Most High God', until Paul, utterly exasperated, ordered the spirit to leave her – which it did, 'that very hour' (16:16–18). Luke adds weight to the story by claiming to have been there himself at the time, an example of *autopsia*.

---

will – you run no risk and lean to neither side (*How to write history* §60, Loeb tr.), quoted by Alexander, 'Fact', 387.

5. The python was the snake that guarded the shrine of Delphi on behalf of Gaia (who has recently won acclaim as the great mother-goddess of the environmental movement). Apollo killed the python, but nevertheless adopted the snake as a symbol of the oracular shrine that Delphi now became, which is what entitled the RSV translators to render the adjective πύθωνα modifying 'spirit' by 'of divination'.

(2) Acts 19:11–20. (Paul's activities in Ephesus, quoted here *in extenso*.)

> And God did extraordinary miracles by the hands of Paul, so that handkerchiefs or aprons were carried away from his body to the sick, and diseases left them and the evil spirits came out of them. Then some of the itinerant Jewish exorcists undertook to pronounce the name of the Lord Jesus over those who had evil spirits, saying, 'I adjure you by the Jesus whom Paul preaches'. Seven sons of a Jewish high priest named Sceva were doing this. But the evil spirit answered them, 'Jesus I know, and Paul I know; but who are you?' And the man in whom the evil spirit was leaped on them, mastered all of them, and overpowered them, so that they fled out of that house naked and wounded. And this became known to all residents of Ephesus, both Jews and Greeks; and fear fell upon them all; and the name of the Lord Jesus was extolled. Many also of those who were now believers came, confessing and divulging their practices. And a number of those who practised magic arts brought their books together and burned them in the sight of all; and they counted the value of them and found it came to fifty thousand pieces of silver. So the word of the Lord grew and prevailed mightily.

For our commentary we turn to the greatly respected Ernst Haenchen. The first of the two passages causes him no great difficulty. Basically, it is a story of an exorcism, and here the traditions are so strong and so widespread that even the rationalist historian must pay them some attention. Here is Haenchen's conclusion:

> The author's freedom … is strange to the modern reader. But it did not occur to any of the great Roman historians simply to say 'how it actually happened'. They all wanted to inform, influence and motivate. Luke would not have broken the tradition of great Roman historical writing … when he narrated the history of the mission in Philippi in his own fashion. The difference between *facta* and *ficta* has not been the same in all ages.[6]

6. *Acts*, 504.

His response to the second passage is very different: it is dismissive, even indignant. He finds the handkerchiefs (v.12) especially repulsive, so much so that they provoke him into a tart criticism of Luke that is clearly theologically inspired:

> He could view Paul ... only with the eyes of his own time: the Paul, already transfigured by legend, who so overflowed with divine power that even the cloths on his body are drenched with it. Such an Apostle is already delivered from weakness. He lives no longer in the sphere of the cross but in that of glory.[7]

Turning next to Jerome Murphy-O'Connor's 1996 biography, we find that in consequence of his decision to rely primarily upon the relatively sparse information that is to be gleaned from Paul's letters he scarcely glances at the more prodigious side of Paul's activities. Of the exorcisms in particular he seizes every opportunity, if one may be permitted the Irishism, to say nothing at all. Murphy-O'Connor is not untypical of modern New Testament scholars, most of whom, when they *have* to comment on the magical elements in Acts, tend to hover between the bland, the disdainful and the fatuous.[8] Yet with the exception of Stephen, all the major players in Acts are exorcists: Peter, Paul, and, between them, the slighter figure of Philip, who actually plays quite an important role in Acts, both geographically, since it is he who carries the word into Samaria (thought of by Luke as situated between Judaea and 'the end of the earth': Acts 1:8),[9] and theologically, since his convert, the Ethiopian eunuch, occupies the conceptual space between Peter's purely Jewish converts and the Roman centurion Cornelius.[10] (Jesus too, of

7. Ibid., 563. I discuss this view of Paul in Chapter 5.
8. A good example of the fatuous is F. F. Bruce's comment on the conclusion of the passage quoted *in extenso* above: 'Such an incident was bound to make a deep impression on minds conditioned to think in magical terms, although modern readers may wonder about the quality of the faith so engendered': *Acts*, 412.
9. The Greek for this is ἕως ἐσχάτου τῆς γῆς, which is actually a quotation from Isa 49:6, as can be seen from Acts 13:47, which cites the whole verse. Theologically (though not geographically) the end of the earth had been reached once Paul turned to a completely Gentile audience in Pisidian Antioch.
10. Nowadays most New Testament scholars pay far more attention to Ethiopic Enoch than to the Ethiopian eunuch. But worth considering is James M. Scott's intriguing suggestion that the missionary programme outlined in Acts 1:8 is

course, was an exorcist, one of the few statements one can make about him with total assurance.)[11] Lastly it should be added that the conclusion to the second excerpt ('So the word of the Lord grew …'), whilst in no way untypical of Luke's style, appears to conflict with his general determination to ascribe the success of the gospel, not to miracles, but to preaching, and especially to Paul's success in proving from the scriptures that Jesus was the Messiah. Insofar as the content of this passage 'goes against the grain' of the author's declared intention we should be the more reluctant to dismiss it.[12] Luke himself obviously believed it.

For our final example of responses to the two excerpts from Acts we turn to A. N. Wilson's biography, so different in almost every respect from that of Murphy-O'Connor. He introduces the story of the Philippian slave-girl with something of the same detachment that we have seen to be typical of ancient historians: 'Luke tells his readers that one day … '; and he comments perceptively in conclusion that

> Most modern readers of the Acts of the Apostles, whether or not Christian believers, would have regarded the activities of the slave-girl as mumbo-jumbo. In the world of classical antiquity, however, most people would have accepted the powers of the unseen; it was simply a question of which demons or gods were better than another, or, if you were Jewish, which were legitimate. … The point at issue in Philippi was not the lawfulness of fortune-telling, still less its efficacy, but who was in charge.[13]

Similarly, referring to the handkerchiefs that gave such offence to Haenchen, Wilson writes:

---

influenced by the Table-of-Nations tradition stemming from Genesis 10. In that case the episode of the Ethiopian eunuch (8:26–40) may represent the extension of the mission to Ham, the second of Noah's three sons, just as the preceding chapters (2:1–8:25) allude to Shem and the succeeding chapters (9:1–28:31) to Japheth. Here are the three 'ends of the earth', with Jerusalem the centre. See chapter 14 ('Luke's Geographical Horizon') of *The Book of Acts in Its Graeco-Roman Setting*, ed. D. W. J. Gill and C. Gempf , 483–544.

11. See Excursus I.
12. For a theoretical discussion of this argument, with some practical examples, see E. P. Sanders and Margaret Davies, *Studying the Synoptic Gospels* (London, 1989), ch. 20, pp. 301–15.
13. *Paul*, 145–7.

It is interesting that Luke should mention these powers of Paul's after his arrival in the city of Ephesus, the city of magic, of demons, of the goddess [Artemis]. The post-Enlightenment sophisticate who reads of Paul's miraculous gift will wish to distinguish, perhaps, between Paul's 'faith healing' – the result of 'pure religion and undefiled' – and the superstitions of the 'pagan' Ephesians. Luke seems to make no such distinction.[14]

Wilson, the brilliant amateur, has a better appreciation of the value of Luke's work than either of the professional New Testament scholars, Haenchen and Murphy-O'Connor (who, as we have seen, ignores these passages completely). If we are looking for scholars with a genuine appreciation of and feel for the magic and miraculous elements in Acts we must turn to historians like Stephen Mitchell and Ramsay Macmullen[15] or to that maverick among biblical scholars, the late Morton Smith.[16] It is surely impossible to get any real understanding of the religious Paul whilst wearing blinkers that shut out the sight of the spiritual and demonic world in which he lived. Both Jews and pagans felt themselves surrounded by spiritual beings, though the latter thought of these as deities (generally benign) and evil demons, whereas the former, though theoretically monotheists, focused their fears on the demons they held responsible for all kinds of miseries, especially diseases and natural disasters. Paul's instinctive horror at the idea of drinking from a cup that had been shared by demons (1 Cor 10:21) betrays his true feelings, despite his notional assent to the proposition that idols do not exist (1 Cor 8:4).

The recognition that many of the events recorded in Acts might not withstand critical scrutiny by scientifically-trained rationalist historians is no reason for dismissing as of no value Luke's less critical narrative. Indeed, to a historian more interested in mood and atmosphere than in facts, the *cultural* historian, as Jacob Burckhardt calls him, the Book of Acts is an invaluable aid. This is what Erich Heller has to say about Burckhardt's penchant, in his great work, *The Culture of the Renaissance in Italy*, for including in

14. *Paul*, 183–4.
15. *Pagans and Christians*.
16. *Jesus the Magician*.

his accounts of the achievements of the great men and women of the *quattrocento* anecdotal stories that do not ring true to a modern ear: are these, he asks, 'worthy of a self-respecting scholar? Have they not the romantic flavour of fanciful dramatizations rather than the authentic ring of precise recording?' His answer is that the source from which Burckhardt takes his anecdotes (he names the partisan and untrustworthy Matarazzo) 'is not chosen for the sake of factual exactitude'. It has for him 'the authenticity of the mind, imagination, and spirit of the Renaissance, and if it yields a negligible *quantity* of the reliable facts, it nevertheless reveals something more important to him: the *quality* of the life of the period, or as he would have called it, the *Geist* of the epoch'.[17]

We can safely leave the last word to Burckhardt himself. Towards the beginning of the first volume of his other great work, the lectures on *The Greeks and Greek Civilization*, he issues a manifesto in defence of what he calls 'cultural history':

> One great advantage of studying cultural history is the *certainty* of its most important facts, compared with those of history in the ordinary sense of narrated events: these are frequently uncertain, controversial, coloured, or, given the Greek talent for lying, entirely the invention of imagination or self-interest. Cultural history by contrast possesses a primary degree of certainty, as it consists for the most part of material conveyed in an unintentional, disinterested or even involuntary way by sources and monuments; they betray their secrets unconsciously and even, paradoxically, through fictitious elaborations, quite apart from the material details they may set out to record and glorify, and are thus doubly instructive for the cultural historian.[18]

17. *The Disinherited Mind* (Harmondsworth, 1961), 60–1.
18. *The Greeks and Greek Civilization*, ed. Oswyn Murray; tr. Sheila Stern (London, 1998), 5.

6
Paul the Prophet

Introduction

Paul the Convert, Paul the Mystic, Paul the Apostle. Now Paul the Prophet. I have suggested that Paul would have been puzzled to have been called a convert, embarrassed to be called a mystic, and gratified to be called an apostle. How would he have responded to the title of prophet? Perhaps by calling for some clarification. When you call me a prophet, he might have said, what do you mean? Confronted by such a challenge most people, perhaps even most Pauline scholars, would find it hard to come up with a fully satisfactory answer. But that is what I propose to attempt in this chapter.

The difficulty is twofold. In the first place, there is only a handful of instances of the use of the word 'prophet' in Paul's authentic writings, less than a dozen all told,[1] and these refer to two quite different groups of people. In the second place, he never uses the term of himself; so in defending the use of the title we need to be quite clear why and in what sense we want to apply it to him.

I want to begin some way off with some general reflections on prophecy and then to move gradually closer to Paul. Eventually I hope to show that he was a prophet in two quite different senses, and to give some consideration to each of these.

Clairvoyants and soothsayers

Ask the man in the street or the woman on the bus what they understand by the term 'prophet', and you would probably get an answer

1. Rom 1:2; 3:21; 11:3; 1 Cor 12:28, 29; 14:29, 32 *bis*, 37; 1 Thess 2:15.

something like this: a prophet is a kind of seer or soothsayer, some-one who predicts the future, someone who, well, *prophesies*. And the ability to predict the future is indeed a very important connotation of the word, one to which we shall have to return. Perhaps we should start, though, by putting to one side tea-leaves, horoscopes and crystal balls, and also by bracketing out some of the other more esoteric kinds of divination, such as chiromancy, pyromancy, necromancy and haruspication. The prophet, we may wish to maintain, is more than a simple clairvoyant. From among a truly remarkable number of techniques for predicting the future the only one we need to retain is the *prophetic oracle*.

The prophetic oracle

What does the concept of oracle add to that of prophecy? It gives it what the Germans call a *Sitz im Leben*, a cultural setting. In pre-classical and classical Greece, and also in the Hellenistic era that followed, the oracular shrine, a sacred site in which people from all walks of life came to seek advice and reassurance from the god who was believed to inhabit it, was very important both socially and politically. What gave the prophets who ministered at these shrines their authority was that *they spoke on behalf of the god*. They could advise, warn, criticize and scold, and sometimes predict the future. However, when they did this, prophesying in the sense in which we have come to understand the term, they did not always bring enlightenment. On the contrary, they often took good care to shroud their predictions in riddling language, thus guarding them-selves against any comeback, especially from the rich and powerful. The Delphic Oracle in particular, the most ancient and revered of all the Greek oracles, was notoriously sibylline. The best example of its characteristic equivocations is Herodotus's story of how Croesus, the ultra-rich king of Lydia, sought advice on whether he should send an army against the Persians. He was told if he did he would destroy a great empire, but not, of course, that the empire in question would be his own (*Hist.* 1.53).

What deserves especial emphasis, however, is the original mean-ing of the word 'prophet'. Speaking for God, the prophet is first and foremost an *intermediary* between God and ordinary mortals, an *interpreter*. From the noun προφήτης comes the verb προφητεύειν. Τίς προφητεύει θεοῦ; asks Xuthus in Euripides's *Ion*: who is speaking for the god, who is to act as his interpreter? (l. 413). And no doubt it was because the word προφήτης carried this meaning that the Alexandrian translators of the Hebrew Bible decided to use it to render the Hebrew נביא, a term which is actually derived from a Semitic root meaning 'to call'. For the most part προφήτης works perfectly well, because the most important role of the prophets of Israel and Judah was to do precisely what the Greek word suggests: to speak on behalf of God. This needs to be stressed, if only because although it is the primary meaning of the term it has rather drifted away from ordinary English usage. Nowadays the only people to retain the connection with the divinity are scholars, both biblical and, less commonly, classical. But in the period that concerns us *all* prophets, Greek, Roman and Jewish, were thought of as speaking on behalf of a (or the) god.

Ecstatic prophets

So far, then, we have discovered two important ideas connected with prophecy: first the idea of prediction, above all *oracular* prediction, and secondly the idea of mediation, speaking *on behalf of* the divinity. But in certain passages of the Hebrew Bible the word נביא and its verbal cognate carry very different associations, making the Greek word look curiously out of place. In spite of this neither the translators of the Septuagint nor the historian Josephus in his free and sometimes idiosyncratic adaptation of these passages made any attempt to look for a more appropriate alternative.

Of the passages in question the most illuminating are two that concern the behaviour of King Saul, behaviour that in both cases (for the passages are variants of the same basic story) prompts the famous question, 'Is Saul too among the prophets?' Here is one of them:

And it was told Saul, 'Behold, David is at Naioth in Ramah.' Then Saul sent messengers to take David; and when they saw the company of the prophets prophesying, and Samuel standing as head over them, the Spirit of God came upon the messengers of

Saul, and they also prophesied. When it was told Saul, he sent other messengers, and they also prophesied. And Saul sent messengers again the third time, and they also prophesied. Then he himself went to Ramah, and came to the great well that is in Secu; and he asked, 'Where are Samuel and David?' And one said, 'Behold, they are at Naioth in Ramah.' And he went from there to Naioth in Ramah; and the Spirit of God came upon him also, and as he went he prophesied, until he came to Naioth in Ramah. And he too stripped off his clothes, and he too prophesied before Samuel, and lay naked all that day and all that night. Hence it is said, 'Is Saul too among the prophets?' (1 Sam 19:20–24; cf. 10:10–12)

It is just possible, I suppose, that the English translators use 'prophets' and 'prophesy' in this passage because they were eager to render the Hebrew evenly throughout. But it is more likely that they were translating with an eye to the Septuagint and missed the real difference in meaning. Otherwise they might have tried to suggest something of the divinely inspired delirium that is clearly what this passage is about. And in that case the episode might have ended not, 'Is Saul among the prophets?' but, 'Is Saul among the ravers?' or possibly '… among the dervishes?'

Josephus too, who cannot be accused of slavishly following either the Hebrew or the Greek, kept the same terminology, but with one extra nuance. Where the Hebrew speaks of 'the spirit of God' (19:23) Josephus says 'the divine spirit' (τὸ θεῖον πνεῦμα: *A.J.* 6.222), but in the earlier version the expression he uses to explain Saul's frenzy is ἔνθεος γενόμενος – coming under the control of God (6.56). The word ἔνθεος is the source of ἐνθουσιασμός (*enthousiasmos*), the term for spirit possession. There is no reason to believe that Josephus wanted to distinguish between (a) suffering the onset of the spirit of God and (b) being divinely inspired or possessed.[2] He uses the term ἔνθεος γενόμενος in other contexts too, to account for Saul's superhuman strength when he encouraged the Israelites to go to war against the Ammonites by dismembering a

---

2. See Rebecca Gray, *Prophetic Figures*, a first-rate study to which I am greatly indebted.

team of oxen single-handed,[3] and to explain Elijah's fleetness of foot when he outran Ahab's chariot all the way from Mount Carmel to Jezreel.[4] Even more significantly, he uses the term of himself, as we shall see, at a crucial moment of his life when he felt impelled to prophesy.

At this point some comment is necessary. The most striking singularity of the exhibition of ecstatic prophecy in which Saul was driven to participate is that the so-called prophets *did not speak*. If they opened their mouths at all, it was, we must assume, with inarticulate raving. The sources agree upon the dominance of the spirit, but these were not prophets in the classic sense of spokesmen for God. Reading these stories dispassionately, and resisting the heavy pressure of the interpretative tradition, we would probably not call them prophets at all but rather corybants or bacchantes.

Nevertheless there is a link, and an important one, with what we might call mainline prophecy. For here too the prophet was often thought to have been seized hold of by God. Nor is this idea confined to the Jewish tradition. When Greek or Roman oracles, as is not uncommon, 'are presented as the direct speech of the inspiring oracular divinity, the psycho-physiological state of possession is presupposed. It was widely believed, for instance, of the Pythian oracle at Delphi that a god or daimon actually took over her speech-organs in order to deliver oracular responses.'[5] And we may recall at this point that the slave-girl who so infuriated Paul at Philippi with her wearisome reiteration of his purpose and identity was credited by Luke with possessing a πνεῦμα πύθωνα: Acts 16:16.

A powerful witness to the fusion of the Greek and Jewish traditions is the Alexandrian philosopher Philo, a generation older than Paul. (He was an old man when he led a Jewish delegation to the emperor Gaius in AD 39/40.) Philo actually describes himself as filled with corybantic frenzy through having been seized by God (ὡς [ὥστε] ὑπὸ κατοχῆς ἐνθέου κορυβαντιᾶν: *Migr. Abr.* 35), and elsewhere speaks of his soul as frequently taken over by God

---

3. *A.J.* 6.73–80 = 1 Sam 11: 5–11, where both MT and LXX have 'spirit of God'.
4. *A.J.* 8.346 = 1 Kings 18:46, where MT and LXX have 'hand of God'.
5. See David E. Aune, *Prophecy*, 33, plus notes 121–5 *ad. loc.*, where he takes issue with certain views of W. D. Smith, 'So-called Possession in Pre-Christian Greece', *Transactions and Proceedings of the American Philological Association* 96 (1965), 403–6.

(εἰωθυῖα τὰ πολλὰ θεοληπτεῖσθαι: *Cher.* 27). In yet another passage (*Spec. Leg.* 1.65) Philo speaks of the prophet as serving simply as the channel for another's insistent prompting. In other words the prophet, at least occasionally, is simply the mouthpiece of God, like a ventriloquist's dummy with no voice of his own – a conception scarcely distinguishable from that found in the Greek oracular tradition.[6]

Finally, it should be observed that this tradition of spirit-inspired prophecy is clearly the source of one important element in Paul's own concept of the nature and function of prophetic activity within the Christian community at Corinth. The only passage in his writings where prophecy is discussed at any length is 1 Corinthians 12–14. (6 out of 10 instances of the noun προφήτης and 9 out of 11 instances of the verb προφητεύειν are found in these chapters.) Prophecy is numbered there among what Paul calls charismata or spiritual gifts, and since it was in any case part of the Greek tradition, it will have been welcomed at Corinth quite readily. Corinth, after all, although on the opposite side of the gulf, is not very far from Delphi. Although Paul himself must have numbered prophecy among his own gifts, his true prophetic calling must be located elsewhere, and I shall postpone any further discussion of the topic of charismatic prophecy until the next chapter.

Paul a prophet?

Before leaving it completely, however, we should note one small problem. If Paul himself, as may be inferred from the general tenor of his discussion at this point, reckoned himself among those gifted with this particular charisma, why is it that he does not actually say so? He does not hesitate to say that he speaks in tongues. Why does he not specifically claim to have the gift of prophecy also? Here as so often we must resort to guesses. My own guess would be this. Paul would readily admit to being a prophet in this restricted sense, but somehow this is not what he really means by the term. Whenever he uses the term outside this passage he does

---

6. For Philo 'prophecy was synonymous with the oracular' (M. E. Isaacs, *Concept of Spirit*, 49).

so in one of two ways. Prophets are either writers of scripture (Rom 1:2; 3:21; cf. 16:26) or else they are martyrs who were put to death by their own people (Rom 11:3; 1 Thess 2:15). Paul was the first but by no means the last Christian writer to speak of the prophets in this way. It is perhaps significant that he does not do so in his letter to the Corinthians. The reason for this is probably that he did not put charismatic prophets in the same category as the great prophets of the past. In his mind these two groups were placed in completely different boxes. No doubt there is some inconsistency here, at least in his use of words; but consistency was never one of his strong points.

So what is the explanation? I think that Paul assumed, probably without giving the matter much thought, that all the inspired writers of scripture and all those brave men who were killed by an ungrateful people for doing what God had commissioned them to do were long dead, indeed that they belonged to a bygone age. In this sense all good prophets, indeed all genuine prophets, are and can only be dead!

He was not the only one to think so. Ben Sira, in the concluding section of his work, beginning with the words 'Let us now praise famous men' (Sir 44–50), gives the distinct impression that prophecy had died out before the construction of the second temple. Josephus evidently thought that the last great prophet was John Hyrcanus, whose thirty-year reign as high priest ended in 104 BC. Josephus says of him that 'so closely was he in touch with the deity that he was never ignorant of the future' (*B.J.* 1.69). This is something he never says of his own contemporaries: he was convinced that this remarkable gift of far-sighted vision that he so admired in the ancient prophets was a thing of the past, which is why he restricts the use of the term 'prophet' almost exclusively to figures from this golden age.[7]

For Josephus, then, as for Paul, the true prophets, the great prophets, the only people really deserving the name, belonged to the past. Calling oneself a prophet then would have been like claiming to be a saint today. However much you may aspire to sanctity, you are going to think very hard before you say you have acquired it.

---

7. See R. Gray, *Prophetic Figures*, 34.

Eschatological prophets

Of the two aspects of Paul's experience that may properly be described as prophetic, by far the more important is that in which his claim to stand within the prophetic tradition is at best indirect. To show this I shall be appealing to evidence in the work of his younger contemporary, the historian Flavius Josephus, whose life, different as it was from Paul's, offers nevertheless some striking parallels.

Like Paul, Josephus began a new career as a result of a mid-life crisis. Whilst continuing to regard himself as a loyal Jew he came to be regarded as a traitor and a turncoat by his former friends and allies. His conversion too, if we may call it that, was precipitated by a revelation (or so he claimed) which he described in language drawn from the prophetic tradition of Israel. In spite of an enduring respect and admiration for this tradition he never actually calls himself a prophet, yet demonstrates time and again by indirect hints and allusions that he considered himself the heir of the prophetic tradition.[8]

The prophets nearest to Josephus's heart were Jeremiah and Daniel. Like Jeremiah, Josephus found himself caught up in a war that could not be won, against insurmountable odds. And like Jeremiah too he concluded that God was punishing his people for their sins. Though he was doubtless convinced that the enemies of Israel would ultimately be overcome, it is significant that in his detailed reconstruction of the history of Israel, at the one point in which there appeared to be a prediction that God himself would finally bring about the collapse of the Roman Empire he resorted to equivocation. The statue with feet of clay in Nebuchadnezzar's famous dream was shattered by a stone 'cut out by no human hand' that eventually 'became a great mountain and filled all the earth' (Dan 2: 31–35). The last great empire, Rome, would eventually founder. God would not allow his people to remain in subjection for ever. Writing, however, for a Roman readership, Josephus prudently refrained from saying so.

8. 'He claims that he was "chosen" (ἐπιλεγόμενος, *B.J.* 3.354) and "sent" (προπεμπόμενος, 3.400) by God to act as his "messenger" (ἄγγελος, 3.400) and "minister" (διάκονος, 3.354). In a speech attributed to Vespasian, Josephus describes himself as "a minister of the voice of God" (διάκονος τῆς τοῦ θεοῦ φωνῆς, 4.626)' (R. Gray, *Prophetic Figures*, 37).

Daniel, as it happened, was the second of the prophets for whom Josephus felt a strong affinity. He too was an interpreter of dreams, and he too ended up in the court of a foreign king whose favours provoked the envy of the local courtiers; so when he came to adapt Daniel's story Josephus made sure to underline this point by inserting a comment to that effect: 'for people are jealous when they see others more highly honoured by kings than themselves' (*A.J.* 10.250).

These examples are enough to illustrate the persistence of the Jewish prophetic tradition and the extent to which it was prized by those who saw themselves to be its heirs. The point is argued fully and convincingly by Rebecca Gray in her book on Jewish prophecy, though she makes no mention of Paul.

The most important parallel, however, between the careers of the two men is undoubtedly the revelatory experience that changed both their lives. Before commenting upon the significance of Paul's account of his own revelation in Galatians, let me say something about Josephus.

In the spring of AD 67, some time after the start of the Jewish revolt, Josephus, who had emerged as one of the leaders of the Jewish forces, took over the command of the Galilean town of Jotapata, a well-fortified mountain stronghold that was about to be besieged by Vespasian. Throughout the siege, which lasted forty-seven days, Josephus was tirelessly devising new stratagems for defeating the Romans; but when the town's defences were eventually breached by a force led by Vespasian's son Titus and the end was in sight, he fled, and took refuge in a nearby cave. After a couple of days his hiding-place was betrayed to Vespasian, who immediately sent messengers urging him to surrender.

Whilst he was trying to make up his mind what to do he had a revelation. This is what he says: 'he was visited once again by those nightly dreams in which God had foretold to him the impending fate of the Jews and the destinies of the Roman sovereign'. He explains that he was an 'interpreter of dreams and skilled in divining the meaning of ambiguous utterances of the Deity'. What is more, he concludes, 'a priest himself and of priestly descent, he was not ignorant of the prophecies in the sacred books, and at that hour he was inspired (ἔνθεος γενόμενος) to read their meaning' (*B.J.* 3.351–3). In determining to give himself up, he convinced himself that his surrender was the recognition of a divine calling, and in the prayer to God which concludes this part of his narrative he describes this in language deliberately reminiscent of the prophetic tradition: 'Since you have chosen me (τὴν ἐμὴν ψυχὴν) to announce what is about to happen (τὰ μέλλοντα εἰπεῖν), I willingly surrender to the Romans and consent to live; but I swear (μαρτύρομαι) that I go not as a traitor, but in your service (ὡς σὸς διάκονος)' (3.354).

We may or may not believe Josephus's account of the reason why he decided to surrender. Rebecca Gray, following Tessa Rajak, puts up a strong case for the defence, but I confess that it leaves me unconvinced.[9] I do know, though, that the human capacity for self-delusion is virtually limitless; so even if we are not prepared to exonerate Josephus from the charge of special pleading, there is no reason to doubt that by the time he came to write the story of the war he had managed to persuade himself that he was telling the truth.

However that may be, what interests us most in Josephus's story is the explanation he gives of his vision into the future. 'Skilled in divining the ambiguous utterances of the Deity', he says, and 'not ignorant of the prophecies of the sacred books, at that hour he was inspired to read their meaning.' The phrase 'ambiguous utterances of the deity' betrays his knowledge of the Greco-Roman tradition of oracular divination. He is conscious that he is about to pronounce an oracle. The source of his insight is the Bible, the sacred books of his own tradition, and although he does not say so we may assume that the book in question was that of Jeremiah, one of the two prophets for whom he felt a special affinity.

The practice of interpreting the sacred writings of the past as if they were intended to refer to the present was well known at Qumran. What has come to be called the pesher method of interpretation is really just another form of oracular prophecy. Josephus says of the Essene sect that it included in its numbers people well-versed in the scriptures and in prophetic sayings: 'seldom if ever', he says, 'do they err in their predictions' (*B.J.* 2.159).

---

9. Interviewed by Vespasian after his surrender, Josephus told him 'that he had fore-told to the people of Jotapata that their city would be captured after forty-seven days and that he himself would be taken alive by the Romans' (*B.J.* 3.406). With such a clear awareness of the futility of resistance, how could he have nerved himself to continue the struggle or have persuaded his fellow-citizens to do the same? This passage alone is enough to demonstrate his untrustworthiness.

Many of the Jewish writings of the second temple period, then, attest the persistence of a tradition of prophetic inspiration that consisted essentially of a special insight into the meaning of scripture. Josephus, as we have seen, describes how the exercise of this gift, under divine impulsion or inspiration (ἔνθεος γενόμενος), led him to the most important decision of his life. Leaving aside the vexed question whether what he describes as a visionary gleam should really be ascribed to hindsight, it remains true that the framework for understanding this experience was given him by the scriptures.

Turning now – at last – to Paul, we may start with the observation that scholars (and I am thinking in particular of David Aune) have discovered quite an array of oracular pronouncements embedded in his writings.[10] Only one of these is oracular in the sense that I have been using the word, that is, dependent upon a special insight into the scriptures,[11] but there is enough evidence to show that Paul continued throughout his career to exercise a gift that has to be called prophetic. A good example is the exclamatory prediction in the chapter on resurrection in 1 Corinthians:

> Lo! I tell you a mystery. We shall not all sleep,
> but we shall be changed, in a moment,
> in the twinkling of an eye, at the last trumpet,
> for the trumpet shall sound,
> and the dead shall be raised imperishable,
> and we shall all be changed.   1 Cor 15:51–2

The passage that I want to discuss next (Gal 2:15–16) does not figure in Aune's list, but it indicates, it seems to me, an oracular insight remarkably similar to that exhibited by Josephus in the story we have just been considering. In describing his revelatory call, Paul, like Josephus, thinks of Jeremiah; although unlike Josephus he did not repeat Jeremiah's message of doom and gloom: what struck

---

10. In a comprehensive survey Aune has detected ('with varying degrees of confidence') about a dozen (including three from 2 Thessalonians): Rom 11:25–26; 1 Cor 12:3, 9; 14:37–38; 2 Cor 12:9; Gal 5:21; 1 Thess 3:4; 4:2–6, 16–17a; 2 Thess 3:6, 10, 12.
11. Rom 11:25–26. This is discussed below.

him, evidently, was the call itself – singled out by God from his mother's womb. For the substance of his message he turned not to Jeremiah but Isaiah. Here is a slightly fuller version of the passage (translated directly from the LXX) to which he is alluding:

> And now the Lord says, who formed me from the womb to be his servant (δοῦλος), to join (τοῦ συναγαγεῖν) Jacob and Israel to him – I will be joined (συναχθήσομαι) and glorified before the Lord, and God will be my strength – and he said to me: 'It is a great thing for you to be called [to be] my servant (τοῦ κληθῆναί σε παῖδά μου) to raise the tribes of Jacob and restore the diaspora of Israel (τὴν διασπορὰν τοῦ Ἰσραηλ): I have appointed you (τέθεικά σε) as a covenant to the people, as a light to the Gentiles, so that you may bring salvation (τοῦ εἶναί σε εἰς σωτηρίαν) to the end of the earth. Isa 49:5–6

This is the burden of Paul's own task: to carry salvation to the end of the earth. The standard Greek edition of the New Testament (Nestle-Aland) signals nearly fifty references in Paul's letters to that part of the book of Isaiah known to modern scholarship as Second Isaiah (chapters 40–55).[12] This sheerly academic distinction would obviously have meant nothing to Paul, but the number of references is quite striking, and proves his extensive knowledge of the section of the book that is particularly focused on Israel's mission to witness to the Gentile world.

In a previous chapter I raised the question whether Paul's sense of his own calling as apostle of the Gentiles came to him in a flash, on the Damascus road, or whether he arrived at it later, by reflecting on the meaning of the scriptures. And as in the case of Josephus, the question is impossible to answer with any assurance. Nevertheless, there are some grounds for believing that in Paul's case the scriptural framework of understanding was actually part of the revelation itself.

Paul, of course, had a practical approach to the scriptures: he usually knew what he was looking for in the way of argument or proof, and being a clever man, he usually found it. But this does not mean that *in every instance* his scriptural exegesis was simply an

---

12. These are conveniently listed by K. O. Sandnes, *Paul*, 62, n. 51.

instrument of argument. If, as is certainly possible, his missionary vocation was part and parcel of his revelatory experience, then there is every likelihood that the passage of Isaiah to which he alludes when describing his call was already bubbling in his brain *before* he had begun to look for the words he needed.

This is particularly the case if Paula Fredriksen is right in her contention that the promise of an approaching end that somehow recognized the need to incorporate the Gentiles in God's providential plan was an integral element in the preaching of the Jewish followers of Jesus whom Paul had been persecuting. The great advantage of this proposal is that it bypasses one otherwise virtually impassable obstacle: the need to find a convincing *theological* explanation for the vindictiveness of the orthodox party. The very word 'orthodox' highlights the problem. As has often been pointed out, the Jewish religion is much more an affair of ortho*praxy* than ortho*doxy*, behaving in the right way rather than believing the right things. And this is especially true of second temple Judaism, which tolerated a variety of different sects, distinguished from one another much more by their behaviour than by their beliefs. The problem is exacerbated by the fact that all the earliest followers of Jesus continued, as far as we can ascertain, to obey all the prescriptions of the Jewish religion. When changes were made they caused problems.

Hence the attractiveness of Fredriksen's suggestion that what really alarmed the persecutors was the disturbing effect of the new message upon Jewish-Gentile relations. It may be helpful to repeat her conclusions here:

> The belief in a Messiah known to have died must have struck many prima facie as odd or incredible; a Messiah without a Messianic age, irrelevant. But the enthusiastic proclamation of a Messiah executed very recently by Rome as a political trouble-maker – a *crucified* Messiah – combined with a vision of the approaching End *preached also to Gentiles* – this was dangerous. News of an impending Messianic kingdom, originating from Palestine, might trickle out via the ekklesia's Gentiles to the larger urban population. It was this (by far) larger, unaffiliated group that posed a real and serious threat. Armed with such a report, they might readily seek to alienate the local Roman colonial government, upon which Jewish urban populations often

depended for support and protection against hostile Gentile neighbours. The open dissemination of a Messianic message, in other words, put the entire Jewish community at risk.[13]

If this is so then the promise of salvation to the Gentiles will have been a constant preoccupation of the persecutors, and therefore of Paul himself, because it was the most important reason for their hostility. The suggestion that he began to be seduced by this idea even before his dramatic conversion is surely not too far-fetched. After all, it had its roots in the writings of the prophet Isaiah that he often quoted in his own letters. And if this is right then it is even more likely that his overwhelming sense of mission was with him from the beginning: the passages from Isaiah that came to have such a strong appeal for him could have been part of the traditional framework of understanding that is an inseparable element, as I have argued, of all mystical experience.

For Paul the future of the Gentiles was inextricably linked with the fate of Israel. He must have reflected long and hard on this question; and his passionate concern for the predicament of his own people was to find expression in three remarkable chapters of his letter to the Romans: some consider these chapters (9–11) to be the real heart of the letter.[14] Starting with an extraordinary outburst of anguish, he ends with an equally extraordinary oracle. 'I could wish', says Paul, 'that I myself were accursed and cut off from Christ for the sake of my brethren, my kinsmen by race' (9:3). Writing this, he is clearly obsessed with the thought that their rejection of his gospel might cause them to miss what he had come to regard as their only true salvation. Yet by the time he has reached the end of a truly tormented discussion he seems to have changed his mind.

This is how Paul states his triumphant conclusion:

I want you to understand this mystery,[15] brethren: a hardening has come upon part of Israel, until the full number of the

---

13. 'Judaism', 556.
14. E.g. Krister Stendahl, *Paul among the Jews and Gentiles*, 4, 85.
15. Only on two occasions, remarks Markus Bockmuehl, 'does Paul disclose to his readers an element of new teaching which he calls a μυστήριον': *Revelation and*

Gentiles come in, and so all Israel will be saved; as it is written:
> The Deliverer will come from Zion,
> he will banish ungodliness from Jacob;
> and this is my covenant with them
> when I take away their sins.   (11:25–27)

This startling volte-face has long exercised the ingenuity of commentators. How could Paul, suddenly confident, and sublimely so, of the ultimate salvation of 'all Israel', have reached this conclusion so quickly? A few commentators (Calvin for one) solve the problem by reinterpreting 'all Israel' to mean the (Christian) church. But 'Israel' is used with its ordinary reference *in the preceding verse*; and in any case since the Christian church cannot possibly be understood to include unconverted Jews, it does nothing to explain how Paul, in such manifest distress at the beginning of chapter 9, has had his anxieties so rapidly allayed.

Adolf Deissmann, one of the earliest commentators to insist on the primacy of religion over theology in Paul's career, cites these chapters as a paradigm example of what he calls Paul's prophetic vision: 'when he lays bare an intellectual problem and sets about solving it we immediately see the lion entangled in the meshes of a net. He becomes more and more entangled, seeking an escape this way and that in passionate defiance, until at the last moment, just as we fancied him caught, with one mighty stroke (*mit einem gewaltigen Prankenhieb*) he rips the net apart.'[16]

Deissmann has a good sense of the sheer vigour of Paul's conclusion, though the problem of which he speaks is surely no less emotional than intellectual. One solution is the proposal that the mystery of which Paul speaks was disclosed to him at the precise moment when he was dictating this part of the letter.[17] The very

---

Mystery, 170. The other is the passage we have just discussed:1 Cor 15:51–55. Bockmuehl comments interestingly on both texts, comparing them with 1 Thess 4:13–17.

16. 'Evangelium', 118.

17. David Aune (*Prophecy*, 252) is clearly attracted by this suggestion, which comes from B. Noack, 'Current and Backwater in the Epistle to the Romans', *ST* 19 (1965), 155–66. In 'Visionary' (165–6) Susan Niditch comments on certain dream reports in rabbinical literature which include the memory of a scriptural text: 'the interpretation thus becomes midrash and dream interpretation all at once'.

term 'mystery' supports this suggestion. Mysteries lie hidden until they are revealed. Paul is clearly speaking here of a revelation, a revelation, moreover, confirmed by a passage from the scriptures (actually a slightly adapted conflation of Isa 27:9 and 59:20–21) used to ground his vision of the ultimate redemption of Israel. It is an oracular saying in the strong sense. And of course although the texts in question are drawn from 'First' and 'Third' Isaiah, this is also a faithful reproduction of the original vision of the exilic prophet we call Second Isaiah, for whom the eventual coming-in of the Gentiles was always secondary to the salvation of Israel.

Biblical scholars spend much of their lives in juxtaposing passages from the scriptures; but at the time Paul wrote this passage we may assume that he was not actually looking for inspiration whilst scrolling through a copy of Isaiah. These were texts that came spontaneously to his mind in the act of writing.

From biblical times onwards believing Jews and Christians have turned frequently to the Bible in search of comfort and inspiration, some casually, others systematically.[18] Among the latter are to be numbered Jewish mystics practising meditation on the first pages of Genesis and Ezekiel.[19] In his comparison of Paul's Damascus road experience with that of the 'merkabah mystics', John Bowker offers a similar instance from the life of Rousseau, urging 'the dramatic effect in Rousseau's experience when he suddenly grasped the full meaning of the Dijon prize essay title, as he reflected on it on the way to visit Diderot at Vincennes; the title posed the question whether the progress of the arts and sciences tended to purify or corrupt morals'.[20] Here is the passage in question:

> If anything was ever like a sudden inspiration it was the impulse that surged up in me as I read that [the title]. Suddenly I felt my mind dazzled by a thousand lights; crowds of lively ideas presented themselves at once, with a force and confusion that threw me into an inexpressible trouble; I felt my head seized with a vertigo like that of intoxication. A violent palpitation oppressed me,

---

18. The most famous single instance is probably Augustine's eventual response to the command 'tolle, lege' (take up and read).
19. See Excursus II: Merkabah Mysticism.
20. '"Merkabah" Visions', 171, n. 1.

made me gasp for breath, and being unable any longer to breathe as I walked, I let myself drop under one of the trees of the way-side, and there I spent half an hour in such a state of agitation that when I got up I perceived the whole of the front of my vest moistened with my own tears which I had shed unawares. Oh, sir, if ever I could have written even the quarter of what I saw and felt under that tree, with what clarity should I have revealed all the contradictions of the social system, with what force would I have exposed all the abuses of our institutions, in what simple terms would I have demonstrated that man is naturally good, and that it is through these institutions alone that men become bad.[21]

Part at least of Bowker's reason for citing this experience of Rousseau is that it took place *on a road*; but it is perhaps more apposite as an illustration of how a visionary experience can be triggered by the reading of a text. And if the title of a prize essay could have such an effect, how much more the memory of a page in the Bible![22]

Surprising as it is, Paul's sudden vision is really only a reversal of the idea that had so angered him when he joined the persecutors of the new Jesus movement. For according to that conception the Gentiles' eventual turning to God did *not* involve conversion in the strong sense, actually becoming Jewish, and therefore, for males, being circumcised.[23] Paul had suddenly realized that Israel too, through the generous benevolence of God, might be saved without formal acceptance of the gospel.

Of course there is a contradiction here. Right up to the point at which Paul discloses the mystery, his entire argument has assumed

---

21. C. W. Hendel, *Citizen of Geneva: Selections from the Letters of J-J. Rousseau* (New York, 1937), 208

22. As Rousseau's experience shows, the Bible is far from being the only text capable of engendering inspiration. The best-known examples in literature are probably the legendary feats of chivalry performed by Don Quixote after his perusal of the tales of Amadis of Gaul and the less glorious behaviour provoked in Emma Bovary by her eager reading of the trashy romances that were the pulp fiction of the 19th century. But my own favourite example of what one might call exegesis in practice is the first kiss of Paolo and Francesca as they were read-ing together the story of Lancelot's love for Queen Guinevere. It was the book and its author, comments Dante, that was the go-between here: 'Galeotto fu il libro, et qui lo scrisse/quel giorno più non vi legemmo avante' (*Inferno*, Canto V, 127–38).

23. See Fredriksen, 'Judaism', 547–8.

that there is a single road to salvation: faith in Jesus Christ. However many or however few are to be saved, this is the road they would have to take. So we are forced to ask whether the startling vision of 11:25–26 involves a retraction of the premise on which not only the previous discussion but indeed Paul's entire career has been based, the imperative need to preach the gospel.

By far the best solution to this problem is to be found in a little book by Ed Sanders in the Oxford Past Master series. Were we to confine ourselves to human history as we know it, the present age, we should be forced to recognize that Paul is confronted by an irresolvable dilemma: 'if faith in Christ is an absolute condition of salvation, why did God choose Israel in the first place?' His solution, Sanders points out, 'involves a triumph of what is now called lateral thinking'. He escapes the dilemma *by changing categories*, by introducing a new dimension into the equation, one that 'transcends the period of human choice and focuses on the boundless mercy of God.... Israel is not singled out for salvation by a separate route and distinguished from Gentiles, only some of whom are saved; Israel is simply a part of God's final victory, which will embrace the entire creation.'

Sanders is fully aware that the elements of his solution cannot easily be reconciled: 'How could Paul, on the one hand, think that it mattered desperately that people came to faith in Christ, say that it determined whether or not they shared Christ's life, and predict destruction for those who rejected his message ... and, on the other hand, say that God would save everyone and everything? What did he really think?'

Sanders's answer is 'both, almost certainly'. But he acknowledges that they cannot both be put into the same logical or theoretical system, largely because, underlying them, there are quite distinct images and figures. On one side there are the images of the judgement seat and of *the athletic contest*: 'When Paul thought in one of these images, he naturally thought in terms of innocence or guilt or winners and losers.' On the other hand there is the image of God as omnipotent king of creation: he created the world and he will save all that he created. 'It is this image which takes control in the closing verses of Romans 11.'[24]

---

24. E. P. Sanders, *Paul*, 125–7.

This is a brilliant solution. I would only add that it is not strictly speaking a *theological* solution. It is less a matter of thought, even lateral thought, than of an oracular insight, one that reverses, or rather complements, the insight with which Paul began. This too came to him as a sudden revelation. This too was grounded in the words of the most universalistic of all Israel's great prophets. Before becoming a theologian, and in the very act of becoming an apostle, Paul undertook the responsibility for putting into effect God's plan for the world. To fail to recognize that this task stemmed directly from Israel's prophetic tradition is to ignore one of Paul's own fundamental insights. Paradoxically, therefore, if we are to do justice to the riches of Paul's religious heritage we must be prepared to bestow on him the grand title of prophet that he was too modest to claim for himself.

7

Paul the Charismatic

The last two chapters will focus on a single topic, huge, elusive, and all-important. This is the topic of the spirit. First we need to consider the operation of the spirit within one of the communities Paul founded, the church of Corinth. In the last chapter, returning to the idea of Paul the shaman, we will turn our attention to the role of the spirit in Paul's own life.

The spirit

One has to start by emphasizing the part spirits – or the spirit – played in the lives of people in the ancient world. Any unpredictable or inexplicable event, anything beyond human control or outside normal categories of explanation, was ascribed, if you were a pagan, to the work of gods, goddesses or demons, or, if you were a Jew, either to the providential power of God or else to the malign influence of wicked spirits or the devil. The sun, the moon and the stars circled the earth without gravity; the clouds clashed in the sky without electricity; and the world had not yet been blessed with sociologists and psychologists eager to explain to men and women the seemingly irrational elements in their own behaviour.[1] At the

---

1. For the evidence from the abundant writings of the early church see the excellent survey by Heinrich Weinel in *Die Wirkungen des Geistes*, a book specifically intended to follow up the similarly entitled work by Hermann Gunkel published a decade earlier. Weinel himself remarks after a preliminary run-through of the material that 'whenever the early church speaks of spirit and spirits it is always a matter of a perception based on frequent occurrences of real experiences. Accordingly any inquiry concerning the Holy Spirit should not proceed

turn of the era neither science nor philosophy, Greek or Roman, had made much headway in any of these areas, and fifteen hundred years later, at the end of the sixteenth century, Hamlet could still complain to Horatio that 'there are more things in heaven and earth' than can be accounted for ('dreamt of') in his philosophy.

Writing of a world in which Christianity had already gained some foothold, Peter Brown remarks upon the increasing importance of a belief in demons: 'Outside Christianity, the demons had remained ambivalent (rather like ghosts). They were invoked to explain sudden and incongruous misfortunes, deviations from normal behaviour such as riots, plagues and inappropriate love-affairs. They were as widely invoked, and caused as little anxiety, as microbes do today. Christianity, however, made the demons central to its view of the world.'[2]

This is not quite true of Paul. Not that his sense of evil was any less than that of his Christian successors, but the demons played a smaller role. For him the enemies ranged against the spirit, that is to say God's spirit, were primarily three: sin, flesh, and (much more equivocally, as we shall see) the law. He does occasionally mention Satan, the great adversary (Rom 16:20; 1 Cor 5:5; 7:5; 2 Cor 2:11; 11:14; 12:7; 1 Thess 2:18); and after dismissing pagan idols as not worth a thought, he cannot suppress a shudder of disgust at the idea of sharing what he calls 'the cup of demons' (1 Cor 10:21). Still, his vision of the world was not quite the one described by Peter Brown, and it seems to me unlikely that he would have fully approved of the warning issued in his name by one of his followers, which anticipates the later Christian viewpoint: 'we are not contending against flesh and blood, but against the principalities, against the powers, against the world rulers of this present darkness, against the spiritual hosts of wickedness in the heavenly places' (Eph 6:12). At the same time Paul was no whit less cautious than the author of Ephesians, no less aware of the dangers that surrounded the fledgling Christian churches.

from teaching or teachings about the spirit, but must *take as its starting-point the experiences* on the basis of which the teaching has arisen or to which it refers', 63 (emphasis in the original).
2. *The World of Late Antiquity*, 54.

The forces of evil, however conceived, were real. Above all, they were *powerful*. Not, though, as powerful as God. Like all good Jews Paul was sure that God controlled from afar the destiny of nations, and that of individuals too. Though remote and, in himself, inaccessible, God frequently intervened directly in human affairs. These interventions, which by their very nature manifested his power, were generally ascribed to his spirit. We have already seen the regular association of spirit and power in Paul's writings.

The Greek word for spirit, πνεῦμα, is neuter. The Hebrew, רוח, is feminine, a grammatical fact exploited by the early Syriac fathers to insert a feminine presence at the heart of the Trinity.[3] (The Latin word, *spiritus*, is masculine, which would have caused Paul no problems.) More important are the associations of the word, for, like 'grace' and 'salvation', the word 'spirit' in his writings resembles a coin whose image has been rubbed away by over-use: it continues to be passed from hand to hand and fills many a blank on many a page, but we have to make a real effort if we are to get any sense of what it meant for Paul, a vivid presence informing all that he wrote, and indeed all that he thought.

The spirit people

Paul was convinced that all Christians possessed the spirit. Writing to the Corinthians, he uses the term ἀρραβών, 'first instalment' (2 Cor 1:22; 5:5).[4] To have the spirit in this way meant that one could bank on the remainder being fully paid later. This would have to wait until the resurrection, because according to Paul, the spirit is only partially available in this life. We may think this metaphor infelicitous, and although it does get part of Paul's meaning across it conveys nothing of the sheer *power* of the spirit. To do this, I

3. See Sebastian Brock, 'The Holy Spirit'; '"Come, compassionate Mother..., come, Holy Spirit"'. The evangelist John, confronted with an analogous situation, was compelled to change the word. Unable to cope with the idea of a female incarnation (for 'wisdom' is feminine in both Greek and Hebrew), he used the term λόγος instead. That is why 'the Word [*not* Wisdom] was made flesh' (John 1:14).
4. Cf. Rom 8:23, where the equivalent term 'first-fruits of the spirit' (ἀπαρχὴ τοῦ πνεύματος) is used.

believe we need to employ a metaphor which was not available to Paul and which in any case he did not need. To enter imaginatively into this strange world there is some advantage, I suggest, in thinking of the spirit as a kind of electricity.

I remember as a boy reading a series of primitive science fiction stories, probably in the *Wizard* or *Hotspur*, about a man who could charge himself up with electricity like a living battery, and then went round helping people who found their normal source cut off. Confronted with a power failure in a hospital, say, or a submarine, or a factory, all he had to do was to grasp a couple of wires and the lights would go on again. Anyone imbued with the spirit, above all Paul himself, has a similar kind of power, one that can be applied in a variety of situations where brute force or manual dexterity is of no avail. Instead of entitling this chapter 'Paul the Charismatic' I might have called it 'Paul the Dynamo', which could be equally well defended on the basis of Paul's frequent use of the word δύναμις, 'power', in connection with the spirit.

How, according to Paul, was the spirit conveyed? How did he manage to transmit this energy to his converts, so as to charge them up? The answer, however surprising we may find it, is quite clear: by preaching the gospel. In his Second Letter to the Corinthians he envisages another preacher approaching them and proclaiming a completely different gospel. By accepting this, he concludes, they would be charging themselves up with a different spirit (2 Cor 11:4). What this other spirit would be like, how its power would be focused, he does not say. In all probability he has not fully imagined this alternative spirit; he is speaking rhetorically. But he is clearly convinced that the gospel was the cable through which the current passed.

Elsewhere, attacking the Galatians for supposing that the spirit was supplied to them as a consequence of their observance of the Jewish law, he tells them the true alternative: what turned on the current was 'the proclamation that has the power to elicit faith' (Gal 3:2).[5] Paul concludes with a question: 'Does the one who now supplies the Spirit to you and works wonders among you do so

---

5. Here and elsewhere when quoting Galatians I make use of J. L. Martyn's translation in his Anchor Bible Commentary, though without always following it exactly.

because you observe the law, or is he working these wonders through the proclamation that elicits your faith?' (3:5). There the one who supplies the spirit (an odd expression, we might think) is either God, or Christ or, as I am inclined to think, Paul himself. In any case Paul is perfectly prepared to admit that the most obvious indication of the presence of spirit is the working of miracles: there could be no more striking proof of power.

The Greek word for miracles here is δυνάμεις (the only instance of the word in Galatians). Earlier, writing to the Thessalonians, he had asserted that his gospel had come to them not only in word, but also 'in power and in the Holy Spirit and with full conviction' (1 Thess 1:5), and I think we may assume that there too the power (δύναμις) was manifested in miracles (δυνάμεις).[6]

According to Paul, then, this huge concentration of supernatural energy was transferred to the new churches through their acceptance of the law-free gospel. How could he possibly think that such a dramatic result could be achieved simply by a shift in religious allegiance? Because he saw this as equivalent to his own much more traumatic conversion years earlier.[7] In fact he seems to have believed that his converts were somehow privileged to share in his own vision of 'the light of the glory of Christ, who is the image of God' (2 Cor 4:4).

Let us look a little more closely at how Paul continued to perceive the role of the spirit in the churches that he founded. The Thessalonians, who caused him no concern in this regard, were urged not to quench the spirit (1 Thess 5:19), the metaphor here being not a wind but a blazing fire. To the Galatians he spoke of a fruit-bearing tree (5:22) and of a harvest from a well-sown field (6:8). But the church that gave him really serious trouble in its response to his teaching concerning the spirit, and consequently prompted the most significant development of his own conception of the spirit, was the church at Corinth. The so-called First Letter to the Corinthians (at

---

6. For an argument that possession of the spirit resulted in observable phenomena see D. J. Lull, *The Spirit in Galatia*.

7. Arguably too, though I do not wish to engage in this debate, the bestowal of the spirit was connected very early with the rite of baptism. This undoubtedly became before long a ritual of formal entry into the community – or, as van Gennep puts it, a rite of passage. But for Paul (*contra* Schweitzer) the sacrament was not the most important thing.

the best estimate one of five or six that he wrote to them)[8] contains both Paul's reaction to various reports that had reached him about their goings-on, and his response to a number of questions that some of them had raised themselves.

For our purposes the most important of these questions is the one he addresses in three chapters towards the end of the letter, 12–14. There is an ambiguity in the Greek phrase that heads these chapters: Περὶ δὲ τῶν πνευματικῶν. Paul's answer shows that he takes the phrase to refer to spiritual gifts, and although initially he avoids the term 'spiritual', preferring instead to speak of gifts, charismata, in chapter 14 he harks back to the language of the original question, and the translator has to acknowledge the shift in terminology by adding the word 'spiritual'. The reference is identical, and there is not much difference in meaning between charismata and spiritual gifts, but it may well be that those who put the question were hoping that he would say something about the self-styled spirit *people* who were causing so much trouble in the community with their pretensions and their posturing.[9]

One of Paul's problems here is that he could not very well object to the name these people had chosen for themselves. Indeed, in other circumstances he might well have coined it himself to refer to all Christians, for this is how he thought of them – as people of the spirit. So he could neither object to the name, nor indeed to their slogan, πάντα ἔξεστιν, 'anything goes', for it was simply an alternative way of proclaiming Christian freedom, a benefit he had been the first to extol. The best he could do by way of riposte, and it is not a particularly good one, is to add the demurrer, ἀλλ' οὐ πάντα συμφέρει, 'but not everything helps': 'anything goes but not everything helps' (10:23). What does not help is clear from the context, which also indicates the nature of the aberrations into which the spirit people had strayed.

In the first instance there follows a denunciation of sexual permissiveness, the frequentation of the brothels for which Corinth was

8. The precise nature of Paul's correspondence with the Corinthians is a complex question that cannot be entered into here. Whether you put the number of his letters at five (Murphy-O'Connor: *Paul*, 52–6) or six (Thrall: *Commentary*, i, 3–49) depends on whether you see 2 Corinthians 9 as a postscript or as a separate letter.

9. The Greek genitive (πνευματικῶν: 12:1) could in principle be either masculine (spirit people) or neuter (spiritual gifts).

renowned from way back in the classical era, when Aristophanes (*fr.* 354) invented the word Κορινθιάζεσθαι to denote precisely this practice. 'Shun fornication', urges Paul: 'Every other sin which a man commits is outside the body. Do you not know that your body is a temple of the Holy Spirit within you, which you have from God?' (6:18–19). It is an extraordinary image, calculated to bring up with a start a group of men (and possibly women also) who prided themselves on the title 'spirit people'. 'You are not your own', Paul concludes: 'you were bought with a price. So glorify God in your body' (6:19–20). He must have found their claim to unfettered freedom particularly galling, inasmuch as he had himself lauded freedom as one of the enormous privileges accompanying the gift of the spirit: 'the Lord is the spirit, and where the spirit of the Lord is, there is freedom' (2 Cor 3:17). Centuries later John Milton experienced a similar sense of outrage: 'Licence they mean when they cry liberty.' One individual in the community had committed incest, a sin even more shocking than fornication.

A very different kind of misdemeanour, involving scandalous behaviour during the Eucharistic meal that Paul had called the Lord's Supper, prompted one of Paul's angriest outbursts. People were bringing their own food without offering to share it with others, and Paul was furious. Invoking the slogan of Christian freedom, 'anything goes', was for him no justification for such selfish and divisive behaviour.

Besides their general sexual permissiveness and their selfishness in ignoring the feelings and needs of those who could not afford to bring their own food to the Eucharistic meal, the spirit people went blithely on eating the meat of animals sacrificed to idols without sparing a thought for the scandal this might cause to those whom Paul called the weaker brethren. Even more seriously, they seem to have considered that their spiritual existence, which was their pretext for indulging in sexual vices, also entitled them to ignore Paul's teaching about the bodily resurrection, perhaps to the point of denying it altogether.

Paul regarded the self-styled spirit people with an anger tinged with contempt. The extent of his anger can be gauged from a bitterly sarcastic passage earlier in the letter. He begins his attack on the 'spirit people' (πνευματικοί) like this: 'I could not address you as spirit people, but as men of the flesh, as babes in Christ. I fed you with milk, not solid food; for you were not ready for it; and even yet you are not ready, for you are still of the flesh' (3:1–3). The πνευματικοί were convinced that they had already reached spiritual maturity, that they were, in Paul's language, τέλειοι, mature or perfect (see 2:6; 14:20). To address them as babes, νήπιοι, was the worst of insults. But Paul is not yet through with them. He concludes his harangue with an outburst of sarcastic invective as extreme as anything in his writings: 'Already you are filled! Already you have become rich! Without us you have become kings! ... We are fools for Christ's sake, but you are wise in Christ. We are weak, but you are strong' (4:8, 10).

We have already observed how Paul thinks in polar opposites: wisdom and folly, strength and weakness, wealth and poverty, maturity and infancy. At this point I want to cut some corners by quoting directly a couple of passages from Paul's near-contemporary, the Jewish philosopher Philo of Alexandria:

> But seeing that for babes (νήπιοι) milk is food, but for grown men (τέλειοι) wheaten bread, there must also be soul-nourishment such as is milk-like, suited to the time of childhood ... and such as is adapted to grown men in the shape of instructions leading the way through wisdom and temperance and all virtue.
>
> *Agr.* 9 (Whitaker)

'The mere infant (νήπιον παιδίον)', he explains elsewhere, 'bears the same relation to the mature man (ἀνὴρ τέλειος) as the sophist does to the sage (σοφός), or school subjects to the sciences which deal with virtues' (*Sobr.* 9).

For Philo wisdom was the ultimate goal, the summit of human attainment: small wonder that he reserves it for the mature. Here is a second passage:

> For wisdom (τὸ σοφόν) is rather God's friend than his servant (δοῦλος) ... But whoever has this portion [wisdom] has passed beyond the bounds of human happiness. He alone is nobly born (εὐγενής) ... the possessor not of riches, but of all riches (οὐ πλούσιος, ἀλλὰ πάμπλουτος) ... not merely of high repute, but glorious (οὐκ εὔδοξος, ἀλλ' εὐκλεής) ... sole king (μόνος βασιλεύς) ... sole freeman (μόνος ἐλεύθερος)....
>
> *Sobr.* 55–7 (Coulson); cf. *Virt.* 174

Even without Philo's help it would be possible to infer from Paul's ironical comments in 1 Corinthians 3–4 how these people saw themselves, and the kind of claims they were making. 'They apparently viewed themselves as being *wise, powerful, nobly born, filled, rich, kings* and *glorious*, as opposed to *foolish, weak, dishonoured* (i.e. σοφοί, δύνατοι/ἰσχυροί, εὐγενεῖς, κεκορεσμένοι, etc., vs μωροί, ἀσθενεῖς, ἄτιμοι).'[10]

Since Paul cannot be held responsible for instilling in the heads of the spirit people ideas that he obviously regarded as shocking and reprehensible, how did they come by them? One possible answer is: from the teaching of Paul's rival Apollos. Described by Luke (Acts 18:24) as λόγιος, that is to say both learned and eloquent, this personage hailed from Alexandria, and so it is a good guess that he will have come under the influence of Philo. If this is so, and if he passed on some of Philo's ideas to the Corinthians, then we have some explanation of the kind of language they were using. Whether Paul himself recognized the allusions to Philo is hard to know.

So much then for the spirit people themselves, and for Paul's way of responding to their claims. We must now turn to his attempt to put an end to the disruption in the community that had ensued both from their rhetorical self-aggrandisement and from their shockingly divisive behaviour.

Building up

Paul had two problems. It was as if, to return to our electrical metaphor, he had to deal with a severed cable that was flailing around and sending off sparks in all directions. To switch off the power altogether was no solution: 'quench not the spirit'. It was a matter of harnessing this abundant but random energy. At the same time there could be no question of renouncing the principle of Christian freedom, for that would have opened the way to a return of the rule of law that he had had to fend off in Galatia. He was

---

10. See Richard A. Horsley, 'How can some of you say?', 205. This is one of a series of fine articles in which Horsley turns to Philo to explain what was causing Paul so much trouble at Corinth. See also: 'Pneumatikos vs Psychikos'; 'Wisdom of Words'; 'Gnosis in Corinth'.

forced to have recourse to the rhetorical skills in which, with a characteristic display of self-deprecation, he would later proclaim himself to be lacking. What he had to do was to find an alternative principle, one to which he could appeal without contradicting the principle of liberty on which he set such store. And this set him a further problem. He could not appeal directly to his own authority. If he did that, he would expose himself to the sneering rejoinder that whilst preaching freedom he was practising oppression. He had to find a kind of interior discipline, one that could be qualified, in Kant's phrase, as a principle of autonomy and not of heteronomy.

First, however, before ordering the gifts, he had to re-establish some kind of harmony in the community. The first of his two lists of charismata, therefore, underlines above all else the fact that they are all manifestations of a single spirit: evil spirits are many and various, but the good spirit, the Spirit of God, has no rivals.

Here is his first list:

> There are varieties of gifts, but the same Spirit; and there are varieties of service, but the same Lord; and there are varieties of working, but it is the same God who inspires them all in everyone. To each is given the manifestation of the Spirit for the common good. To one is given through the Spirit the utterance of wisdom, and to another the utterance of knowledge according to the same Spirit, to another faith by the same Spirit, to another gifts of healing by the one Spirit; to another the working of miracles, to another prophecy, to another the ability to distinguish between spirits, to another the interpretation of tongues. All these are inspired by one and the same Spirit, who apportions to each one individually as he wills   (1 Cor 12:4–11)

The community bubbles and seethes, like a saucepan on the boil. No one knows when or where the next convulsion will occur. Each convulsion is different, but each displays the driving energy that informs the whole. It would be pointless to try and put the lid on, and Paul would not dream of doing so.

'To each is given the manifestation of the Spirit', and if spirit then, *ipso facto*, a kind of authority. There is then no easy distinction to be drawn between power and authority. Paul, obviously enough, is anxious to establish his authority, but he cannot place it outside, and certainly not above, the spiritual power from which it is derived.

It is instructive at this point to compare Paul's nuanced view of charismatic authority with the composite picture built up by Max Weber in the section of his *Sociology of Religion* where he sets prophet against priest as exemplifying two alternative strategies of authority in religious communities. Weber gets the word 'charism' from Paul, and in his wide-ranging discussion he mentions 'the carefully cultivated postulate that the apostle, prophet or teacher of ancient Christianity' (note the deliberate allusion to 1 Cor 12:28) must be careful to give his services free, or, as Weber puts it, 'must not professionalize his religious proclamations'[11] – a clear allusion to Paul's argument in chapter 9 of the same letter. Yet the idea of the prophet who 'exerts his power simply by virtue of his personal gifts' as opposed to the priest who derives his authority solely from his hierarchical office is hard to square with Paul's determination to impose a structure within the various manifestations of the spirit and not to replace these with an external, institutionalized authority. There are no priests in Paul's churches.

Instead, Paul attempts to bring the people who manifest these gifts into line by stressing the need for them to function harmoniously together like the various parts of the body. Accordingly he produces a finely developed metaphor of the model community, in which each individual respects and values the rest; just as the eye never says to the hand 'I have no need of you' and the head never says to the feet 'I have no need of you' (12:21). At the same time it is obviously not lost on Paul that the ideal is not matched by the reality. One has the distinct impression that when he speaks of the respectful treatment accorded to what he calls the less honourable (ἀτιμότερα) parts of the body he may have particular people in mind. Quite conceivably this is a kind of parable *à clef* that his readers will know how to interpret.

Having dealt with the divisiveness in the community by establishing a principle of harmony, Paul now has to find a principle of order. He starts by drawing up a list of people endowed with 'spiritual gifts': 'God has appointed in the church first apostles, second prophets, third teachers, then workers of miracles, then

11. *The Sociology of Religion*, 48.

healers, helpers, administrators, speakers in various kinds of tongues' (12:28). The most bothersome of these gifts is the last, glossolalia, speaking in tongues. This has nothing to do with having a gift for languages or indeed with any kind of articulated speech. It is at best a kind of melodious babble, and people giving utterance in this way may have no idea at all what they are saying: hence the need for an interpreter.[12] Paul sees nothing wrong with glossolalia as such; in fact he thanks God that he speaks in tongues 'more than you all' (14:18). It bothers him in the first place because there is no guarantee that it will be understood by other members of the congregation. 'If lifeless instruments, such as the flute or the harp,' he says, 'do not give distinct notes, how will anyone know what is played? And if the bugle gives an indistinct sound, who will prepare for battle? So with yourselves; if you in a tongue utter speech that is not intelligible, how will anyone know what is said?' (14:7–9). It bothers him in the second place because it is evidently the gift most flaunted by the spirit people and has the effect of setting those able to exercise it apart from (and, in their own opinion, above) everybody else. After complaining about the sheer incomprehensibility of this strange speech, he concludes: 'since you are eager for manifestations of the spirit, strive to excel in building up the church' (14:12).

Here he has found the principle of organization he has been looking for. He uses the word οἰκοδομεῖν, literally translated into Latin as *aedificare*. (The English borrowing from the Latin, 'edify', has a very different resonance.) He will rate one gift higher than another if it is of service to the whole group; so, quite logically, the ability to *translate* the glossolalia is reckoned to be superior to the actual speaking in tongues. At the heart of his discussion he places the famous chapter on love, ἀγάπη. Although missing from the two lists of charismata given in the preceding chapter (12:7–11, 28–30), love obviously has a strong cohesive force: it builds up; which is why, hard on the heels of the panegyric on love, Paul continues with the exhortation: 'make love your aim, and earnestly desire the spiritual gifts, especially that you may prophesy' (14:1).

Yet behind the ostensible deprecation of the more flamboyant spiritual gifts there lies a not-so-sneaking admiration. Paul does not

12. See Felicitas Goodman, *Speaking in Tongues*; and the comments of Philip Esler in *First Christians*, 40–51.

let the Corinthians forget that he speaks in tongues more than all of them (14:18). Nor should we forget that he ascribes his success in winning converts to the most spectacular gift of the lot, the power to work miracles. As he drew up his list of spiritual gifts it cannot have escaped him that many of his readers will have responded by reflecting admiringly how well the list illustrated the numerous services that he himself had performed for the community. There is not an item on his list in which he was not supreme. 'Are all apostles?' he asks, 'Are all prophets? Are all teachers? Do all work miracles? Do all possess gifts of healing? Do all speak with tongues? Do all interpret?' (12:29–30). The answer of course is 'no, not all', but also, tucked away, 'Paul, certainly'. What a man! Behind the facade of deconstruction, if I may be permitted a final Irishism, Paul is actually assembling an elaborate argument to buttress his own position. I do not doubt that his central concern is what he says it is: the building-up of the community. ('It is in the sight of God that we have been speaking', he tells the Corinthians in his second letter, 'and all for your upbuilding [*aedificatio*]' (2 Cor 12:19).) But to achieve this aim he needs to write the kind of letter that he was to describe, somewhat wryly, as 'weighty and strong' (2 Cor 10:10). The effectiveness of what he writes largely depends upon his readers' recognition of his authority. And that authority is, in the strongest possible sense, a *spiritual* authority, deriving from his own exercise of the spiritual gifts he is listing and assessing in these very chapters. As Hans Windisch puts it: the apostle's ἐξουσία [that is to say, both his power and his authority] is spiritual (*etwas Pneumatisches*), an indefinable spiritual entity.[13] It has to be, for it is inseparable from the spiritual gifts of which, though he would never dream of saying so, Paul is the supreme exponent and the supreme master. Equally, these gifts are inseparable from the spirit itself – the spirit of God, the spirit of Christ, the spirit that 'has been poured into our hearts' (Rom 5:5).

A further proof of the spiritual nature of Paul's authority is the fact that it could be exercised at a distance: 'For though absent in body I am present in spirit, and being present (ὡς παρών) I have already pronounced judgement in the name of the Lord Jesus...' (1 Cor 5:3–4). 'Present in spirit' is such a familiar expression that it

13. *Paulus und Christus*, 176.

may fairly be called a cliché. But we have only to glance at the context in which it was first employed to see that Paul felt able to project his presence across the Aegean Sea all the way from Ephesus, which is where 1 Corinthians was composed.

J. H. Schütz, in a much-praised book,[14] has developed a subtle argument designed to show that the 'legitimacy' of Paul derives from the gospel. But if that is true it is true precisely because the gospel, as Paul sees it, is what confers or, as he quaintly puts it, 'supplies' the spirit. Without his mastery of spiritual gifts, his power to perform cures and miracles, his prophetic and interpretative skills, his speaking in tongues – all powers that constituted him as a shaman or at least as a shaman-like figure – Paul's authority, as he was only too aware, would vanish, and with it his ability to assist in the building-up, the *aedificatio*, of the community.

Paul's authority

Before long, as it happens, his authority did come under threat, once again in a manner that he found hard to counter. In 1 Corinthians, as we have seen, he had established his authority quite subtly, by reminding his readers of his own supremacy in the domain of spiritual gifts. But the spirit people, who must have been infuriated by his attack, responded by questioning whether there was any basis for his claims. Either they themselves or else some outsiders who had succeeded in impressing them by the extent of their own spiritual powers[15] actually had the effrontery to borrow the proudest of Paul's titles, that of apostle; with the result that Paul now began to speak, ironically no doubt, but with some bitterness also, of 'super-apostles' (ὑπερλίαν ἀπόστολοι, 11:5; 12:11). Moreover, he had had to pay the price for his sarcastic mockery of the spirit people by himself becoming the target of some unpleasant jokes. His enemies were even brutal enough to make scathing remarks about his physical appearance: 'His letters are weighty and

---

14. *Paul and the Anatomy of Apostolic Authority*.
15. Many scholars, Murphy-O'Connor among them, think that the 'super-apostles' were Judaizers, welcomed by the spirit people as useful allies. This is a plausible view, but hard to prove.

strong, but his bodily presence is weak, and his speech of no account' (2 Cor 10:10). Not nice! Not nice at all!

Worst of all, though, was the threat to his authority. One indication of his concern is the extraordinary frequency of the verb συνίστασθαι in this letter,[16] a word generally used of self-commendation. 'Are we beginning to commend ourselves again?' he asks in 3:1; to which the answer can only be: 'You are indeed!' The truth is that he has rather painted himself into a corner. His heavy emphasis on the spiritual gifts, along with the unspoken implication that he outdid everybody else not just in glossolalia (which he mentions specifically) but in all the others too, had proved, from the rhetorical point of view (that is to say as an exercise in persuasion), utterly disastrous; and he obviously realized that it was no use simply repeating these claims. That would be like trying to win an argument by shouting louder.

On the other hand he could not go back on what he had already said. He had been accused of vacillation when he changed his travel plans and deferred a second visit: 'Do I make my plans like a worldly man, ready to say Yes and No at once? As surely as God is faithful, our word to you has not been Yes and No' (1:17–18), a remark that is best interpreted as an indignant rebuttal of the charge of way-wardness. So if Paul was not prepared to shift his ground, he had to find a way of 'commending himself' without appearing to do so. He could not go back on his previous letter by denying altogether the value of spiritual gifts; nor could he continue to convince the Corinthians of his superiority in that domain.

His solution to this dilemma is remarkable. The disparaging comments about his personal appearance were easy enough to shrug off. The spirit people will have found it difficult to counter Paul's clever rejoinder, one that Philo, something of a hero to the spirit people, would certainly have applauded, that it is not the body, fragile as a piece of crockery, that counts, but what it contains: 'we have this treasure in earthen vessels, to show that the transcendent power belongs to God and not to us' (4:7). Much more worrying was the charge of self-aggrandisement, self-proclamation, a charge that may

---

16. 3:1; 4:2 *bis*; 5:12; 6:4 *bis*; 7:1; 10:12, 18 *bis*; 12:11. Elsewhere 5 occurrences at most: Rom 3:5; 5:8; 16:1; Gal 2:18. (In Col 1:17 the word has an entirely different meaning.)

well have been provoked by his earlier letter, the accusation that he had been motivated throughout by a determination to establish his own authority, to regain control. This he simply denies: 'for what we proclaim is not ourselves, but Jesus Christ as Lord, with ourselves as your servants, for Jesus' sake' (4:5).

Although he may have come to regret the way he tackled the pretensions of the spirit people, he could not back off completely. Above all, he had to continue to maintain the authority and power of the spirit itself. His solution was the reversal of values which we considered in Chapter 4, the discovery of *power in adversity*: 'I will all the more gladly boast of my adversities, that the power of Christ may rest upon me. For the sake of Christ, then, I am content with adversities, insults, hardships, persecutions, and calamities; for when I am weak, then I am strong' (12:9–10). Regarded simply as a rhetorical ploy, this is a brilliant move, trumping all his opponents' aces. But I have to say in conclusion that I think it is more than that. No one would have put up with the incredible hardships that Paul had to endure simply in order to win an argument. Nor did Paul ever really believe that spiritual authority resided in the ability to dazzle people with conjuring tricks. To get to the heart of his *teaching* about the spirit we must abandon theology and return to our central theme of Paul's *religion*. That will be the theme of the final chapter.

8

Paul the Possessed

In the preceding chapter we noticed that the all-important topic of the spirit has two distinct aspects. There is first of all the part played by the spirit in the lives of Paul's converts and in the way he established his ἐξουσία (power and authority) over them: we concluded that this must be seen as something essentially spiritual. In the second place there is the role of the spirit in Paul's own life. This remains to be considered. Despite an extended discussion of Paul's vision and call on the Damascus road, I have thus far said virtually nothing about the part played by the spirit (or the spirits) at that critical moment of his career. This is where it is necessary to return to a theme that has been touched upon only incidentally in the last five chapters: the comparison with shamanism.

In order to avoid the difficulties, both practical and theoretical, that accumulate as soon as one tries to establish a *genealogical* (or *convergent*) connection between Paul and shamanism, I want to use this comparison here as, in J. Z. Smith's phrase, 'a disciplined exaggeration in the service of knowledge'. Anyone offended by the suggestion that Paul was a shaman is welcome to think of it as a metaphor.

Where Paul particularly resembles the typical shaman is in his relation to the spirit world, and I hope I will be forgiven for repeating here the statement of Hermann Gunkel that first encouraged me to embark on this project: to Paul, he says, his life was an enigma whose solution lay for him in his teaching regarding the πνεῦμα (spirit): 'to us [Paul's] teaching regarding the πνεῦμα is an enigma whose solution is to be found in his life and only in his life'.[1]

---

1. *Influence*, 105–6.

Juxtapose this with the authoritative conclusion of M. S. Shiroko-goroff, that

> In all Tungus languages this term ['shaman'] refers to *persons of both sexes who have mastered spirits, who at their will can introduce these spirits into themselves and use their power over the spirits in their own interests, particularly helping other people who suffer from the spirits; in such a capacity they may possess a complex of special methods for dealing with the spirits.*[2]

And he adds: 'The shaman is supposed to have, at the beginning of his career, at least one spirit (usually, a complex one) with the help of which he may master other spirits, or at least know them.'

Paul, as we have seen, only ever speaks of one spirit, that is the holy spirit: when he evokes the possibility of a different spirit, conveyed by 'a different gospel' (2 Cor 11:4), he is speaking ironically. The expression 'unclean spirit', common in the gospels, is missing from Paul's letters. He does occasionally refer to the devil, and he is fully aware of the demons conjured up in pagan sacrifices; but his favourite word for the power of evil, always used in the singular, is 'Sin'. This he envisages as a kind of cosmic force doing battle with grace on a global scale, and possessing the frightening capacity of taking up residence in the human soul. For Paul the real world, to an extent which is seldom realized, is a world populated by spirits. If we wish to enter imaginatively into this world one possible route is that of shamanism.

When developing this point in Chapter 2 I focused more particularly on Paul's activities as an exorcist. We saw that this feature of his ministry, shared by shamans of all periods and all societies, can be traced in Christian history right back to the life of Jesus.

In Chapter 4 we turned the spotlight on Paul's mystical experiences, especially the ecstatic rapture of which he speaks in 2 Corinthians 12. Like some other mystics, he was reluctant to say much about this, but he does speak in the same context of other visions and 'an abundance of revelations'. The trances in which such visions occur are a feature of the Jewish *Hekhalot* that continued the tradition of *merkabah* mysticism within which Paul's experiences

---

2. *The Psychomental Complex of the Tungus*, 269 (italicized by the author).

must be placed. According to Mircea Eliade they also characterize shamanistic activity all over the world.

There remains, however, one further phenomenon that frequently crops up in the discussion and description of shamanism. The phenomenon of spirit-possession, a topic on which I have said little thus far, relates to two distinct phases of Paul's life, the troubled period immediately preceding his conversion and the whole of his subsequent religious experience 'in Christ'.

Agony on the Damascus road

Let us start with Ioan Lewis's observation, tossed out almost casually in the middle of a discussion of shamanism: 'While some shamans', he remarks, 'are summoned by dreams or visions to their calling, this is by no means the universal pattern of recruitment. Very commonly, as with St Paul, the road to the assumption of the shaman's vocation lies through affliction valiantly endured, and, in the end, transformed into spiritual grace.'[3]

I have already suggested that there is only one passage in Paul's writings that could have prompted this comment: Romans 7: 13–25. Here, as in Chapter 4, I propose to place my own translation, spiced with a few Greek quotations, alongside the RSV:

RSV	JA
13 Did that which is good, then, bring death to me? By no means! It was sin, working death in me through what is good, in order that sin might be shown to be sin, and through the commandment might become sinful beyond measure. 14 We know that the law is spiritual; but I am carnal, sold under sin. 15 I do not understand my own actions. For I do not do what I want, but I do the very thing I hate. 16 Now if I do what I do not want, I agree that the law is good. 17 So then it is no longer I that do it, but sin which dwells within me. 18 For I know that nothing good dwells within me, that is, in	Did that which is good, then, turn out to be death for me? Certainly not! Rather it was sin, working death in me through what is good, in order that sin might be unmasked and though the commandment become sinful beyond measure. We know that the law is spiritual; but I am carnal, sold as a slave to sin (ἐγὼ δὲ σάρκινός εἰμι πεπραμένος ὑπὸ τὴν ἁμαρτίαν). I do not understand why I behave as I do. For I do not do what I want, but I do the very thing I hate. Now even if I do what I do not want, I agree with the law: it is right (καλός). So now it is no longer I that do it, but sin dwelling within me

3. *Ecstatic Religion*[2], 60.

my flesh. I can will what is right, but I cannot do it. 19 For I do not do the good I want, but the evil I do not want is what I do. 20 Now if I do what I do not want, it is no longer I that do it, but sin which dwells within me. 21 So I find it to be a law that when I want to do right, evil lies close at hand. 22 For I delight in the law of God, in my inmost self, 23 but I see in my members another law at war with the law of my mind and making me captive to the law of sin which dwells in my members. 24 Wretched man that I am! Who will deliver me from this body of death? 25 Thanks be to God through Jesus Christ our Lord! So then, I of myself serve the law of God with my mind, but with my flesh I serve the law of sin.

(ἡ οἰκοῦσα ἐν ἐμοὶ ἁμαρτία). For I know that nothing dwelling within me, that is in my flesh, is good. Willing is within my power (τὸ γὰρ θέλειν παράκειταί μοι), but not the performance of what is right. For I do not do the good I want, but the evil I do not want is what I do. Now if I do what I do not want, it is no longer I that do it, but sin dwelling within me. So I find it to be a law that when I want to do right, evil attends me (ἐμοὶ τὸ κακὸν παράκειται). For in my inmost self I delight in the law of God, but I see in my members another law at war with the law of my mind and making me captive to the law of sin which dwells in my members (αἰχμαλωτίζοντά με ἐν τῷ νόμῳ τῆς ἁμαρτίας τῷ ὄντι ἐν τοῖς μέλεσίν μου). Wretched man that I am! Who will deliver me from this body of death? Thanks be to God through Jesus Christ our Lord!

This passage is unquestionably one of the most puzzling and, for that reason, most fiercely debated paragraphs that Paul ever wrote. The reading I wish to defend, however obvious it may seem to an anthropologist like Lewis, is not one likely to be found in a scholarly commentary. In order to defend it, in fact, I am compelled to resort to a device that I actually find somewhat uncongenial, and which I usually regard with a suspicion not unmixed with hostility.[4] This is the device of deconstruction.

How does this work? From a grammatical perspective the passage is quite straightforward: first person, singular number, and, up to the cry for release in the penultimate verse, present tense. The trouble is that many scholars, in fact the majority, take the 'ego' in this passage to refer to mankind in general rather than to Paul in particular; and there is a widespread opinion that, despite the use of the present tense, the passage is really about the past, and specifically about the pre-Christian past, before the deliverance that the writer pleads for in the penultimate verse has actually come about. Consequently there are four possible lines of interpretation: (1) if Paul is speaking about himself then he could be describing his struggle with sin *before* the experience on the Damascus road; alter-

4. 'Je m'en méfie', a French friend of mine remarked, 'comme de la peste.'

natively (2) he might be speaking of his desperate efforts *after* his conversion to live, as he puts it in the next chapter, 'according to the spirit' rather than 'according to the flesh'. Many people believe, however, that the 'ego' in this passage is not an individual ego – Paul – but a rhetorical device for projecting onto the screen an internal struggle that is the common lot of humanity. And in that case the picture might be either (3) a representation of the pre-Christian self throughout the long reign of Sin before she was finally ousted by Christ, or lastly (4) the description of a never-ending battle with Sin that Christians are engaged in all their lives. That of course is the classic Lutheran position, and it is still held by a handful of New Testament scholars.[5]

The best explanation of the continuing disagreement, I suggest, is that no single reading really works. There is something to be said, perhaps, for each of the four types of interpretation; but my own view is that Paul had at least two of the possible scenarios in mind: probably not all four, and certainly not just one. He was thinking first, I suggest, of the appalling struggle he had to endure before the blinding revelation on the Damascus road propelled him into a new life. But he was also thinking, I believe, of the Divided Self, classically encapsulated in a couplet from Ovid's *Metamorphoses*: 'Video meliora proboque, deteriora sequor' ('I see and approve of the better course, but pursue the worse') (7.20–21). Unfortunately, since it is quite impossible to reconcile the two readings I wish to defend, I am compelled to resort to deconstruction, which is quite precisely a way of disclosing contradictions. The discovery of irre-concilable meanings in a text might be thought an unsatisfactory outcome of any exegetical endeavour; but one main purpose of the deconstructionists is to promote feelings of uneasiness and irritation in readers of a more traditional bent.[6] Yet in spite of some residual discomfort, I see no alternative here. I will begin by expounding one of the possible interpretations that I shall eventually discard.

(a) *Luther in modern dress*

The first thing to note is that in the preceding half-dozen verses Paul has been telling a story. One quite attractive view of this story is that

5. Notably J. D. G. Dunn, *Romans 1–8*. For a philosophically more interesting version of this position, see Hans Jonas, 'Philosophical Meditation'.
6. See my remarks in *Studying John*, 200–4.

although spoken in the first person it is really about the fall of Adam, eating the forbidden fruit in the garden after being tempted by the devil. Paul assumes (quite a common assumption in Jewish readings of Genesis) that the command not to eat the fruit was actually one of the ten commandments given to Moses on Mount Sinai: 'thou shalt not covet'. The story has a grim ending and a clear moral. The ending is death, for the sentence of mortality pronounced on Adam implies that in one sense, the spiritual sense, he is already dead. Hence the conclusion: 'Sin, taking advantage of the commandment, deceived me and by it killed me' (7:11). Then follows the moral: 'so the law is holy and the commandment is holy and just and good' (7:12). Immediately after the story and its moral comes something completely different: a kind of intimate personal diary. The mood has changed from dramatic excitement to febrile anxiety, the inner anguish of someone – still called 'I' but now, obviously, no longer Adam – wrestling with his inability to perform what he knows to be right: 'for I do not do the good I want, but the evil I do not want is what I do' (7:19).

Along with the change of mood comes a change of tense. What confronts us in this passage is the consequence of the story that has just been told. Paul does not draw attention to the shift from past to present, but it must be significant. What is past is past; but we, all of us (for we are provisionally assuming that the ἐγώ has a universal application), have to live with the consequences of Adam's fall, the total incapacity of the ἐγώ to cope unaided with its own evil desires. Even from the point of view of his Christian present Paul cannot look upon the ravages of Sin as finished with and swept aside. They are now part and parcel of the make-up of the ἐγώ, which is thus 'captive to the law of Sin which dwells in my members' (7:24). Yet there is an important proviso: Sin no longer has things all her own way, because between the conclusion of the story of Adam and the present of which Paul speaks there has been a dramatic intervention, that is to say, the coming of Christ. This means that there is now a new power operating on the side of good. Hence the experience of the Divided Self described so graphically here. Although in a sense the victory has already been achieved, and the transfer of allegiance (from Sin to Spirit) already carried through, both before and after this passage (in chapter 6 and again in chapter 8) Paul repeatedly exhorts his Christian readers to act 'according to the spirit', making it clear that the struggle is not yet over. In his account of the Divided Self Paul shows himself prepared to confront the negative side of Christian existence before displaying the positive, triumphant side in the following chapter.

An important phrase in this passage is the one translated 'the inmost self' (ὁ ἔσω ἄνθρωπος) : 'I delight in the law of God in my inmost self' (7:22), with the result that 'I of myself serve the law of God with my mind', but Paul adds (it is where the chapter ends): 'with my flesh I serve the law of sin' (7:25). Although enabled by God's grace to delight in the law of God, the Christian (even in his true, innermost self) has not thereby stepped out of his fleshly integument or somehow sloughed it off like a serpent's skin. On this reading Romans 7, from v. 13 onwards, is not about the past, but about the present.

The summarizing conclusion of chapter 7 picks up the word σάρξ (flesh), which has been a key word throughout. As a consequence of having been, as Paul puts it, 'sold as a slave to Sin', the ἐγώ is carnal, σάρκινος (7:14), embedded or embodied in the flesh, which is corruptible and destined to return to dust. The epoch inaugurated by Adam's sin is not yet over. In principle, no doubt, both Sin and Death have been defeated by Christ, but one would have to be blind not to see that both continue to make their presence felt. There is quite unmistakably an overlap. Hence the radical division or split which is the central subject of this passage. It is exhibited in various ways: the fact that we cannot draw any clear line between the epoch of Adam and that of Christ means that the law is split too, belonging in a negative way to the pre-Christian era, where it is seized on by Sin for the purpose of bringing Death; but in a positive way to the present, Christian era, where it can actually be categorized as πνευματικός, spiritual. This is why Christian existence, or rather the Christian self, is also split down the middle, with, to mix the metaphor slightly, a foot in both camps.

For Paul the practical problem is clearly what exercises him most, but the theoretical explanation of it that he gives here is also of considerable interest. He manages to preserve the balance –and the tension – between two alternative accounts: one of which would disown all personal responsibility completely by assigning all the blame to an alien power, be it Sin or the devil; the other refusing to acknowledge the irrational element in much human behaviour. Sin is always envisaged 'as a power exercising great compulsion on the individual but [is] sometimes more easily conceptualized as a force bearing upon one from without (social pressures, constraints of tradition etc.),[7] at others as a force rising up from within (psychological addiction of ingrained habit, hereditary traits etc.)'.[8] In any event, to repeat, this is all real – it is a part of the present, not of a remote, mythical past that we are relieved to be rid of.

That we are *not* rid of it is amply demonstrated by the cry of frustration at the end of the chapter, where, for the first time, Paul turns to the future tense: 'who *will* deliver me from the body of this death?' He knows the answer, of course: 'thanks be to God, through Jesus Christ our Lord' (7:25). 'There is nothing in [this] formula to indicate that it is a deliverance already accomplished which is in view; on the contrary, the closest parallel (1 Cor 15:57) indicates the anticipation of eschatological deliverance.'[9] But until this is accomplished, as the last words of the chapter make clear, 'the split continues, epochally between old epoch and new, personally in the believer. The divided "I" continues to experience the divided character of the law: "I" as mind, "I" united with Christ in his death, experience the law as the law of God; "I" as flesh, not yet united with Christ in his resurrection, experience the law as the law of sin.'[10]

This, then, is an up-to-date version of Luther's reading of Paul,[11] one he took over from the later Augustine, and adapted here from a much longer exegesis of the Durham scholar, James Dunn. I want to underline its significance with one further quotation. One of the most outstanding New Testament scholars of the twentieth century (and his life has spanned most of it) is the Norwegian Nils Alstrup Dahl. Nils Dahl's studies of Paul are frequently cited; but I know of no other scholar prepared to turn for illumination to *Roald* Dahl,

---

7. Hence the imagery of sin as a virtually military force in the preceding section (vv. 8 and 11) or here (v. 23), or as a slave owner (v. 14).
8. Hence the notion of sin as taking up residence in the ἐγώ (v. 17). Much of the argument in the preceding section is drawn from J. D. G. Dunn, *Romans*, ad loc., though I have not always used his words.
9. Ibid., 397.
10. Ibid., 411.
11. This was seen by Wrede as long ago as 1904: 'The truth is, the soul-strivings of Luther have stood as model for the portrait of Paul' (*Paul*, 146).

and specifically to the concluding poem from a collection entitled *Dirty Beasts*. The poem is called *The Tummy Beast*.

> One afternoon I said to mummy,
> 'Who is this person in my tummy?
> 'He must be small and very thin
> 'Or how could he have gotten in?'
> My mother said from where she sat,
> 'It isn't nice to talk like that.'
> 'It's true!' I cried. 'I swear it, mummy!
> 'There *is* a person in my tummy!
> 'He talks to me at night in bed,
> 'He's always asking to be fed,
> 'Throughout the day, he screams at me,
> 'Demanding sugar buns for tea.
> 'He tells me it is not a sin
> 'To go and raid the biscuit tin.
> 'I know quite well it's awfully wrong
> 'To guzzle food the whole day long,
> 'But really I can't help it, mummy,
> 'Not with this person in my tummy.'
> 'You horrid child!' my mother cried.
> 'Admit it right away, you've lied!
> 'You're simply trying to produce
> 'A silly asinine excuse!
> '*You* are the greedy guzzling brat!
> 'And that is why you're always fat!'
> I tried once more, '*Believe me*, mummy,
> 'There *is* a person in my tummy.'
> 'I've had enough!' my mother said,
> 'You'd better go at once to bed!'
> Just then, a nicely timed event
> Delivered me from punishment.
> Deep in my tummy something stirred,
> And then an awful noise was heard.
> A snorting grumbling grunting sound
> That made my tummy jump around.
> My darling mother nearly died.
> 'My goodness, what was that?' she cried.

At once, the tummy voice came through,
It shouted, 'Hey there! Listen you!
'I'm getting hungry! I want eats!
'I want lots of chocs and sweets!
'Get me half a pound of nuts!
'Look snappy or I'll twist your guts!'
'*That's him!*' I cried. '*He's in my tummy!*
'So now do you believe me, mummy?'

But mummy answered nothing more,
For she had fainted on the floor.

My reason for quoting *The Tummy Beast* is that it underlines more effectively than any detailed argument what I conceive to be the crucial weakness of the Lutheran interpretation: its failure to take seriously enough the language of *occupancy* in this passage. In many ways the interpretation is a persuasive one, catching most effectively the very common experience of the Divided Self. But Paul goes on (in 8:2) to speak of *liberation* from the law of Sin and Death, whereas what he had been talking of up to then was a state of enslavement (7:25) and, what amounts to the same thing, as having been sold [so as to be] under Sin, a phrase that evokes the image of being knocked down to Sin under the auctioneer's hammer (7:14).[12] Paul's general conception of the Christian life certainly includes the idea of a continuous struggle. Equally, though, it is irreconcilable with the picture he gives (in 7:17 and 20) of someone completely in thrall to Sin, who is portrayed as having taken up residence in the self and exercising absolute control. The deconstruction of the Lutheran view is not the result of arbitrary nit-picking by the interpreter, but something demanded by the text itself. In the next chapter the Christian is warned not to act κατὰ σάρκα (according to the flesh), showing that Sin has not altogether relinquished control. But this is quite different from the expression ἐν τῇ σαρκί μου (in my flesh) in chapter 7, which implies a state of

---

12. In translating the key phrase, πεπραμένος ὑπὸ τὴν ἁμαρτίαν, as 'sold *under* sin' RSV follows mechanically the standard rendering of ὑπό with the accusative. But the phrase suggests a sale *to* sin [as a slave]. So, rightly, Fitzmyer: 'sold in bondage to sin': *Romans*, 472.

such extreme carnality that the true self, the inner self, has no chance whatever of winning through.

A further objection, one that involves a quite literal exercise in deconstruction, concerns the peculiar fashion in which the chapter ends: 'So then, I of myself serve the law of God with my mind, but with my flesh I serve the law of Sin.' This conclusion has always puzzled commentators, because it jars so badly with the triumphant cry that immediately precedes it. Dunn's explanation is that although the writer knows how he will eventually be delivered, and says so quite clearly, the actual deliverance is still to come. But the immediate lapse into misery is decidedly disconcerting.

The best explanation is still that of Rudolf Bultmann, following Adolf Jülicher and Friedrich Müller.[13] He regards the final sentence as a gloss. Trying to make sense of what precedes, a copyist added his own summary of the argument in a marginal note. A later copyist, mistakenly assuming the marginal gloss to be part of what Paul wrote, inserted it in the text as best he could: hence the confusion.[14] Without this ending Dunn's thesis is obviously weaker, but even if Bultmann's ingenious suggestion is disallowed the Lutheran view espoused by Dunn cannot be maintained against the argument from the occupancy of Sin.

(b) *The Divided Self*

For all the objections that can be marshalled against this classically Lutheran position, one cannot ignore the sense Paul conveys of the agonizing struggle to which the ego is subjected as it is torn confusedly this way and that in its vain effort to do what is right.

Just how human beings can choose to do what they know to be

13. See *TLZ* 72 (1947), 197–202. Bultmann thinks that 8:1 is a gloss too. Another example of a gloss in Paul's writings, more widely accepted, is 1 Cor 15:56: 'The sting of death is sin and the power of sin is the law.'

14. Fitzmyer, p. 477, notes that this is a logical suggestion, 'but suspect', he adds, 'for that very reason'! It is all too easy for a word or phrase one thinks one has deleted to creep back into the text. An example of how an author's own gloss can be included by mistake is to be found in the first printed version of one of Robert Louis Stevenson's early poems. Looking years later through the notebook that contained it, and amused by its somewhat grandiloquent style, he scribbled the ironic comment, 'quite so, jes so', words the editor wrongly assumed to be part of the original poem. See Janet Adam Smith in *The New York Review of Books*, March 3, 1994, p. 31.

wrong and in fact often do so choose is both an intriguing philosophical puzzle at least as old as Plato and a practical problem abundantly illustrated in both Jewish and Western literature. (The
Qumran *Hodayoth*, Ovid's *Metamorphoses*, and the writings of
Epictetus are frequently cited, and the rabbinic concept of the war-
ring impulses in human nature, the יצר רע and the יצר טוב, offers
an especially close parallel.)[15]

It is largely on the basis of this passage in Romans 7 that Stanley
Stowers has been able to argue that Paul's purpose in this letter is to
commend to his readers a route to self-mastery.[16] Although this
thesis has serious weaknesses, it is hard to deny that here at least
Paul is acknowledging the continuing difficulty of remaining faithful
to one's own ideals. Yet the price to be paid for placing it at the
centre of Paul's concerns is to shut one's eyes to his real argument.
The only theory that can assume and absorb it without difficulty
is Luther's, and there are, as we have seen, insuperable objections
to this. Hence the necessity of some kind of deconstructionist
interpretation, admitting the presence of the Divided Self but
recognizing that there is also a strong autobiographical element in
this difficult passage.

(c) *Paul's struggle with the Law*

Before defending an alternative interpretation that moves out of the
general into the particular by arguing that Paul is really describing
his own inner struggle before this was put an end to by the revelation on the Damascus road, I want to say something about how the
passage under discussion fits into the general context in Romans. Ed
Sanders rightly points out that the precise topic at this point is 'What
is the relationship between the law and sin?'[17] This is the question
that the preceding discussion makes so urgent. It is an extraordinary
question, asked as it is by a man who had faithfully observed the law
from childhood. The question had become inescapable as early as
5:20, when Paul has the law 'sidle in' ($\nu\acute{o}\mu os$ $\delta\grave{e}$ $\pi\alpha\rho\epsilon\iota\sigma\mathring{\eta}\lambda\theta\epsilon\nu$) to
give its backing to Sin and 'increase the trespass'.

---

15. See M. Hengel, *Judaism and Hellenism*, 140–1 and the literature cited in nn.
224–6.
16. S. K. Stowers, *A Rereading of Romans*.
17. *Paul, the Law*, 77

Now by the time Paul wrote Romans he had long been convinced that God had planned from the outset to reconcile mankind to himself not through the law but through faith in Christ. This, as Sanders points out, created for him 'a theological problem of the first order of magnitude: What was God up to before Christ? What was the point of the law?' Sanders thinks it far more likely that Paul was driven to passionate expression of these 'real problems' than that the cause of his torment was personal angst or his analysis of the existential plight of humanity: 'These may be real problems for moderns, but I doubt that they were for Paul.'[18]

But what if Paul had been driven by the course of his argument in these chapters to reflect on the critical period in his own life when he was forced to make the choice for himself? This was when he was beginning to have doubts about the wisdom or rectitude of his persecution of the Jesus movement. The fact that he elsewhere claims to be 'blameless' with regard to 'righteousness under the law' (Phil 3:6) may be a decisive argument against the view that he had to wrestle continually with a sense of his own worthlessness, but it is perfectly easy to reconcile with the very different view that at a certain point in his life he was coming to regard the law as more of a hindrance than a help in the decision he was soon to have to take. Indeed, if he had had no serious problem hitherto in obeying all the provisions of the Jewish law, his anguish at the moment when he foresaw that he would have to abandon it is all the more comprehensible. But in that case a new, very different problem arises: why, having sacrificed the law in favour of a law-free gospel, does he still feel compelled to defend it as 'holy and just and good' (7:12)?

It is in fact impossible to be sure what sense to attach to the word νόμος, 'law', in all its occurrences (twenty altogether in chapter 7, half of them in this particular section). Paul uses this word very frequently, and in the great majority of instances he is clearly referring to the Mosaic law. Some exegetes tie themselves into knots in an attempt to retain the same reference throughout the passage. Their task becomes even harder if they want to include the triumphant proclamation at the beginning of the next chapter: 'For

---

18. Ibid., 78–9.

in Christ Jesus the law of the spirit of life has set you [me?][19] free from the law of Sin and Death' (8:2).

The bulk of Romans 7, from v. 7 onwards, is an attempt to justify and explain the conclusion Paul had just reached: 'now we are discharged from the law, dead to what held us captive, so that we serve not under the old written code but in the new life of the Spirit' (7:6). But Paul is not content with this formulation and feels the need both to modify it and to explain it. Why so? Because it presents the law in too negative a light. Paul has found himself dragged along by his own argument to a point where he is on the brink of identifying the law, that is the Mosaic law, the nerve-centre of the Jewish faith, with sin. He cannot bring himself to do this. Teetering on the brink, he takes a decisive step backwards: 'What then can we say? Is the law sin? Perish the thought!' (7:7). Yet he is sure of one thing: between the law and Christ you have to choose – you can't have both. There was a point in his own life when he found himself confronted with the choice, and it was the hardest choice he ever had to make. As we have seen, he had been a follower of the law, religiously speaking (and there can have been few people more religious than Paul) blameless: the law had been at the centre of his life. Is it any wonder that this fervent Jew, wrestling with the growing conviction that he would have to abandon all that hitherto had given his life any meaning, and terrified by the thought that not to do so would be the unpardonable sin, came to identify the hold the law still had on him as an evil which he must somehow escape? Rationally, he knew perfectly well that the law was God-given and therefore good – 'spiritual', he says (7:14): nothing he says anywhere about the law is more paradoxical than this. Yet experientially and existentially, for him personally, *the law was sin*. And Sin had come to occupy his soul as an alien presence: he had been sold and was now a slave. 'Wretched man that I am! Who will deliver me from this body of death?' (7:24). It is a cry of despair. We have already seen the answer: 'The law of the Spirit of life in Christ Jesus has set me/you free from the law of Sin and Death' (8:2).

---

19. The MSS are divided between σε (you in the singular) and με (me) at this point.

'The law of Sin and Death': in a single substantive phrase, Paul groups together the three powers to which he felt himself enslaved. The immense sense of relief that permeates this passage comes from Paul's assurance that the dominating presence in his life is now no longer the law but the Spirit.

Nevertheless, the occupying force that caused Paul such anguish until the actual moment of liberation was not the law, but Sin. The modern reader, accustomed to thinking of sin as a single wrong action, finds it hard to appreciate the extraordinary weight that Paul attaches to the term. Replacing 'Sin' with 'the devil' would bring us closer to Paul's meaning. For as we have seen, he thinks of Sin either as a kind of cosmic force, which, as in Romans 5, can be ranged against grace in an epic struggle for control over the destiny of the human race; or else, as in the passage we are considering, as an alien intruder, sinister and malign, and impossible to dislodge without the assistance of an even more powerful supernatural force.

Worth recalling here is the gospel saying about the unclean spirit which, after being ejected from a particular individual, passes through waterless places seeking rest, but finds none. Then he says: 'I will return from my house from which I came' (Matt 11:44–45). Here the metaphor is fully developed: we remember that the spirit returns to find his house swept and garnished, which gives him the idea of inviting 'seven other spirits more evil than himself' to share this nice clean home. To demythologize this story too quickly, or to conclude that it has nothing to do with what Paul is saying, would be to forfeit a valuable aid to understanding. Paul, unlike Matthew, does not elaborate upon the metaphor, but that does not entitle us to ignore it. Probably our best chance of reaching back to Paul's horror and dismay at his own helplessness is to project upon our own mental screen the images of films like *Alien* (1, 2, or 3). The unease we feel as we scroll these images through our minds helps us to put aside our own rational selves for a while and to empathize with the disarray of what Peter Brown calls Late Antique man, over whose religious and intellectual life hung, as he puts it, 'the sharp smell of an invisible battle…. To sin was no longer merely to err: it was to allow oneself to be overcome by unseen forces. To err was not to be mistaken: it was to be unconsciously manipulated by some divine

power.'[20] The battlefield could be the world, but Brown is thinking of the human soul.

Where does the law come in here? After a long argument
beginning at the end of chapter 5, Paul reaches the conclusion that
'now we are discharged from the law, dead to what held us captive,
so that we serve not under the old written code but in the new life
of the Spirit' (7:6). We have already remarked that the reason for
Paul's dissatisfaction with this formulation and his desire to modify
and explain it, is that it presents the law in too negative a light. In
what follows, therefore, the alien occupancy is attributed not to the
law but to Sin. Yet in spite of his real reservations Paul's first way of
putting the matter, where he expresses his sense of servitude under
the law, is probably a true reflection of what he really thinks. In
describing his own shift of allegiance it is obviously more accurate to
contrast his present allegiance to Christ with his previous service of
the law – of the law, not of Sin. His temporary sense of helplessness
under the control of Sin is different from his conscious allegiance to
the law. The close association between Sin and the law in the key
passage, an association verging upon identification, suggests that
the confusion reflects a period of turmoil in Paul's life in which the
need to abandon the law had become painfully evident to him; so
much so that to have continued to cling to the law would have been
equivalent to rejecting the call of Christ: he could imagine no
greater sin.[21] Looking back later on this distressing time he saw his
initial refusal to reject the law as a proof of the domination of Sin in
his life. No wonder he was confused.

No account of Paul's conversion can be fully satisfactory if it does
not acknowledge that the visitation of the Risen Christ must have
been preceded by an intense inner struggle. For Paul, as Daniel
Boyarin puts it, 'the agony preceded the ecstasy';[22] equally the
ἀγωνία preceded the ἔκστασις.

---

20. *The World of Late Antiquity*, 54.
21. Worth emphasizing is the conjunction of 7:20 and 21: 'Now if I do what I do
    not want, it is no longer I that do it, but sin dwelling within me. So I find it to
    be a law (Εὑρίσκω ἄρα τὸν νόμον) that when I want to do right, evil attends
    me (ὅτι ἐμοὶ τὸ κακὸν παράκειται)'. Here the law (ὁ νόμος) is equivalent to
    'principle', but the use of the definite article makes it look at first as if Paul is
    referring, as usual, to the Mosaic law: 'so I find the law – that evil attends me'.
22. *A Radical Jew*, 122. Cf. H. Weinel, *St Paul*, 148–9.

Life in the Spirit

We noticed earlier how Ioan Lewis distinguishes between two paths to the shaman's vocation, one involving a long and painful struggle, the other a visionary call. But there is no reason why the two should not represent successive episodes in the shaman's call.

It is now time to take another look at Paul's tantalizingly brief account of his call in the letter to the Galatians. Worth stressing is that there is no dispute over the fact that he interpreted this as a revelatory experience: he insists that he did not receive the gospel from a human teacher but by a revelation of Jesus Christ: δι' ἀποκαλύψεως Ἰησοῦ Χριστοῦ (Gal 1:12); and a little further on he uses the verb ἀποκαλύπτειν, to reveal: 'But when he who had set me apart from my mother's womb and had called me through his grace was pleased to reveal his Son in me, in order that I might preach him among the Gentiles' (1:15–16).

If the revelatory nature of Paul's call is uncontested, the same cannot be said about the phrase I have just translated 'to reveal his Son in me'. 'In me' is a literal translation of the Greek ἐν ἐμοί but by this time the preposition ἐν was sometimes added to the dative as an optional extra, without altering the meaning. So the more usual translation, 'to reveal his son *to* me', cannot be excluded. There are, however, three reasons for continuing to prefer the alternative: 'in me'. The first is that it is much the easiest and most natural rendering of the Greek, and so should be allowed to stand as long as there are no overriding arguments against it. The second reason is that it enables us to see more clearly that a change of occupancy is involved. Up to that moment, as we may infer from Romans, the occupant of Paul's ἐγώ was Sin: from now on it was 'the Son'. In the third place, a little further on Paul goes on to tell the Galatians that 'it is no longer I who live, but Christ who lives in me' (Gal 2:20), a verse in which the ἐν ἐμοί can brook no other translation:[23]

---

23. One modern commentator who supports this interpretation is Hans-Dieter Betz: 'The "in me" corresponds to Gal 2:20 ("Christ ... lives in me") and 4:6 ("God has sent the Spirit of his Son into our hearts"). Paul does not explain how the three passages are related to each other, but we may assume that they complement each other. This would mean that Paul's experience was ecstatic in nature, and that in the course of this ecstasy he had a vision (whether external

For I through the law died to the law, that I might live to God. I have been crucified along with Christ; it is no longer I who live but Christ who lives in me; and the life I now live in the flesh I live by faith in the Son of God, who loved me and gave himself for me.   Gal 2:19–20

Paul's assertion that he died to the law and was crucified along with Christ is generally given a purely theological explanation; even the ugly term crucifixion, like grace and salvation, has been dulled by familiarity. Here if anywhere we are in what Hugh Kenner calls 'the whispering forest of traditional poetry, where the very words to which millions of minds respond have helped to form the minds that respond to them'.[24]

This is why our eyes slide over this passage with none of the shocked puzzlement that must have affected its first readers. Most present-day Christians are probably more familiar with the beautiful portrayals of the crucified Christ typical of, say, Raphael than with the hideously contorted victim gasping out his pain from the altarpiece of Raphael's contemporary, Matthias Grünewald. Yet Grünewald's picture is unquestionably a more faithful evocation of the grim reality.

Stephen Moore, one of a handful of modern scholars to reflect seriously on the sheer horror of this barbarous form of execution, comments, in the first chapter of his book *God's Gym* (headed 'Torture: the Divine Butcher'), on 'the restraint exercised by the evangelists in their accounts of Jesus' crucifixion'.[25] This is

---

or internal or both – "I do not know, God knows" [cf. 2 Cor 12:2, 3])' (*Galatians*, 71). See ch. 3, n. 17, *supra*.

24. *The Pound Era* (London, 1972), 521.

25. p. 6. Also worth remarking upon is the rarity of the depiction of the crucifixion in early Christendom. The symbol of the cross is much less common in the catacombs than, say, the fish, the shepherd, or the dove. The crucifixion is even rarer, and remains so in the 4th and 5th centuries (in the abundant Christian sarcophagi, for example) long after the discovery of the true cross by Constantine's mother Helena, and is missing altogether from the mosaics in the basilicas of Rome and Ravenna. The earliest portrayals of the crucifixion show an open-eyed, calmly triumphant Christ, with no trace of suffering. The first truly realistic crucifixion scene comes in a Syriac gospel manuscript known as the Rabula miniature, dating from the end of the 6th century. See *DACL* III/2 (Paris, 1913–14), 3045–131.

particularly true of John. The act of hoisting the cross onto its supporting plinth must have been accompanied by an agonizing jolt, but John turns it into a symbol of glorification (ὑψοῦν).[26]

Luke too averts his gaze from the cross, which remained for him a bewildering truth that he could only accept as a necessary (though still incomprehensible) part of God's plan. The Messiah, unquestionably, had to suffer before entering his glory (Luke 24:26; cf. Acts 17:3; 26:23); but if it had been left to Luke to choose a slogan summarizing Paul's gospel it would have been the Risen, not the Crucified Christ, Paul's own succinct statement of a message he knew to be 'folly to the Gentiles' (1 Cor 1:23), and which he acknowledges later on in the letter we are now considering to be a stumbling-block to the Galatians (5:11). Yet Luke tells us that in his address to the Athenians on the Areopagus Paul spoke not of the cross but of the resurrection (Acts 17:21).

So we have to ask what prompted Paul to choose the term συνσταυροῦσθαι (be crucified along with) to introduce his affirmation that 'I live, no longer I, but Christ lives in me'.[27] It is sometimes explained as a metaphorical expression for the sufferings he subsequently endured in the course of his apostolic ministry. But this is not how he referred to them himself, and he must have realized that these, however severe, were little more than pin-pricks compared with the tortures of the cross. Any suggestion to the contrary would have represented such a gross and improbable insensitivity on his part that we must look elsewhere for an explanation.

It is to be found, I suggest, in his actual experience of an agonizing death that preceded a new kind of life. This is in fact what Paul says (!); but the clue to *understanding* what he says, if we could only see it, comes from a very dissimilar religious tradition, that of shamanism. In asserting that he died to the law and was crucified with Christ, Paul is referring to the anguished struggle that preceded the blinding revelation of his call. This was the necessary preliminary of the new life he now leads. The event that the two verbs allude to

---

26. See my *Understanding*, 363–6.
27. The only other occasion that Paul uses the term is in Rom 6:6, referring more generally to the death of the old self (ὁ παλαιὸς ἡμῶν ἄνθρωπος). Here the usage *is* metaphorical.

is the traumatic experience that led up to his decision to abandon the law, the indispensable precondition of the call itself, and also its negative or obverse side. The abandonment of the law is now seen as a death *to* the law. In shamanistic terms it was the victorious outcome of a terrible struggle. Sin, like a malign demon, had seized on the law as an instrument with which to keep Paul in subjection.[28] Paul had just had a vision of the Crucified and Risen Christ. It was natural for him to describe his own terrifying experience in terms that recalled this vision. Whatever it was that had previously been at the centre of his life, the new centre is Christ. Looking back on his pre-Christian past, he generally sees it to have been dominated by the law. Only in Romans 7, where he describes the struggle itself, does he see the temptation to cling to the law as the consequence of the occupancy of Sin. From now on, though, it is Christ, not Sin, who lives in him.

How are we to make sense of this extraordinary statement? No rational human being can think of himself as being occupied by another. Whatever name we give to Paul's conviction, it unquestionably depends on his awareness that Christ is no longer an ordinary human being but a spirit. In accounts of possession the occupying spirits are frequently given names. The name Paul gives to the spirit that has now taken hold of him is Χριστός: the Anointed One.

It is not the only name he uses: when thinking of his new life, based on a new relationship, Paul sometimes refers to the occupying presence quite specifically as a spirit – in Romans 8:2 as the 'spirit of life'. This should be linked with the term 'life-giving spirit' that he applies to Christ in a passage defending the truth of the resurrection (1 Cor 15:45). Christ's risen body is no longer animated by an ordinary soul (ψυχή), but by a spirit: it is in fact a spiritual body, σῶμα πνευματικόν. In virtue of the resurrection Christ has been transformed into a spirit, not just a living spirit but a *life-giving* spirit, which guarantees the actuality of the new era ushered in by Christ.

Apart from the brief reference to Paul's call in Galatians the most important passage concerning spiritual occupancy is to be found in

28. This passage should be compared with Phil 3:7–11, and with the extracts from Eliade's *Shamanism* cited in my exegesis of that text in Chapter 4.

Romans 8. We should not forget that this follows almost immediately upon the cry of triumph at the end of the previous chapter. There Paul had described the awful sensation of being occupied by Sin. Following the liberation brought by Christ there is now a new occupant in the house of the inner self. That Paul now broadens his vision to include the Roman Christians he is addressing should not blind us to the connection between the two passages: 'you are not in the flesh; you are in the spirit, if in fact the Spirit of God dwells in you (εἴπερ πνεῦμα θεοῦ οἰκεῖ ἐν ὑμῖν).[29] Unless a person has the Spirit of Christ, he/she is not truly his. But if Christ is in you, the body may be dead because of sin but the spirit is alive because of righteousness (τὸ δὲ πνεῦμα ζωὴ διὰ δικαιοσύνην). If the Spirit of him who raised Jesus from the dead dwells in you, he who raised Christ from the dead will enliven (ζῳοποιήσει: bestow life upon) your mortal bodies also through his indwelling Spirit in you (διὰ τοῦ ἐνοικοῦντος αὐτοῦ πνεύματος ἐν ὑμῖν)' (Rom 8:9–11).

In this passage the language of possession or occupancy (οἰκεῖν ἐν, ἐνοικεῖν) is too insistent to miss. 'God's Spirit', 'Christ's Spirit', 'Christ' and 'the Spirit of him who raised Jesus from the dead' are used interchangeably to refer to the indwelling spirit who had become the source of Paul's mastery of all other spirits in his work of evangelization. And Paul sees the same spirit as the dynamic principle in the lives of other Christians too. This conviction is much more than a logical inference based on his experience. It is part of that experience, surely the most vital part. To repeat what I have insisted on time and time again in the course of this book, this is a matter of religion, not of theology.[30]

Commenting on Paul's boast that the Galatians received him 'as the angel-messenger of God, as Christ himself (ὡς ἄγγελον θεοῦ ἐδέξασθέ με, ὡς Χριστὸν Ἰησοῦν) (Gal 4:14), Georg Bertram says that this is the key to Paul's self-understanding (*Selbstbewußtsein*): 'He is entitled to speak in this way because Christ is manifested in

---

29. Seeing the human psyche as being partly carnal and partly spiritual, Paul constantly urges his converts to behave 'according to the spirit' and not 'according to the flesh'. If the flesh is that element in the psyche that permits the occupancy of Sin, it is the (human) spirit that affords access to the (divine) Spirit of God.

30. Ernst Käsemann is able to say: 'The Spirit is our present participation in eternal life, but we can possess him and participate in his gift only as he possesses us' (*Essays*, 65). But what does he mean by this?

him, in his body or in his missionary work.'[31] Bertram encapsulates this phenomenon in the term 'Christophoros' – Christ-bearer: 'Anthropologically speaking, the clearest way of expressing this concept is to say that the spirit of Christ, or the spirit-Christ or the Christ-spirit (all three must be taken into consideration), comes to inhabit and control the man.'[32]

For a final comparison with a shamanistic society I turn to an African society that has so far received no mention in this book, that of the Nuer of the Southern Sudan, basing myself on E. E. Evans-Pritchard's classic study *Nuer Religion*.

Evans-Pritchard thinks that shamans (whom he calls 'prophets')[33] are relatively recent arrivals among the Nuer. He does not speculate on their provenance but clearly implies that the Nuer incorporated them without difficulty into the structures of their own religion.

The opening chapter of *Nuer Religion* is entitled, quite simply, 'God'. The Nuer word *kwoth* actually means spirit, and Evans-Pritchard remarks that it carries the same connotations (of breath and wind) as the Hebrew *ruah*, the Greek *pneuma*, and the Latin *spiritus*. In one sense God inhabits the sky, but in another sense he is ubiquitous: 'He is with [the Nuer] because he is Spirit and being like wind or air is everywhere, and, being everywhere, is here now.'[34]

Another important concept for the Nuer is that of 'the spirits of the air'. These are not clearly distinguished from the supreme spirit, God, but are seen rather to represent God in his dealings with men, much in the same way as 'wisdom' and 'spirit' in the Hebrew Bible. The spirits of the air abide in the sky but have the power of coming down and occupying human beings: 'Spirit in the form of spirits can enter into men, the human being expelled, as it were, and the divine taking its place. There is in the idea the suggestion of the natural man being changed into the spiritual man.'[35]

---

31. 'Paulus Christophoros', 34. This article, little-known and hard of access, is a rare attempt to tackle what the writer calls an *anthropological* problem – a term that includes psychology as well as anthropology.

32. Ibid., 35–6.

33. Ioan Lewis comments upon the general reluctance of British anthropologists to employ the term 'shaman' even where the phenomenon of shamanism is clearly present (*Religion in Context*, 78–80).

34. *Nuer Religion*, 9.

35. Ibid., 60.

Besides the spirits of the air there are other spirits for which the Nuer term is *colwic*. These are spirits which were once individual human beings, distinguished from all others by the fact that their deaths are attributable to the direct intervention of God: they are people who have been struck by lightning, carried off in a whirlwind or, occasionally, discovered dead in the bush for no apparent cause. (*Col* is both the spirit of lightning and a collective representation of the *colwic* spirits in general.) A *colwic*, then, is a man that has been transformed into a spirit. The Nuer say of him that *coa kwoth*: 'He has become Spirit'.

'Having become Spirit the soul of the dead person is now not only a spirit but, as a spirit, part of God, who is all Spirit, and also, when Nuer think of the manner and instrument of death, of God conceived of in his hypostasis of *col*, the spirit of lightning.... Each *colwic* spirit is quite distinctive being, bearing, if it is remembered and revered, the name it had on earth as a person.' Nevertheless, the *colwic* spirits are not clearly distinct from God. Their relation to God 'is not a disjunction, an either … or, but a conjunction, a both … and. A *colwic* is itself and it is also God.'[36]

According to Evans-Pritchard, 'seizure of a man by the spirit may be temporary or permanent. When it is permanent the possessed person becomes a prophet.'[37] He has been given 'powers of healing, divination, exorcism, and foresight.... Nuer call such a charismatic person *gwan kwoth*, owner or possessor of Spirit.... He is also referred to as the *guk* of the spirit, a word meaning a leather bag. The prophet is a bag containing the spirit. '"Possessor" might seem to be here an inappropriate translation of *gwan* ("father", "owner", or "master") since the spirit possesses the man rather than the man the spirit, but the man does own the spirit in the sense that it is in him and gives him spiritual power ordinary people lack.'[38] Much later in his book, Evans-Pritchard sums this up by saying that 'the possessed is thus also the possessor'.[39]

---

36. Ibid., 61.
37. Ibid., 34. The distinction between temporary and permanent possession, picked up and underlined by Mary Douglas (*Natural Symbols*, 121), is called into question by Ioan Lewis (*Religion in Context*, 83–6).
38. *Nuer Religion*, 43–4.
39. Ibid., 303.

In thus summarizing what Evans-Pritchard says about spirit-possession among the Nuer, I have deliberately selected passages that highlight the resemblances between Paul's relation with the spirit of Jesus (Christ) and that of the Nuer prophets with the *colwic* spirits or the spirits of the air. There are, it has to be admitted, numerous differences too, not least the manner of life of the Nuer prophets. Not only do they live apart, shaggy and unkempt, from their fellows, but they are often, seemingly, venal and corrupt. For all that, the esteem in which they are held, their spiritual authority, and above all their relationship with God and the spirits who represent him, need to be underlined.

I want to end by quoting the conclusion of Ioan Lewis's masterly chapter on 'The Shaman's Career', where he expresses the hope that his 'exercise in unpacking an ethnically specific term [shaman] for what is actually the very epitome of charismatic authority may ... contribute to a more informed understanding of universal religious roles, which for too long have been treated as though they represented different species beyond the reach of effective comparative analysis'.[40]

---

40. *Religion in Context*, 92–3.

Conclusion

Dominating the present book is the conviction that one important path to the understanding of Paul has been largely neglected. Hermann Gunkel's insight, expressed as long ago as 1888, that Paul's own life must provide the key to the enigma of his teaching concerning the spirit, has never been followed up.

The reasons for this neglect are primarily three. First and foremost there is the seemingly unassailable conviction – based on nothing but an unexamined assumption – that the concepts and categories of systematic theology are perfectly well-suited to the analysis and understanding of Paul's letters. From this it is but a small step to thinking of Paul as a systematic theologian himself; and despite occasional demurrers this is how he is usually treated whenever his 'thought', 'theology', 'mysticism' (Schweitzer) or 'religion' (Sanders) is under consideration.[1]

The roots of this conviction are buried deep in the history of the Protestant Reformation. In the very first paragraph of his book *Paul and His Interpreters*, first published in German in 1911 under the title of *Die Geschichte der paulinischen Forschung*, Albert Schweitzer comments upon the tendency of the Protestant Reformers to scan Paul's letters for proof-texts of Lutheran or Reformed theology. Not surprisingly, that is what they found. Reformation exegesis, he concludes, 'reads its own ideas into Paul in order to receive them back clothed with Apostolic authority'.[2]

---

1. Of course there are many studies of Paul that are not affected by this criticism. Chief among them are those which rely upon sociological theory and the study of ancient rhetoric. Other scholars adopt a historical approach that bypasses theology completely.
2. *Paul*, 2.

One consequence of this way of approaching Paul (which no one, apparently, called into question) is that the proponents and practitioners of critical exegesis in the nineteenth century followed Baur in organizing their work on Paul according to the topics (or *loci*) of dogmatic theology. The scheme they adopted was more or less closely based on Reformation dogmatics, with the consequence that they assumed a priori 'that Pauline theology can be divided into practically the same individual doctrines as that of Luther, Zwingli and Calvin'.[3] 'In general', comments Schweitzer, 'these scholars are quite unaware of the decisive importance which attaches to the arrangement of the material', and he concludes with some asperity that it has 'always been [a] weakness of theological scholarship to talk much about method and possess little of it'.[4]

It is worth noting that Schweitzer, unlike Adolf Deissmann, never reproaches his predecessors for treating Paul as a theologian, for despite the title of his own later study, this – as we have seen – is what he does himself. His complaint is rather that they fail to treat Paul as a coherent thinker, that they never find the 'red thread' that would guide them through the labyrinth of motifs and concepts in Paul's writings, and that in none of the various ways in which the material is parcelled out is there any satisfactory explanation of the phenomenon of what he himself calls Paulinism.

Not just in the nineteenth century but in the twentieth century also (and no doubt in the twenty-first) any extended treatment of Paul's theology can hardly avoid parcelling out the material under various headings. This is true of Bultmann and, more recently, of the even lengthier treatment of James Dunn. And it is no doubt also the case that Catholic scholars like Joseph Fitzmyer are in this respect the heirs of the Protestant prejudice that governed the exegesis of the early Reformers.

But what of Schweitzer himself? Does he succeed in evading the trap which he has watched his predecessors tumbling into one after another? The answer to this question, I think, is that in one important respect he does. His earlier book was clearly intended as a prolegomenon to *Die Mystik des Paulus*. Twenty years before the appearance of this he had already found what he considered to be a

3. Ibid., 33.
4. Ibid., 34.

satisfactory answer to the question concerning Paul's leading conception or guiding thread. This answer, in a word, is eschatology.

I have already (Excursus III) given a detailed critique of Schweitzer's position. What I want to emphasize here is the fact that his whole discussion is dominated by his sense of Paul as, above all else, a *thinker*, the patron saint (*der Schutzheilige*) of Christian thinking, and Schweitzer's own starting-point is not an experience but a concept.

In refusing to chop up what he regarded as the consistently unified pattern of thinking in Paul's writings, Schweitzer succeeded in stepping out of the vicious circle in which he saw the successors of the Reformers to be trapped; but because he nevertheless continued to regard Paul as a master thinker, he had no interest in looking to his life for an explanation of his teaching. And he specifically rejected any suggestion that the best starting-point for understanding Paul is the Damascus road experience.

Martin Dibelius's extensive review of Schweitzer's *Mystik* (1931), significantly entitled 'Faith and Mysticism in Paul' (*Glaube und Mystik bei Paulus*), picks up on the word mysticism, beginning not with an argument but an affirmation: 'It seems to be widely acknowledged', he says, 'that mysticism in Paul is neither simple, primary, nor essential.' He goes on to distinguish two main strands of piety or devotion (*Frömmigkeit*) in what he calls the higher religions, the mystical and the prophetic.[5] He locates Paul among the latter and rejects Schweitzer's description of Paul's Christ-mysticism as 'a solidarity (*Zusammengehörigkeit*) with Christ our Lord that is both grasped in thought and experienced in life'.[6] Dibelius is clearly anxious to hobble the concept of mysticism so as to prevent it from straying into sacrosanct areas of Protestant theology where it might do some real damage. He opens the concluding section of his review by asserting that 'any question

---

5. He derives this distinction from Friedrich Heiler's *Das Gebet*. See his later article, 'Paulus und die Mystik', 136, n. 6, which starts by making the same point. One might conclude that it had never crossed his mind that prophets can be mystics too (what of Isaiah, say, or Jeremiah, or Ezekiel?) but for the fact that a little further on (p. 151) he evokes the possibility of the propinquity (*das Nebeneinander*) of the prophetic and the mystical. Yet he immediately denies that this is applicable to Paul himself.

6. 'Glaube', 97.

regarding Paul's mysticism must start with an awareness of the thoroughly *un*mystical structure that is characteristic of the apostle's theology': all talk of mysticism must be carried out within this framework. This holds, he says, for a formula such as 'in Christ', for the reciprocal formula 'known' and 'be known', for terms like gnosis, sharing in suffering, vision, transformation, and for concepts like putting on Christ, dying, being buried or rising with him, and rebirth (*sic*).[7] Not mysticism, then, but faith.

Dibelius's review of Schweitzer brings us to the second important reason for the neglect of Paul's life as a key to his teaching. This is the traditional Protestant distaste for the mystical, a distaste (even a horror) that goes right back to Luther. As it happens, Dibelius's rejection of any genuinely mystical element in Paulinism, coming as it does in a review of Schweitzer, is completely off-target. Schweitzer himself would agree with most of it. The effect of Dibelius's criticism is simply to leave Pauline studies where they were before Schweitzer, that is to say with Christian dogma as the only guiding thread. And this is where they remained for the time being: all the heavyweights of the German theological establishment, Barth, Bultmann, and Dibelius, expressed their opposition to mysticism, regarding it as inconsistent with true Christian faith, which they held to be a response, not to an experience, but to the word of God. The very idea of attributing mystical experience to Paul, despite the clear evidence in 2 Corinthians 12, was universally shunned.[8]

There is still a residual reluctance in certain quarters, as may be seen from J. L. Martyn's 1997 commentary on Galatians, to see Paul as a 'religious' figure; and it is a matter of conjecture how far other scholars, especially Christians, are likely to be swayed by such obviously ideological objections.

---

7. 'Glaube', 111.
8. Dibelius dismisses the evidence from 2 Corinthians 12 in a paragraph ('Paulus', 154–5). Catholic scholars too failed to recognize the depth and nature of Paul's mysticism. Alfred Wikenhauser is mainly concerned with what he calls 'a physico-accidental union between Christ and his faithful' (whatever that may mean) and when he comes to speak of Paul's conversion argues weakly that the true beginning of Paul's union with Christ was not the Damascus road experience but his baptism (see *Christusmystik*, 58 and 94–6). And the French scholar Lucien Cerfaux says that what really excites Paul's interest (the word he uses is *passionner*) is not some vague mysticism but precise theological themes (*Le chrétien*, 326).

So far we have been looking at the *theological* reasons for the lack of interest in Paul's religion. This is partly a matter of academic inertia – the persistence of the early division of the various ideas into theological *loci* – but an equally strong reason is the Protestant distaste for the mystical, inspired by the conviction (expressed with especial clarity by Dibelius) that to speak of Paul's *mysticism* is equivalent to challenging his *faith*.

There remains, however, a third, quite separate reason for the long-lasting neglect of Paul's religion. This is the widespread conviction that he was strongly influenced by Hellenistic religions. The interest of German scholars in Hellenism preceded the founding of the history of religions school in the 1880s. Otto Pfleiderer, regarded by some as its founder-father, was one of those who stoutly maintained this theory, and Schweitzer felt able to say that the predominant opinion of German scholars from Baur onwards was that Paul 'was not only influenced by Jewish Hellenism but also derived some of his ideas directly from Greek thought'.[9] This conviction continued throughout the relatively short life of the history of religion school and is still evident in the work of Bultmann.

Schweitzer himself, of course, did not share this view; otherwise he could not have defended the central place of eschatology in Paul's thinking. Anyone who looks to Hellenism for the sources of Paul's thought, he says, is like a man going to look for water in a distant pool and carrying it back in a leaky can in order to sprinkle a garden lying beside a stream. The final page of the long chapter headed 'From Baur to Holtzmann' is of particular interest. After stating categorically that the relation between Paulinism and Greek thought is one of total opposition and that had Paul been influenced in any way by Hellenism he could never have conceived his system as he did, he continues:

> Nevertheless it is possible to understand how theology came to class his doctrine as Greek. The mysticism which enters into it bears a certain analogy to that which springs from Greek religious thought and feeling. Since Judaism, *itself guileless of any mysticism*, produced nothing of the kind, could not create out of itself anything of the kind, the only possible alternative seemed to be

9. *Paul*, 65.

to explain it as due to Greek influence, and to explain the essential character of Paulinism in accordance with this hypothesis.[10]

How far Schweitzer's ignorance of merkabah mysticism was shared by his predecessors and contemporaries I have not attempted to discover.[11] But had much attention been paid to it he would surely have known about it. What he would have made of such a discovery is impossible to say. But it is obviously the case that until scholars searching for Christian origins were prepared to turn away from Hellenism and to look to Judaism instead (especially its apocalyptic and mystical traditions) they were likely to continue rolling in the same rut.

Two early dates are important: 1941, which saw the publication of Gershom Scholem's *Major Trends in Jewish Mysticism*; and 1947, the year of the discovery of the Dead Sea Scrolls. Conclusive proof that merkabah mysticism (see Chapter 3) was practised by at least some of those responsible for the Scrolls is contained in a document known as 'Songs of the Sabbath Sacrifice'. This was not published until 1985; but as early as 1971 John Bowker had put forward the strikingly original suggestion that Paul's vision on the Damascus road occurred whilst he was engaged in precisely this practice; and in 1980 Seyoon Kim's doctoral thesis, *The Origin of Paul's Gospel*, established a link between the key chapter of merkabah mysticism, Ezekiel 1, and the passage in 2 Corinthians where Paul talks of 'the light that shone in our hearts' (see Chapter 3). Kim had been able to consult an earlier version of Christopher Rowland's *The Open Heaven* (1982), in which the impact of the Jewish apocalyptic and mystical traditions upon early Christianity was demonstrated

---

10. *Paul*, 99 (my italics).
11. Evidently none of the scholars named by Morray-Jones (ch. 4, n. 9) can be accused of such ignorance; but it was certainly shared by Dibelius, who whilst acknowledging that Paul bases the mystical language he employs in 2 Cor 3:7–18 upon a midrash of Exod 34:29–35 says that insofar as it is mystical it must be hellenistic! ('Paulus', 140). He does envisage the possibility that even as a Jew Paul may have been acquainted with certain elements of 'gnostic-mystical piety'. But then he adds, significantly: 'Until we get further information from sources that have still to come to light (Jewish prayers for example) the question concerning mystical piety in Paul's Jewish period must remain unanswered' ('Paulus', 158). This essay was first published (in Munich) in 1941, the same year as the appearance (in Jerusalem) of the first edition of Gershom Scholem's *Major Trends in Jewish Mysticism*.

beyond dispute. Others who have followed a similar direction are the Jewish scholar Alan Segal and Rowland's doctoral student, Christopher Morray-Jones. (Although my own project was conceived long before I had become acquainted with the studies of Kim, Segal or Morray-Jones, I am pleased to acknowledge the stimulus I have found in their work.) The theoretical implications of this new approach are huge, but the theological establishment, largely no doubt for the reasons outlined above, is a long way from having grasped them.

The hardest task confronting any New Testament scholar is to come up with an idea or an argument that is at the same time fresh, interesting, and not too far-fetched. New in this book is the suggestion that a comparison of certain aspects of Paul's life and experience with the phenomenon of shamanism may shed light on his religion. (It is this suggestion that makes the book an appropriate outcome of a series of lectures advertised under the heading of 'The Wilde Lectures on Comparative Religion'.) The hunt for a *genetic* link between Paul and earlier shamans proved inconclusive, and I was consequently forced to consider the possibility that the observed resemblances between Paul and the typical shaman were merely coincidental. I concluded nevertheless that the study might nevertheless be worthwhile, partly because it was likely to shed light on the history of early Christianity, partly because it would highlight a number of religious features of Paul's career that were all too often ignored.

Whatever value I may wish to claim for my own analysis, which has been conducted from the perspective of a historian of religion, with some aid from comparative anthropology, it is put forward as an alternative to the theological interpretations of other exegetes. The writings of Paul upon which it is mainly grounded have been endlessly discussed and debated, and what the Germans call their *Wirkungsgeschichte*, their impact upon others throughout history, is certainly too strong to be affected by the findings of one isolated scholar, even if the approach that I have adopted were to be credited with any validity. But I hope that this book, if it is noticed at all, will at least serve to remind the theologians that theirs is not the only path to the understanding of Paul the Apostle.

Bibliography

Alexander, L., 'Fact, Fiction and the Genre of Acts', *NTS* 44 (1998), 380–99.

Alexander, P., 'Incantations and Books of Magic' in E. Schürer, *The History of the Jewish People in the Age of Jesus Christ*, iii.1, ed. G. Vermes, F. Millar, M. Goodman (Edinburgh, 1986) 342–79.

Alter, S. G., *Darwinism and the Linguistic Image: Language, Race, and Natural Theology in the Nineteenth Century* (Baltimore and London, 1999).

Ashton, J., *Studying John: Approaches to the Fourth Gospel* (Oxford, 1994).

——, *Understanding the Fourth Gospel* (Oxford, 1991).

Aune, D., *Prophets and Prophecy in the Ancient Mediterranean World* (Grand Rapids, 1983).

Barth, K., *Church Dogmatics*, i, part 2: *The Doctrine of the Word of God* (Edinburgh, 1956).

——, *The Epistle to the Romans* (Oxford, 1933).

Baur, F. Ch., *Paulus der Apostel Jesu Christi* (Stuttgart, 1845).

Beasley-Murray, G. R., *Baptism in the New Testament* (London, 1972).

Bertram, G., 'Paulus Christophoros: Ein anthropologisches Problem des Neuen Testaments' in *Stromata: Festgabe des akademischen Verreins zu Giessen im Schmalkaldener Kartell anläßlich seines 50. Stiftungstages* (Leipzig, 1930), 26–38.

Betz, H. D., *Galatians: A Commentary on Paul's Letter to the Churches in Galatia*. Hermeneia Commentary (Philadelphia, 1975).

Black, M., *Models and Metaphors* (Ithaca, NY, 1962).

Blacker, C., *The Catalpa Bow* (London, 1975).

Boas, F., 'The Limitations of the Comparative Method of Anthropology' in *Race, Language and Culture* (Macmillan: New York, 1948), 270–80.

Bockmuehl, M. N. A., *Revelation and Mystery in Ancient Judaism and Christianity* (Tübingen, 1990).

Bousset, W., *Kyrios Christos: Geschichte des Christusglaubens von den Anfängen des Christentums bis Irenaeus* (Göttingen, 1964)⁵ [1913].

Boyarin, D., *A Radical Jew: Paul and the Politics of Identity* (Berkeley, 1994).

Bowker, J., '"Merkabah" Visions and the Visions of Paul', *JSS* 16 (1971), 157–73.

Brock, S., '"Come, compassionate Mother ..., come, Holy Spirit"; a forgotten aspect of early Eastern Christian imagery', *Aram* 3 (Oxford, 1991), 249–57.

——, 'The Holy Spirit as feminine in early Syriac literature' in *After*

Eve: Woman, Theology and the Christian Tradition, ed. J. M. Soskice (London, 1990), 73–88.

Brown, P., *The World of Late Antiquity from Marcus Aurelius to Muhammed* (London, 1971).

Bruce, F. F., *The Acts of the Apostles: The Greek Text with Introduction and Commentary*[3] (Grand Rapids, Michigan, 1990).

Bultmann, R., *Die Geschichte der synoptischen Tradition*[7] (Göttingen, 1967) [1921].

——, 'The Historical Jesus and the Risen Christ' in *The Historical Jesus and the Kerygmatic Christ*, ed. C. Braaten & R. Harrisville (Philadelphia, 1964).

——, *Theology of the New Testament i* (London, 1952).

Burkert, W., 'ΓΟΗΣ. Zum griechischen "Schamanismus"', *Rheinisches Museum* 105 (1962), 36–55.

Cerfaux, L., *Le chrétien dans la théologie paulinienne* (Paris, 1962).

Charles, R. H., *The Book of Enoch* (Oxford, 1893).

Chernus, I., *Mysticism in Rabbinic Judaism* (Berlin, 1982).

Clark, J. M., *Meister Eckhart: An Introduction to the Study of his Works with an Anthology of his Sermons* (Edinburgh, 1957).

Dahl, R., *Dirty Beasts, with illustrations by Quentin Blake* (London, 1984).

Deissmann, A., 'Evangelium und Urchristentum' in *Beiträge zur Weiterentwicklung der christlichen Religion*, ed. A. Deissmann et al. (Munich, 1905), 77–138.

——, *Light from the Ancient East* (London, 1927) [1910].

——, *The Religion of Jesus and the Faith of Paul* (London, 1923).

——, *St Paul: A Study in Social and Religious History* (London, 1912) [1911].

Dibelius, M., *An die Thessalonicher I, II. An die Philipper*[3] (Tübingen, 1937).

——, 'Glaube und Mystik bei Paulus' in *Botschaft und Geschichte: Gesammelte Aufsätze ii: Zum Urchristentum und zur hellenistischen Religionsgeschichte*, ed. G. Bornkamm (Tübingen, 1956), 94–116 [1931].

——, 'Paulus und die Mystik' in *Botschaft und Geschichte*, 134–59 [1941].

Dodds, E. R., *The Greeks and the Irrational* (Berkeley and Los Angeles, 1951).

——, *Pagans and Christians in an Age of Anxiety: Some Aspects of Religious Experience from Marcus Aurelius to Constantine* (Cambridge, 1965).

Donaldson, T. L., 'Israelite, Convert, Apostle to the Gentiles: The Origin of Paul's Gentile Mission' in *The Road from Damascus: The Impact of Paul's Conversion on His Life, Thought, and Ministry*, ed. R. N. Longenecker (Michigan/Cambridge UK, 1997), 62–84.

——, *Paul and the Gentiles: Remapping the Apostle's Convictional World* (Minneapolis, 1997).

Douglas, M., *Natural Symbols: Explorations in Cosmology*[2] (Harmondsworth, 1973).

Dupont, J., *ΣΥΝ ΧΡΙΣΤΩΙ: L'Union avec le Christ selon saint Paul* (Paris, 1952).

Dunn, J. D. G., *Romans 1–8* (Dallas, 1988).

——, *The Theology of Paul the Apostle* (Edinburgh, 1998).

Edsman, C.-M., 'A Swedish Female Folk Healer from the Beginning of the 18th century', in *Studies in Shamanism*, ed. C.-M. Edsman (Stockholm, 1967).

Eliade, M., *Le Chamanisme et les techniques archaïques de l'extase*[2] (Paris, 1968); ET= *Shamanism: Archaic Techniques of Ecstasy* (London, 1964).

——, *Rites and Symbols of Initiation: The Mysteries of Birth and Rebirth* (New York, 1965).

Elliger, W., *Paulus in Griechenland: Philippi, Thessaloniki, Athen, Korinth* (Stuttgart, 1978).

Esler, P. F., *The First Christians in their Social Worlds: Social-Scientific Approaches to New Testament Interpretation* (London/New York, 1994).

——, *Galatians* (London, 1998).

—— (ed.), *Modelling Early Christianity: Social-Scientific Studies of the New Testament in Its Context* (London/New York, 1995).

Evans-Pritchard, E. E., *Nuer Religion* (Oxford, 1956).

Fitzmyer, J. A., *Romans: A New Translation with Introduction and Commentary* (London, 1993).

Fredriksen, P., 'Judaism, the Circumcision of the Gentiles, and Apocalyptic Hope: Another Look at Galatians 1 and 2', *JTS* 42 (1991), 532–64.

Freyne S., 'The Charismatic' in *Ideal Figures in Ancient Judaism: Profiles and Paradigms*, ed. G. W. E. Nickelsburg and J. J. Collins (Chico, CA, 1980), 223–58.

Gadamer, H.-G., *Kleine Schriften*, i (Tübingen, 1967).

——, *Truth and Method* (London, 1975).

Gennep, A. van, *Les rites de passage* (Paris, 1909).

Gill, D. W. J. and Gempf, C., ed., *The Book of Acts in Its Graeco-Roman Setting* (Grand Rapids, Michigan, 1994).

Gooder, P., 'Only the Third Heaven? 2 Corinthians 12:1–10 and Heavenly Ascent.' A Thesis submitted to the Faculty of Theology in the University of Oxford for the Degree of Doctor of Philosophy (1998).

Goodman, F. D., *Speaking in Tongues: A Cross-Cultural Study of Glossolalia* (Chicago, 1972).

Goodman, M., *Mission and Conversion: Proselytizing in the Religious History of the Roman Empire* (Oxford, 1994).

Goulder, M. D., 'The Visionaries of Laodicea', *JSNT* 43 (1991), 15–39.

Graves, R. and Podro, J., *The Nazarene Gospel Restored* (London, 1953).

Gray, R., *Prophetic Figures in Late Second Temple Jewish Palestine: The Evidence from Josephus* (Oxford, 1993).

Gruenwald, I., *Apocalyptic and Merkavah Mysticism* (Leiden/Cologne, 1980).

Gunkel, H., *Die Wirkungen des heiligen Geistes nach der populären Anschauung der apostolischen Zeit und der Lehre des apostels Paulus* (Göttingen, 1888).

Haenchen, E., *The Acts of the Apostles: A Commentary* (Oxford, 1971).

Harrell, D. E. Jr., *All Things are Possible: The Healing and Charismatic Revival in Modern America* (Bloomington, 1975).

——, *Oral Roberts: An American Life* (Bloomington, 1985).

Hengel, M., *Judaism and Hellenism* (London, 1974).

——, *Zur urchristlichen Geschichtsschreibung*[2] (Stuttgart, 1994).

Horsley, R. A., 'Gnosis in Corinth: 1 Corinthians 8.1–6', *NTS* 27 (1981), 32–51.

——, '"How can some of you say that there is no resurrection from the dead?": Spiritual Elitism in Corinth', *NT* 20 (1978), 203–31.

——, 'Pneumatikos vs Psychikos: Distinctions of Spiritual Status among the Corinthians', *HTR* 69 (1976), 269–88.

——, 'Wisdom of Words and Words of Wisdom in Corinth', *CBQ* 39 (1977), 224–39.

Horton, R., 'On the rationality of conversion' (*Africa* 49), 373–99.

James, W., *The Varieties of Religious Experience* (New York, 1929).

Jervell, J., 'Der schwache Charismatiker' in *Rechtfertigung: Festschrift Ernst Käsemann*, ed. J. Friedrich, W. Pöhlmann, P. Stuhlmacher (Tübingen/ Göttingen, 1976), 185–98.

Jonas, H.,'Philosophical Meditation on the Seventh Chapter of Paul's Epistle to the Romans' in *The Future of our Religious Past: Essays in Honour of Rudolf Bultmann*, ed. J. M. Robinson (London, 1964), 333–50.

Jordan, L. H., *Comparative Religion: Its Genesis and Growth* (Edinburgh, 1905).

Käsemann, E., *Essays on New Testament Themes* (London, 1964).

——, 'Die Legitimität des Apostels: Eine Untersuchung zu II Korinther 10–18', *ZNW* 41 (1942) 33–71.

Kapelrud, A. S., 'Shamanistic Features in the Old Testament' in *Studies in Shamanism*, ed. Carl-Martin Edsman (Stockholm, 1967), 90–6.

Katz, S. T., 'Mystical Speech and Mystical Meaning', *Mysticism and Language*, ed. S. T. Katz (New York/Oxford, 1992).

Kee, H. C., 'The Terminology of Mark's Exorcism Stories', *NTS* 14 (1967/68), 232–46.

Kim, S., *The Origin of Paul's Gospel*[2] (Berlin, 1984), 193 [1980].

Kollmann, B., *Jesus und die Christen als Wundertäter: Studien zu Magie, Medezin und Schamanismus in Antike und Christentum* (Göttingen, 1996).

Lane Fox, R., *Pagans and Christians* (Harmondsworth, 1986).

Lestienne, M., *Premier Livre des Règnes: La Bible d'Alexandrie* (Paris, 1997).

Lévi-Strauss, C., *Anthropologie structurale*[2] (Paris, 1974).

——, *La Pensée sauvage* (Paris, 1962).

Lewis, I., *Ecstatic Religion: A study of shamanism and spirit possession* (Harmondsworth, 1971); 2nd edition, London, 1989.

——, *Religion in Context: Cult and Charisma* (Cambridge, 1986).

Lienhardt, G., 'The Situation of Death: An Aspect of Anuak Philosophy' in *Witchcraft: Confessions and Accusations*, ed. M. Douglas (London, 1970).

Lieu, J., '"The Parting of the Ways": Theological Construction or Social Reality', *JSNT* 56 (1994), 101–19.

Loisy, A., *L'Évangile et l'église*[2] (Paris, 1903).

——, *Autour d'un petit livre* (Paris, 1903).

Lubbock, Sir John, *The Origins of Civilisation and the Primitive Condition of Man: Mental and Social Condition of Savages* (London, 1870).

Lyell, C., *A Manual of Elementary Geology or The Ancient Changes of the Earth and its Inhabitants, as Illustrated by Geological Monuments*[3] (London, 1851).

McKnight, S., *A Light among the Gentiles: Jewish Missionary Activity in the Second Temple Period* (Minneaoplis, 1991).

MacMullen, R., *Christianizing the Roman Empire, AD 100–400* (New Haven/ London, 1984).

——, *Paganism in the Roman Empire* (New Haven/London, 1981).

——, 'Two types of conversion to early Christianity,' *Vigiliae Christianae* 37 (1983), 174–92.

Marett, R. R., *Anthropology* (London, 1911).

Martyn, J. L., Galatians: A New Translation with Introduction and Commentary. The Anchor Bible 33A (New York, 1997).

——, *Theological Issues in the Letters of Paul* (Edinburgh, 1997).

Meeks, W. A., *The First Urban Christians: The Social World of the Apostle Paul* (New Haven/London, 1983).

Metzger, B. M., 'Considerations of Methodology in the Study of the Mystery Religions and Early Christianity', *HTR* 48 (1955), 1–20.

Meuli, K., 'Scythica', *Hermes* 70 (1935), 121–76.

Mitchell, S., *Anatolia: Land, Men, and Gods in Asia Minor*, ii (Oxford, 1993).

Momigliano, A., *On Pagans, Jews, and Christians* (Middletown, CT, 1987).

Moore, S. E., *God's Gym: Divine Male Bodies of the Bible* (London, 1996).

Morray-Jones, C., 'Paradise Revisited (2 Cor 12:1–2): The Jewish Mystical Background of Paul's Apostolate', *HTR* 86 (1993), 177–217; 265–92.

Murphy-O'Connor, J., *Paul: A Critical Life* (Oxford, 1996).

Niditch, S., 'The Visionary' in *Ideal Figures in Ancient Judaism: Profiles and Paradigms*, ed. G. W. E. Nickelsburg and J. J. Collins (Chico, CA, 1980), 153–79.

Odeberg, H., *The Fourth Gospel: Interpreted in its relation to contemporaneous religious currents in Palestine and the Hellenistic-Oriental world* (Uppsala, 1929).

Oursler, W., *The Healing Power of Faith* (New York, 1957).

Radcliffe-Brown, A. R., 'The Comparative Method in Social Anthropology' in *Selected Essays*, 108–29.

——, 'The Methods of Ethnology and Social Anthropology' in *Selected Essays*, 3–38.

——, *Selected Essays in Social Anthropology*, ed. M. N. Srinivas (Chicago, 1958).

Räisänen, H., 'Paul's Conversion and the Development of His View of the Law', *NTS* 33 (1987), 404–19.

Ramsay, W. M., *The Bearing of Recent Discovery on the Trustworthiness of the New Testament* (London, 1915).

——, *St Paul the Traveller and the Roman Citizen* (London, 1895).

Reitzenstein, R., *Die hellenistischen Mysterienreligionen nach ihren Grundgedanken und Wirkungen*[3] (Leipzig/Berlin, 1927).

Riesner, R., *Die Frühzeit des Apostels Paulus* (Tübingen, 1994).

Roberts, O., *My Story* (Tulsa/New York, 1961).

Robinson, J. A. T., *The Body: A Study in Pauline Theology* (London, 1952).

Rohde, E., *Psyche: Seelencult und Unsterblichkeitsglaube der Griechen*[9/10], ii (Tübingen, 1925).

Rose, H. J., *Concerning Parallels* (Oxford, 1934).

Rowland, C., *The Open Heaven* (London, 1982).

Sanders, E. P., *Jesus and Judaism* (London, 1995).

——, *Paul* (Oxford, 1991).

——, *Paul, the Law, and the Jewish People* (Philadelphia, 1983).

——, *Paul and Palestinian Judaism: A Study of Patterns of Religion* (London, 1977).

Sandmel, S., 'Parallelomania', *JBL* 81 (1962), 1–13.

Sandnes, K. O., *Paul – One of the Prophets? A Contribution to the Apostle's Self-Understanding* (Tübingen, 1991).

Schoeps, H.-J., *Paul: The Theology of the Apostle in the Light of Jewish Religious History* (London, 1961).

Scholem, G., *Major Trends in Jewish Mysticism*[2] (New York, 1946) [1941].

Schütz, J. H., *Paul and the Anatomy of Apostolic Authority* (Cambridge, 1975).

Schweitzer, A., *Geschichte der paulinischen Forschung von der Reformation bis auf die Gegenwart* (Tübingen, 1911): ET = *Paul and his Interpreters* (London, 1912).

——, *Die Mystik des Apostels Paulus* (Tübingen, 1931): ET = The *Mysticism of Paul the Apostle* (London, 1956).

——, *The Quest of the Historical Jesus: A Critical Study of its Progress from Reimarus to Wrede* (London, 1910).

Segal, A. F., 'Conversion and Messianism: Outline for a New Approach' in *The Messiah: Developments in Earliest Judaism and Christianity*, ed. J. H. Charlesworth (Minneapolis, 1992), 296–340.

——, *Paul the Convert: The Apostolate and Apostasy of Saul the Pharisee* (New Haven and London, 1990).

Sharpe, E. J. *Comparative Religion: A History* (London, 1975).

Sherwin-White, A. N., *Roman Society and Roman Law in the New Testament* (Oxford, 1963).

Shirokogoroff, M. S., *The Psychomental Complex of the Tungus* (London, 1935).

Smith, C. G., 'The Foible of Comparative Literature', *Blackwood's Magazine* 169 (Edinburgh, 1901), 38–48.

Smith, J. Z., 'Adde Parvum Parvo Magnus Acervus Erit' in *Map Is Not Territory: Studies in the History of Religions* (Leiden, 1978), 240–64.

——, *Drudgery Divine: On the Comparison of Early Christianities and the Religions of Late Antiquity* (London and Chicago, 1990).

——, 'In Comparison a Magic Dwells' in *Imagining Religion: From Babylon to Jonestown* (Chicago, 1982), 19–35.

——, 'Religion, Religions, Religious' in *Critical Terms for Religious Studies*, ed. M. C. Taylor (Chicago and London, 1998), 269–84.

Smith, M., 'Ascent to the Heavens and the Beginnings of Christianity', *Eranos Jahrbuch* 50 (1981), 403–29.

——, *Jesus the Magician*[2] (Wellingborough, 1985).

——, 'On the History of *ΑΠΟΚΑΛΥΠΤΩ* and *ΑΠΟΚΑΛΥΨΙΣ*' in *Apocalypticism in the Mediterranean World and the Near East*, ed. D. Hellholm (Tübingen, 1983), 9–20.

——, 'The Origin and History of the Transfiguration Story', *Union Seminary Quarterly Review* 36 (1980–81), 39–44.

Spencer, H., *An Autobiography*, i (London, 1904).

Stendahl, K., *Paul among Jews and Gentiles* (Philadelphia, 1976).

Stowers, S. K., *A Rereading of Romans: Justice, Jews, and Gentiles* (New Haven/London, 1994).

Tabor, J. D., *Things Unutterable: Paul's Ascent to Paradise in its Greco-Roman, Judaic, and Early Christian Contexts* (Lantham, MD, 1986).

Taine, H., *Philosophy of Art* (London, 1865).

Taylor, R. P., *The Death and Resurrection Show: From Shaman to Superstar* (London, 1985).

Templeton, D. A., *Re-exploring Paul's Imagination: A Cynical Laywoman's Guide to Paul of Tarsus* (Eilsbrunn, 1988).

Theissen, G., *Psychological Aspects of Pauline Theology*, tr. John P. Galvin (Edinburgh, 1987).

Thrall, M. E., *A Critical and Exegetical Commentary on the Second Epistle to the Corinthians*, i (Edinburgh, 1994).

Toynbee, A., *A Study of History*, vii (Oxford, 1960).

Tylor, E. B., *Primitive Culture: Researches into the Development of Mythology, Philosophy, Religion, Art, and Custom*, i (London, 1871).

——, *Researches into the Early History of Mankind* (London, 1865).

Vermes, G., *The Complete Dead Sea Scrolls in English* (London, 1998).

——, *Jesus the Jew: A historian's reading of the Gospels* (London, 1973).

Vitebsky, P., *The Shaman* (Boston/New York/Toronto/London, 1995).

Wallace, R., and Williams, W., *The Three Worlds of Paul of Tarsus* (London/New York, 1998).

Ward, R., 'Languages and genes in the Americas' in *The Human Inheritance: Genes, Language and Evolution*, ed. B. Sykes (Oxford, 1999), 135–57.

Watson, F., *Paul, Judaism and the Gentiles* (Cambridge, 1986), 28–38.

Weber, M., *The Sociology of Religion* (London, 1965).

Wedderburn, A. J. M., *Baptism and Resurrection: Studies in Pauline Theology against its Greco-Roman Background* (Tübingen, 1987).

Weinel, H., *St Paul: The Man and His Works* (London/New York, 1906).

——, *Die Wirkungen des Geistes und der Geister im nachapostolischen Zeitalter bis zum Irenäus* (Freiburg i. B./Leipzig/Tübingen, 1899).

Wikenhauser, A., *Die Christusmystik des Apostels Paulus²* (Freiburg-im-Breisgau, 1956) [1928].

Wilson, A. N., *Paul: The Mind of the Apostle* (London, 1997).

Windisch, H., *Paulus und Christus: Ein biblisch-religionsgeschichtlicher Vergleich* (Leipzig, 1934).

Wrede, W., *Paul* (London, 1907) [1904].

General Index

Index of Biblical References

OLD TESTAMENT

NEW TESTAMENT